BECOMING
A TEACHER
THROUGH
ACTION
RESEARCH

BECOMING A TEACHER THROUGH ACTION RESEARCH

Process, Context, and Self-Study

DONNA KALMBACH PHILLIPS AND KEVIN CARR

Routledge
Taylor & Francis Group
New York   London

Book design: Scott Santoro; Worksight

Published in 2006 by
Routledge
Taylor & Francis Group
270 Madison Avenue
New York, NY 10016

Published in Great Britain by
Routledge
Taylor & Francis Group
2 Park Square
Milton Park, Abingdon
Oxon OX14 4RN

Printed in the United States of America on acid-free paper
10 9 8 7 6 5 4 3 2 1

International Standard Book Number-10: 0-415-95237-9 (Softcover)
International Standard Book Number-13: 978-0-415-95237-8 (Softcover)
Library of Congress Card Number 2005023809

Library of Congress Cataloging-in-Publication Data

Phillips, Donna Kalmbach.
  Becoming a teacher through action research : process, context, and self-study / Donna Kalmbach Phillips, Kevin Carr.
    p. cm.
  Includes bibliographical references and index.
  ISBN 0-415-95237-9 (pb : alk. paper)
  1. Teachers--Training of. 2. Action research. I. Carr, Kevin. II. Title.

LB1707.P55 2006
370'.71'1--dc22
                                                                                    2005023809

Taylor & Francis Group is the Academic Division of Informa plc.

Visit the Taylor & Francis Web site at
http://www.taylorandfrancis.com

and the Routledge Web site at
http://www.routledge-ny.com

TABLE OF CONTENTS

ACKNOWLEDGMENTS

Acknowledgment: A thing done or given in recognition of something received; a declaration or avowal of one's act of a fact to give it legal validity . . . an open declaration of something (as a fault or the commission of an offense) about oneself . . . see CONFESSION. —*Merriam-Webster Online Dictionary, 2005*

And so we acknowledge that we have been given much by many and are unable to make a complete account for this generosity; we cannot trace completely the wonder of weblike lines leading to people, places, and situations influencing the writing of this book, or of the many discourses playing, seducing, and commanding our written words. We confess to writing this textbook while living somewhere in a zone of contradiction (Whitehead, 1989), practicing inquiry not only as stance (Cochran-Smith & Lytle, 1999), but as a run, a ride, a trek, and a resting place—as a koan whose answer we have not yet worked through.

We wrote this book over a two-year period while one of us wrote and managed grants, organized outdoor star viewing parties, and knelt cramped beside computers, nudging, consoling machine and humans only to race across campus in time for the "Ten Greatest Physics Experiments" (Carr, 2005). The other one of us wrote while in conversations with students—"Should it be *Witness*, *Esperanza Rising*, or maybe, *Granny Torrelli Makes Soup*?"—while earnestly arguing for department budgets, catching a cell-phone appointment during the commute, and living a night life of writing polices and programs. We wrote to the rhythm of hallway conversations with colleagues, and the tunes of Pat Metheny and Pink Martini. We wrote even while conferencing, chatting, joking, and e-mailing (very late at night) with our students Carrie, Christy, Cindy, Julie, Kelly, and Michael (whose work is featured here), but also with many more who gave us permission to use pieces of their work and their quotes in this text, provided invaluable comments as we drafted sections, and even eagerly tested the software used for this project. Their framed pictures on our office walls remind us, in the words of Archbishop Oscar Romero, "We are prophets of a future not our own." We confess: we do not know where their words become our words and therefore encompass the text of this book.

We confess we wrote this book while "doing" life: two long-distant road-bike rides; long winter backcountry ski treks; an extra 30 minutes of gym time and an extra mile of running to find time to think, ask questions of life, and try to find and make connections. One of us wrote to a new baby crying, a happy preschooler asking "how many more days will you be doing this project?" and a third small voice singing "Tomorrow" with great earnestness. Another wrote to "It's Wednesday night—got to get ready for *the* group"; a trek in Peru; the sawdust and displacement of remodeling; and soy, extra-shot lattes. We wrote during a dark election, the call for peace, the sound of war, and in the silence of a long line of candles on a winter night.

One of us wrote this book in memory of the Oregon Writing Project, reading Nancie Atwell's *In the Middle* (1987, the first edition), banning the big teacher's desk from her middle school classroom, and reading, writing, and doing action research that transformed because Elena, Nora, Randy, Robbie—all of us (with and without our labels)—published *Somewhere in the Jungle*; and, yes, we all *believed*.

We confess we wrote this book while reading and rereading our favorites, the work of our distant colleagues. For Donna these were Elizabeth Ellsworth (1997); Shoshana Felman (1987); Jennifer Gore (1993); Patti Lather (1991, 1992, 1994, 2004); Erica McWilliam (1994); Elizabeth St. Pierre (1997, 2000, 2001); and a collection by Sharon Todd (1997), finding some deep resonance of message in their words in constructing this text. And when academic words came to their limit, she turned to riverbanks and wild geese with Kathleen Dean Moore (1995, 1999) and Mary Oliver (1994, 1997) and a line from a Sue Monk Kidd novel, "There is nothing perfect . . . there is only life" (2003, p. 256). For Kevin, the voices were those of James Gleick (1987), Henri Nouwen (1996), Parker Palmer (1993), and Mike Rose (1989), and for stress relief and escape, Jon Krakauer (1997), Leo Tolstoy (1901), Jason Moore (2003), and Aron Ralston (2004).

In the words of C. S. Lewis, "We read to know that we are not alone." We have not been alone in writing this book.

And we acknowledge our struggle with the wise words of Lao Tzu, "In pursuit of knowledge, every day something is acquired; In pursuit of wisdom, everyday something is dropped." And we know we could not have completed this project were it not for the gracious gift of time from our spouses John and Lisa; our friends; colleagues like Mindy, who read drafts even while completing her dissertation; the many others who responded to our talk and ideas; the potential seen by the editors at Routledge; and a grant from George Fox University.

Yes, we acknowledge that we wrote this book while "doing" life; while in question; while teaching with conviction/doubt, passion/apathy, and hope/despair, believing in our students even as they and others gave us the gift of believing in us. We acknowledge the words of Maxine Greene (2001) in our own practice, for our "notions of teaching are much involved with notions of human relationship, intersubjectivity, the pursuit of various kinds of meaning, and *the sense of untapped possibility—of what might be, what ought to be, what is not yet*" (p. 82—emphasis added).

We write this acknowledgment in gratitude—for relationships, changing subjectivities, the cacophony/harmony of life, for the named and unnamed influences here; for the irony/illusion of wholeness that is found in incompleteness, for *the sense of untapped possibility*.

AN INTRODUCTORY GUIDE AND INVITATION

If this book could be more—if this book could touch, smell, argue, exclaim, sigh, even dance—then it might be more representational of action research as we have come to know it.[1] However, it is *a book*, and as such it is bound by linear structures of thinking that do not always reflect the cyclical and even messy processes of doing action research. Just the same, we have attempted to create a book that allows space for you to interact, to talk back, and that recognizes that as a reader you are always engaged, whether you are connecting with text or significantly bored with the content. (We, of course, hope the latter is *not* true of the present volume!) This book is unique in formatting—here are some general guidelines for organizing your journey and navigating the content.

Who Is This Book Written For?

The title, *Becoming a Teacher Through Action Research: Process, Context, and Self-Study*, encapsulates both the book's purpose and audience. While *Becoming a Teacher through Action Research* (*BTAR*) may be useful in a wide variety of settings, it is written especially for people who are formally becoming teachers for the first time.

Becoming a Teacher . . .

The United States and many other countries offer teacher education programs for students working toward their first teaching certification or license in precollege teaching. We use the term *preservice teacher* for the student pursuing teaching licensure for the first time. Most preservice teacher education programs include a substantial field experience component (often called *student teaching*). *BTAR* is designed for preservice teachers who are or will be engaged in teaching.

We believe that preservice teacher education programs and other routes to becoming a teacher create scaffolds for a critical phase in professional life, one that includes not only technical training in teaching but significant transformation of identity as well. You will not be the same after becoming a teacher. This book acknowledges, supports, and intertwines teaching's technical and transformational elements; ultimately, what you bring to the book and take away is part of the individual/collective journey you travel.

. . . Through Action Research

Many preservice teacher educations programs include an action research project, capstone project, teaching improvement project, or some other experience that could be framed as *action research*. We believe that preservice action research has the potential to shape teacher identity in powerful ways. You will become a different teacher by doing your action research project. The central purpose of this text is to scaffold your action research process, not only to make the journey successful, but to make it transformative.

---

[1]   We have borrowed the format and the sentiment of Gary Paulson, young adolescent writer, in his description of the limitation of text as described in the preface to *The Winter's Room* (1989).

Process, Context, and Self-Study

BTAR will support your preservice action research journey in three critical ways. First, and foremost, *BTAR* will guide you through the action research (AR) process in a linear fashion, from understanding the process, finding an area of focus, designing a study and collecting data, analyzing and interpreting the data, and communicating your findings to others. In addition, *BTAR* includes critical side roads that you may follow to explore the larger context of AR, as well as the inner life of teacher action research. Think of *BTAR* as a travel guide that includes not only critical information and instructions for completing your trip, but suggests many interesting side roads and detours that may, depending on time and inclination, provide additional richness and depth to your journey.

Organization and Navigation

This volume is divided into three sections. Think of these sections as the roads you will travel to your final destination, a completed action research project. The main road leads you in a linear fashion through the steps involved in carrying out an action research project. You may move sequentially through these steps and arrive at the end with an action research project. You will know you are on this main road because the sections are marked by this icon: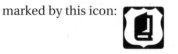

Cultural Context: Introduction to the Cultural Context Activities

The school and community in which we work provide the living environment for our professional context (Gay, 2000). This strand of *Becoming a Teacher Through Action Research: Context, Process, and Self-Study* will help you place teaching and action research within a greater cultural context. Even as you plan your lessons, design your research project, and daily attend a school site for a practicum experience, the larger cultural environments are present and powerful. Such influences are hard to define or categorize, but one can analyze, synthesize, deconstruct, and thus theorize about the influences around us. Taking a closer look at these forces allows us to re-create our own images, values, and beliefs about teaching and research.

We believe that this process of re-creation requires active, critical thinking and personal reflection. Therefore, the content of this strand comes largely in the form of questions rather than answers. You will be asked to observe, analyze, and interpret the cultural space around you to find clues about the nature of the context where you are journeying. These skills are, not accidentally, the same skills teachers use in implementing action research.

The activities in this strand serve as a tangible reminder that we do not teach and do research in isolation. Our lives are connected through social histories, invisible genealogies that grow to tell the stories of teaching. These collective stories, be they interpreted as truth, myth, or merely fiction, swirl around conversations of education. This strand is a space in which to consider these stories more closely as part of your action research process.

Throughout the activities, deliberately resist the desire to say, "This is right," "This is wrong," or, "What's the problem with

continues →

Many times we need to travel the main road to get where we need to go. But often we gain more from the journey if we take the time to travel some side roads along the way. We believe that action research is not done in isolation and requires consideration of context. At the same time action research is intensely personal and requires introspection and self-reflection. To support work in these areas *BTAR* includes two side roads that are accessible from the main road: *Cultural Context* and *Self-Study*. These side roads will appear on the sides of the page and be marked with the icon ◗ for cultural context and ⌕ for self-study.

This book is *not* written for the passive reader; we want you to interact with the text. Read with a dedicated spiral notebook or journal close by. Throughout the text, there will be specific places for you to respond; these are marked with this icon: ◖ Taking time to respond will allow you to better construct your own meaning of action research.

Alternatives Modes of Travel

Traditional printed books can be limited in the kind of materials, ways of communication, and interactivity they can offer. To create alternatives, this volume includes interactive textware

this?" The goal is *not* to determine "rightness," but to deeply consider public images, values, and beliefs about teaching and research. By identifying these themes among the discourse of dominant culture, we can better choose our own course of action: Why do we accept or reject these themes? What other alternatives exist to define ourselves and our chosen profession? Do we wish to blend what we discover into some "new" construction for ourselves and our teaching identity? What will these new images, new stories be like?

Many of these activities will ask you to interpret data on some small scale. This is the same kind of interpretation you will be doing in your action research project. Don't be too concerned with being "objective" in these interpretations. Because of the way we are both consciously and subconsciously influenced by our culture, experiences, ethnicity, gender, and class, we cannot totally escape ourselves to be "objective" in the purest sense of the word. As one of our colleagues often says, "It's hard to separate *you* from you." In order to develop trustworthiness in our judgments about the world around us, we must constantly and critically examine our own motives, bases, and desires.

on a companion CD. The *BTAR* textware allows you to interact with the text dynamically through a variety of text entry, drawing, highlighting, and mapping tools. Work done while interacting with the *BTAR* textware is saved electronically so that the CD materials become individualized as you travel. *BTAR* interactive textware runs on your computer (see the CD for minimum hardware requirements) without any special software. The CD also includes supplementary materials, examples, and illustrations that are too unwieldy to include in the appendixes of the printed book. To access the optional CD-based *BTAR* activities, insert the CD into your computer's CD drive. When the CD opens, find the desired *BTAR* activity in the list and click on its icon with your mouse. You will be sent to the desired activity. There are many ways of using this textbook and supplementary CD as directed by your course instructor or other mentor. Even if the CD materials are not assigned, you may find them helpful for doing additional learning and work in some areas. Any work completed from the CD can be printed or saved on your own computer. For some, doing the activities in a technology lab or a coffee shop with others adds yet another dimension to the use of this text. Just remember that the interactive textware is not an integral part of the book; please consider our prompts to use the CD as invitations to explore further. That said, here are three possibilities for using the text and CD materials in tandem:

1   You may use the printed book and a personally dedicated notebook or journal for activities within this volume, and use the CD only to access, view, and print (if applicable) supplementary charts, data sets, examples, and videos.

2   You may use the printed book and *BTAR* interactive textware together, using the CD to complete and save work on selected activities or in certain settings (such as your school's computer lab or on a laptop), as an alternative to your own paper or the spaces in the text. When reading the paper text, references to the CD are indicated using this icon: (icon)

3   You may use the *BTAR* interactive textware in place of the printed book, using the book as a backup or in settings where computers are not available or do not function properly. The interactive textware includes the full text, seamlessly integrated with interactive activities and supplementary materials.

Taken as a whole, our intent is that this text, with its main road and scenic side roads both within the text itself and in the interactive textware, will serve as a flexible travel guide for your own journey in becoming a teacher through action research. You will fill in the blanks, more than likely color outside the lines, and thus complete the details of the story. Because there is more than one way to approach this book, we encourage you to

Self-Study: Introduction to Self-Study Activities

Self-study is a term used in educational research circles to describe teaching and researching practices in order to "better understand: oneself; teaching; learning, and the development of knowledge about these" (Loughran, 2004, p. 9). Self-study can take many forms, ranging from the simple keeping and study of a personal diary or journal to carrying out a more thorough examination of self and practice such as an "autoethnography" (Ellis & Bochner, 2003). What all self-study research has in common is its autobiographical perspective—you the teacher/researcher become the subject of the study. Such study is embedded with deliberate acts of reflection that result in transformation of self, practices, and/or systems (Carr & Kemmis, 1986; LaBoskey, 2004; Schon, 1990; Zeichner & Liston, 1996). The self is not studied in isolation; rather, "understanding of teaching and learning derives from contextualized knowledge, by a particularly reflective knower in a particular teaching situation" (Bass, Anderson-Patton, & Allender, 2002, p. 56).

Self-study and action research share commonalities such as an emphasis on improving practice, interactive collaboration, and the primary use of qualitative methods (Feldman, Paugh, & Mills, 2004; LaBoskey, 2004). A certain amount of self-study is part of any action research project; after all, your own experiences, perceptions, and growth are all intimately entwined with your teaching practice.

This is especially true as a preservice teacher—you will be transformed as a result of stepping into the classroom and working through the process of action research. Schulte (2002) defines the transformation process as the "continuous evolution of one's own understanding and perspectives in order to better meet the needs of all students. It is marked by a disruption of values or cultural beliefs through critical reflection with the goal of more socially just teaching" (p. 101).

Documenting and reflecting upon this transformation process is an important component of doing action research as a

continues ➡

find the way that best fits your style and cultural and personal approach to learning and apply it here.

Whether you choose to wander the side roads or only travel the straight highway of your action research project, our invitation is for you to use this book to become a critically thinking, empowered teacher who can use action research to listen, observe, interact, and engage— and thus, *teach*—all students.

preservice teacher. It requires risk on your part, and finding some space and time to open yourself up to such interrogation; take a first step with the personal interview that comes later in the self-study activities in this book. O'Reiley (1998), writing about the power of quiet reflection on teaching, notes, "Sometimes I'm scared to do these quiet things because I might stumble on some data I didn't count on" (p. 15). Yet such data discoveries may be the beginning of a transformation.

CHAPTER 1
BECOMING A STUDENT TEACHER / ACTION RESEARCHER

 Images of Teacher and Researcher

You want to be a teacher. You come to this decision with your dreams and visions of what a "teacher" is. You aspire to certain standards, expectations, and desires. You know it will be hard work, but that's not a concern right now. You're focused on your dreams of what teaching will be like. Maybe you remember your favorite teacher: the third grade teacher who inspired you to become a mathematician, the middle school teacher who convinced you that you were an artist, or the high school teacher who took you trekking along fault lines and created a passion for geology. Or, perhaps what motivated you to become a teacher are your worst memories: you do *not* want to be like your boring ninth grade history teacher, the seventh grade teacher who used put-downs, or the first grade teacher who didn't believe you could read. You want to be different. You want to make a difference. We want you to make a difference as well, and we think the process of action research is one way of helping you achieve your dreams.

That's why we've written this book about teaching and research. It is not an "authoritative" account of either teaching or research, in which we as "experts" define for you teaching and research. Rather, it is designed to guide you through your individual process of *becoming* a teacher, a process that is different for everyone, and one in which we the authors are ourselves engaged. We've written in this fashion because we believe that action research is a powerful way of not only documenting your journey in becoming a teacher, but also a powerful way of *being* a teacher. The text is designed to be interactive, since this is how we view teaching and learning and researching—as interactive process of discovery and inquiry. It is a process that involves opening up possibilities through a reexamination of taken-for-granted ideas. This process involves risk with the potential for both personal and collective transformation.

In this book, you will learn about *action research*, a kind of research that is in a category of its own but can be defined and interpreted in many ways. We will be discussing the term *teacher/ researcher*, or the teacher as the *intelligent inquirer*, throughout this book. But these discussions often require a paradigm shift: the teacher as a researcher is *not* an image our culture gives us. Rather, *teacher* and *researcher* are often constructed as figures in opposition, having very different traits, interests, and values.

It seems we all come to education with images and definitions of what "good teacher" and "good researcher" represent: how they act, look, and think. It is important to consider what our images are and how these images are shaped by our culture, gender, and ethnicity; our community and family values; and our experiences. Education courses and school experiences often change our ideas of what a "good" teacher and researcher is. Wherever you are in the journey of becoming a teacher, it is critical to consider your own response to the questions, "What is a good teacher?" and "What is a good researcher?"

What is a Good Teacher?

Begin with your image of a "teacher." Start by defining a "good teacher" in your notebook or journal. Brainstorm as many different qualities, attributes, and skills you associate with someone who is a "good teacher."

Compare and contrast your text definition to figures 1–1.8 completed by preservice teachers of a "good teacher." (If you have never drawn your own picture of a "good teacher," it may be an interesting activity for you to complete at this time.)

Drawings like these reflect the social values that surround us. In this case, the drawings of teacher mirror values portrayed in popular culture (Weber & Mitchell, 1995). Anthropologists have written extensively about how our perception of reality is shaped by media and literature. These sources teach us what is "normal" or "acceptable." In this way, such perceptions limit our boundaries of what is possible. How does your own definition of a "good teacher" both limit and provide possibilities of who you might become as a teacher?

Further analyze your definition and the drawings by preservice teachers by responding to the following questions:

> What themes appear among the drawings? What do the drawings have in common?
>
> What might be useful and dangerous about these themes?
>
> What is *not* included in these drawings?
>
> How do your ideas about a "good teacher" compare with those shown?
>
> In your definition of a good teacher, did you include any attributes you might associate with *research*?
>
> Are there any words representing analysis, decision making, or synthesizing of information?
>
> Is the concept of "research" one you associate with the act of good teaching?

FIGURES 1.2– 1.5: Teacher Drawings

What is a Good Researcher?

Now consider your image of a "researcher." Start by defining "good researcher" in your notebook or journal. Brainstorm as many different qualities, attributes, and skills you associate with someone who is a "good researcher."

Compare your definition to drawings of researchers we have collected from preservice teachers in our classes.

Analyze both your definition and the drawings above by responding to the following questions:

> How does your definition of "researcher" compare or contrast with your idea of "teacher"?
>
> What themes seem to be present?
>
> What might be useful or dangerous?
>
> Why do you think these similarities or differences exist?
>
> What experiences have you had that define "teacher" and "researcher" for you?

In analyzing these drawings you have engaged in *deconstruction*, a key element of doing action research that will appear as a theme throughout this book.

Exploring "Action" and "Research"

Having considered the terms *teacher* and *researcher*, begin now to form a definition of *action research*, the genre of research this book explores.

Activity: Exploring "Action" and "Research"

This activity may be completed by using the tools on the companion CD.

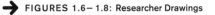

FIGURES 1.6– 1.8: Researcher Drawings

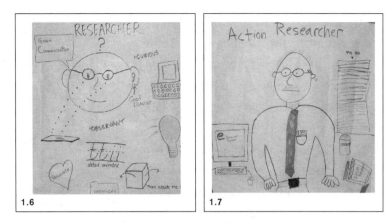

1.6

1.7

1.8

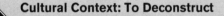

Cultural Context: To Deconstruct

The term deconstruction is often associated with the French philosopher Jacques Derrida, who used it to refer to a "strategic device" used in reading, interpretation, and writing (Derrida, 1983). This "strategic device" may be thought of as a "way of thinking"; as a way of thinking, deconstruction avoids asking what is "right" or "wrong," but instead asks "about the danger of what is *powerful* and *useful*" (Spivak, as cited in Lather, 1992, p. 120; emphasis added). To deconstruct often means looking at oppositional or apparently contradictory ideas (sometimes called binaries) and resisting the tendency to think about them in either/or terms. For example, student teachers often find themselves facing these kinds of binary dilemmas:

continues ➡

Instructions

🔬 In your notebook, create two "webs," one around the word *action* and the other around the word *research*. Try to connect the two webs showing the interrelationships between the two words as you conceive them (figure 1.9).

Use the terms from your webs to create a Venn diagram of the two concepts.

Based upon the webbing activity, write your initial definition of the term *action research*. Your definition will con-

➡ **FIGURE 1.9:** Action Research/Venn Diagram

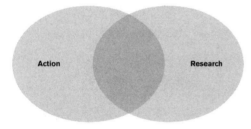

tinue to emerge as you continue to work through this section. You will be asked to recall and revise your initial definition as you encounter new ideas. Even then, consider this a "working definition." Allow it to evolve as you engage with the process of conducting your own action research project.

Action research is most simply defined as a form of research that is practitioner based. In other words, it is done by teachers in their own classrooms with the goal of improving simultaneously pedagogy and student learning. We asked some of our former students to define action research after they had graduated from their teacher education program

teacher: friend/authority

learning: fun/boring

curriculum: textbook/no textbook

teaching method: inquiry/direct instruction

classroom environment: control/ chaos

Many student teachers (and in-service teachers) feel the need to be on one side or the other of such binaries. For example, they must be either a friend or an authority; their lessons are either fun or boring; they must have control or risk chaos. With each of these, there is a sense that one of the sides is right and the other side is wrong. The side must then be defended; each side is isolated from the other. The result is a stagnant, single-view argument that is difficult to grow or expand.

To deconstruct these binaries, we might instead make a list of what is dangerous and useful about each perspective. Consider the assumptions we are making about each term: what values, beliefs, and cultural influences frame our interpretations? The goal of examining our assumptions in this way is to tease something out of the text (and our own thinking) that we may not have noticed before. Such deconstruction allows us to start all over again and to consider the dilemma from another viewpoint. In Lather's words (1991), this means to "keep things in process, to disrupt, to keep the system in play" (p. 13). By doing this, we are continually revisiting dilemmas and discovering alternative ways to approach them. Rather than being "stuck" in one way of thinking, we open up possibilities for approaching such issues. This is particularly important in the classroom.

For example, much has been written about the "reading wars." Such debates often play out as "reading: phonics/ whole language." When this happens, teachers, academics, researchers, and politicians line up on one side or the other, each with their own stacks of "evidence." The result is a stagnant, entrenched, and ongoing debate that doesn't move forward (or even backward). The war metaphor of entrenchment is used here intentionally. Often, this "debate" isn't even a dialogue or conversation: it is simply the two sides shouting at one another.

continues ➡

and while they were in their first year of teaching. This is what they said:

I believe that action research is the ability to daily recognize areas in your classroom that need improvement and then seeking to discover methods that will help make a needed change. I feel that it is a process that you are constantly going through by testing and trying out different methods and documenting what will help your students succeed. —Cole

Action research is everything a good teacher does . . . only documented! As a teacher, it is my job to identify a problem, make a plan of action, and watch carefully to see how my action influences the initial problem. If I never examine my work to see what worked and what didn't, both on a day-to-day basis, and in the larger spectrum of a year, then I am not teaching well. —Natasha

Right now I am researching how to survive my first year of teaching! Really, I am discovering when to rest, when to stay up past midnight to complete my work, how to learn from my fellow staff members, how to keep track of all the paperwork, and how to serve students from a background of neglect and abuse. Every day I am looking up ideas on the Internet, finding the right resources on my shelf of "teacher books," looking for student work or talking with my peers. I am always analyzing my practice. —Elena

Expand your definition of action research by reading the following brief descriptions of projects our teacher education students have conducted:

Yet we know as teachers that each child approaches reading in unique ways, although patterns of reading development do emerge. To be solely on one side or the other is to shut down possibilities of learning for some children. To deconstruct this debate, we begin asking questions. What is useful and dangerous about phonics? What is useful and dangerous about whole language? In addition, we might look at the language being used on each side of the "war." How is each side describing reading, and what do these descriptions assume? What social and power structures benefit from the arguments put forth? Again, the goal is not to arrive at one answer and stay there; the goal is to keep the dialogue moving, thus generating new understanding. "It is not a matter of looking harder or more closely, but of seeing what frames our seeing" (Lather, 1994, p. 38); when we deconstruct, we consider the context and social relationships that influence our seeing. Deconstruction, in this way, "provides a corrective moment, a safeguard against dogmatism, a continual displacement" (Lather 1991, p. 13). When we begin to see these assumptions then we can begin to deconstruct and view classroom dilemmas from various viewpoints.

Here is a more personal account of deconstruction and how it might be used in the classroom. Donna remembers the first time a student stood up in the back of her class and told her in no uncertain terms with an obscene gesture exactly what she could do with her life. At that point, there was a showdown. Donna felt the need to assert her authority. The student had the same need. Although the student was sent from the classroom, no one "won." At first, Donna considered the student as "insolent" and "defying authority." By assuming and thus categorizing the student as "bad," and, therefore, other students as "good," the process of finding ways to work with the student was greatly diminished. Fortunately, Donna had a mentor who talked her through the incident, deconstructing the situation so that she could hear other points of view (like the student's) and begin to construct a learning environment where both she and the student were affirmed and able to learn together.

continues →

Anna

Anna was a student teacher in a third grade classroom where most of the students were below grade level in writing, according to the state writing exam. Anna noticed how the students who had the most difficult time with writing were also those who had a difficult time just getting started. She wanted to explore how prewriting exercises might assist these struggling writers. Anna began to implement several prewriting strategies. She collected three kinds of data: student compositions (each composition was scored using the state required scoring guide), student self-evaluations (inquiring about the writing process), and instructor observations with anecdotal notes.

At the conclusion of Anna's action research project, she wrote the following about what she had learned:

My research project was a journey that took me many places I had not previously envisioned. I not only learned more about how students write and how to assist them in becoming better writers, but also about my own teaching and learning practices. I am more confident in my abilities to assess the needs of a particular class and to adjust the lesson and assignment to meet those needs. . . . I am confident my teaching career will follow a similar journey with new discoveries and unexpected side trips. The process of learning how to evaluate the progress of my class and my progress as a teacher has been invaluable.

Claire

Claire was a student teacher in a seventh grade social studies classroom with 22 students representing a wide variety of learning styles, learning challenges, and reading levels. Claire wondered how history/culture simulations

As a way of thinking, deconstruction takes practice. Unfortunately, we are far more practiced in taking sides, "digging in," and "holding the line." However, through the action research process, learning to use deconstruction can be a powerful tool for thinking about teaching and learning.

A Way of Deconstructing

Deconstruction initially requires that we identify the opposites (or binaries) and then consider assumptions, values, and cultural influences that frame our thinking of these binaries. For example, suppose you collect data about the on- or off-task behavior of students during teaching. You are surprised to find that many more students are off task than you think is appropriate. Yet, this data is confusing because the students seem to be well-engaged in successful learning. At first, you simply take the data at "face value" and conclude that something in your teaching practice needs to be changed in order to promote more on-task behavior. But later, you begin to ask yourself questions: What does on- or off-task behavior actually look like? What assumptions about teaching and learning and "well-behaved" students frames my view of on- or off-task behavior? How might my assumptions about gender, age, and ethnicity frame my definition of "on-task" behavior? What is dangerous and useful about my assumptions? What other story might be told about this data?

By considering such questions, you are able to view on- or off-task behavior from different angles through deconstructing your own assumptions. There are numerous opportunities to practice the skill of deconstruction in the activities in this strand. As you practice, connect the stories and theories you create from the activities back to your own journey of becoming a teacher. How is the cultural context, the prominent power structures, shaping your experience of learning to teach, your image of teacher, student, and school?

might facilitate learning for *all* students. She planned an action research project based upon six triangulated data sets; each data set included observations, student work, and student focus-group interviews.

Claire discovered that simulations are beneficial for students in six specific ways. They provide focused learning; challenge students to take ownership of their learning; engage higher level thinking; increase student engagement; trigger emotion, which in turn leads to increased learning; and encourage learning for diverse learning styles and intelligences. But she also learned things she did not expect. Here is an excerpt from her final reflection:

I discovered that action research is more about improving my abilities as a teacher and, in turn, improving the lives of my students than it is about becoming an expert in one specific area. Although I certainly learned much about the benefits and drawbacks of simulations as a teaching tool, the greatest lessons came in the areas of managing the classroom, being prepared for class, and redesigning lessons to meet individual needs. Not to mention the lessons I learned about Ryan's incredible acting abilities, Melissa's (who is at third grade reading level) capacity for reading difficult materials when she found purpose, and Sadie's sensitivity to being placed in a lower age-level class. Action research is not so much about the ultimate destination, but about the journey and the many companions, such as the three students just mentioned, who accompanied me on that journey.

 Self-Study: Personal Interview

To begin the self-study process, we suggest that you complete this self-interview. This interview probes the question of why you are becoming a teacher and who you are as you begin this process. Ask yourself the following questions, and save your responses for later use in other activities.

- Think back over your decision to become a teacher. What are the top five reasons for making this decision?
- Who and what kind of systems, situations, and experiences inform the above reasons?
- Consider your own career as a student. If you had to choose, what are five "critical moments" from your own schooling? How do these "critical moments" influence your image of a teacher?
- Describe your own cultural, ethnic, and socioeconomic background. How does this background influence your decision to become a teacher?
- Describe in as little or as much detail how gender roles were determined in your family. How does this background influence your decision to become a teacher?
- Describe major factors in the development of your current belief/value system. How do these responses influence your view of what a teacher should be and the role of education in today's society?
- Do any of your responses indicate that part of the teaching process includes doing research? Why or why not?
- Why do you, or don't you, believe research should be/can be part of the teaching process?
- What, in your opinion, would make classroom research both beneficial and ethical?
- Do you want to become a teacher/researcher? Why or why not?

Read through the responses you have given in this self-interview. As you read, note and highlight any repetitive words, phrases, or ideas in your responses. Summarize what the highlighted words, phrases, and ideas indicate about your image of a "good teacher." If possible, share your summaries with a critical colleague; analyze similarities and differences in your decision to become a teacher.

Self-Study Activity: Personal Interview

This interview may be completed on the companion CD.

Abby

Abby was a student teacher in English at a large suburban high school. She was interested in emphasizing critical thinking over content knowledge in her two American literature classes. She believed that Socratic questioning—one-on-one interrogative dialogue between student and teacher about literature—was the best way to facilitate critical thinking. But how could she hold one-on-one dialogue with 54 students within the confines of standard class time and space? She decided to implement online communication between herself and her students about class material, and study the interactions for clues about how critical thinking can be developed in such an environment.

Abby's results illustrated a three-stage critical thinking development process of "aesthetic response," "dialogical analysis," and "dialectical evaluation." Aesthetic response and dialogical analysis were successfully facilitated online—especially the latter. She discovered, through carefully studying and reflecting on the online dialogues she carried on with students, a depth of student experience and thinking that would not have taken place otherwise.

How do the definitions of former students and the examples of these action research projects inform your emerging definition of action research? How is action research similar or different to what you imagined? Add to these student voices the definitions from published writers in the field of action research. As you read through these definitions, note words and phrases that either reinforce or challenge your concept of action research:

[Action research is a] form of teaching; a form of reflective practice and professional learning founded on an ethical commitment to improving practice and realizing educational values. AR involves individuals and groups identifying areas for improvement, generating ideas, and testing these ideas in practice. (Arhar, Holly, & Kasten, 2001, p. 285)

Action research is any systematic inquiry conducted by teacher researchers, principals, school counselors, or other stakeholders in the teaching/learning environment, to gather information about the ways that their particular schools operate, how they teach, and how well their students learn. This information is gathered with the goals of gaining insight, developing reflective practice, effecting positive changes in the school environment (and on educational practices in general), and improving student outcomes and the lives of those involved. (Mills, 2000, p. 6)

Action research . . . is about taking everyday things in the life of education and unpacking them for their historical and ideological baggage. . . . It highlights process with content, rather than content alone. It allows for a focus on teaching, in addition to student outcomes, and on the interplay between the two. (Noffke, 1995, p. 5)

Action research is a comparative research on the conditions and effects of various forms of social action, and research leading to social action. Research that produces nothing but books will not suffice. (Lewin, 1948, pp. 207–208)

Action research is systematic. . . . It involves a self-reflective spiral of planning, acting, observing, reflecting and re-planning. It requires teachers to be acutely aware of a sense of process, and to refine their perceptions to account for that process. . . . Action research raises to a conscious level much of what is already being done by good teachers on an intuitive level. It enables teachers to identify and come to grips with their practice in a humane way which is at once supportive and critical. (McNiff, 1988, p. 7)

As we read through these definitions, we see common themes. Action research

> involves a systematic or organized approach to problem-solving
>
> requires active engagement and interaction between groups of people
>
> insists upon reflection, critical analysis, and revolving assessment
>
> analyzes systems of power; deconstructs taken-for-granted assumptions
>
> results in *Action* as a practical outcome, as in transformation, as in a rediscovered or new sense of self and other, as in empowered teaching and learning
>
> relies upon democratic and ethical principles that value and respect all participants
>
> focuses on a single place of inquiry

Our definition merges with the thoughts of other writers, our own experiences as action researchers, and the experience of the preservice teachers with whom we work and learn. In alignment with the focus of becoming a teacher through action research, we've written our own definition of action research specifically for *preservice teacher action research*. The definition continues to evolve—we think this is indicative of the process of inquiry. At this time, our definition reads like this:

Action research for preservice teachers is a process of learning with community to think and act critically, to recognize and negotiate political systems, and to focus passion growing in one's identity as a teacher. Such a process evolves out of a desire to become a caring, intelligent, transformative educator and includes honing the art and science of planning, assessment, and a critical reflective practice that includes the interrogation of one's own paradigm while in active exploration of ways of thinking and acting beyond those said boundaries. The result of action research for preservice teachers is the beginning of a journey in becoming a teacher living the teaching/research life to simultaneously improve teaching practice, student outcomes, and systems of schooling to be more just and equitable for all children and adolescents.

Here is a metaphor we use to think about preservice action research: Action research is like budget travel. We know the destination conceptually and we anticipate arrival. We lay out everything we are going to take with us; then, we leave much behind and take only the essentials. We include our camera and journal: photos will give context, and our written words will document the events, people, and places we visit and our reactions to them. Action research requires that we pack light, laying aside some of our assumptions and being willing to learn from those we meet along the way. We plan to pick up such souvenirs as language and experience along the way. We expect to come home changed because of our travels; in the end, we may find the destination is not what we thought and that arrival is an illusive concept.

Return now to your definition of action research. Add or delete text based upon the descriptions you have read. In the previous section, you defined the term *researcher*. As a closing activity for these first two sections, we suggest you revise your definition of a teacher/researcher based upon your new understanding of this term.

Philosophical Underpinnings of Action Research

Like our images of teacher and researcher, action research is the product of cultural history and takes its place among many other forms of research in the universe of possibilities. *Research*, in its broadest sense, could be used to name any systematic way of knowing. But not all research is the same. Each different genre of research was developed at its own point in history, incorporating its own set of philosophical assumptions and cultural norms. These assumptions and norms mediate to some degree how school has looked during different time periods. The work of philosophers, artists, scientists, and musicians provide us a window into cultural thought and paradigms. During times of transition, work in these fields often heralds changes that come much later in education. As teacher/researchers, we, too, reflect our collective and individual cultural time and place.

Activity: Paradigm Chart

To understand this concept better, visit the interactive paradigm chart on the companion CD.

A condensed version of the paradigm chart is provided for in figure 1.10.

Cultural Context: Images of School and Society

Have you ever said to someone, "I am going to be a teacher," and they replied, "You sure do look like a teacher"? Maybe this hasn't happened to you yet, but as authors of this text, we have heard this kind of a statement before. When we hear this, we ask, What does a teacher look like?

Perhaps you have found yourself making this kind of observation with your peers. For example, when meeting your fellow colleagues in the teacher-education program, did you find yourself more or less assuming someone "looked like" an English major, an art teacher, or a first grade teacher? What kinds of clues "told" you this? Where might you have learned such perceptions?

This activity looks at popular images of the "teacher." Again, you may agree or disagree with what you find, but we urge you to consider instead what might be dangerous or useful in the images you find and how these images influence the way you think about teaching.

continues ➡

➡ FIGURE 1.10: Paradigm Chart

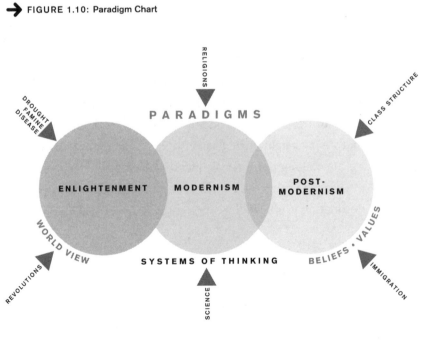

The chart depicts three historical movements, or paradigms, of Western culture: the Enlightenment, modernism, and postmodernism. Each paradigm has defined and redefined a "good education" and has influenced the way educational research is conducted.

The Enlightenment was a time of intense knowledge production as Western civilization began to stress a secular foundation rather than religious belief as the cornerstone of thought. The scientific method of deductive reasoning and logic still resonate in research today as the "objective observer" seeks to understand the world via the senses. Classic art of this time reflects this kind of logic. Clean, orderly, and presenting a vision of clarity, it often reinforced the belief in rationality and the proper order of things. In education, German Empiricist Johann F. Herbart (1776–1841) applied psychology as a science to education. Science, in this way, was thought of as the means of developing students of good moral character.

The modernist period begins with the intensification of Enlightenment principles of rational thought as a way to pursue and find truth. Building upon the deterministic foundation laid by Isaac Newton and others, science constructed a universal structure of theory that seemed unassailable in its ability to predict and control nature. Charles Darwin's *On the Origin of the Species* (1859) provided the ground work for behavioral psychology, which in turn further influenced the concepts of coming to know through objective observation and the rejection of nonempirical evidence. The

Cultural Context Activity: Deconstructing the Public Image of the "Teacher"

This activity may be undertaken using tools and charts on the companion CD.

In this activity you will search for, analyze, and interpret public images of the "teacher." The goal is to find as many images of teachers as possible and look for patterns and commonalities that provide clues into public perception of, and discourses surrounding, "teacher."

Instructions

Log on to the very popular Google search engine (or another search engine of your choice). If using Google, choose the "images" button so you are only searching for Internet pictures.

Search for images of "teacher"; or you can be more specific and search for "elementary teacher" or "high school teacher." (If you do not have Internet access, you may use the data we collected; see appendix B. We have chosen Google for this activity because at the time of publication, it is a powerful and popular search engine, storing millions of images and other resources. As such, it represents a collective cultural museum of popular thought. It is one way we can find data to analyze about Western culture's perceptions of "teacher.")

As you peruse the images, look for the following:

Is the teacher pictured male or female?

What is the teacher's ethnicity?

Is the teacher in the center of the picture, placed in a prominent position?

Is the teacher in a nontraditional setting?

Are there any pictures of students teaching students?

Considering the Results

What do you think the data you collected might say about the public image of "teacher"? How do these collections of images define a teacher? What are the attributes of a teacher? What words would you use to describe the collective, dominant

continues →

individual is characterized as having choice. The subjectivity of personal experience was seen through the objective and rational eye of the senses. Empirical educational research is still firmly rooted in beliefs from the modernist time period. Horace Mann (1796–1859) proposed during this period the "common school," suggesting that public education serve as the "great equalizer." School could be the place where, through group education, all children could learn to be moral, thinking citizens. Art began to reflect some of the dilemmas of this thought. Édouard Manet's *Olympia* (1863), for example, depicts the human body no longer perfect or rational but maintains the scientific tradition of "objectivity" by attempting to show truth through stripping the subject of emotion and moral judgment.

World Wars I and II devastated many of the hopes of the modernists. In the words of Kurt Vonnegut (1970), "Scientific truth was going to make us *so* happy and comfortable. What actually happened when I was twenty-one was that we dropped scientific truth on Hiroshima." Existentialists began to question the role of free will. Albert Einstein had reformulated Newton's laws into a new theory of gravity; his theories led to troubling problems in the field of physics, mapping a new view of the universe through quantum physics. The ideal of an "objective observer" was questioned, and the concept of the individual as a unified whole began to crumble. Art by Pablo Picasso, such as *Weeping Woman* (1937), questions the "truths" of rationality and objectivity, exposing the limitations of

image of a teacher from your Google search? Write down your responses and be prepared to share them with your colleagues.

Through Google we searched for "elementary teacher" and reviewed 38 images. Of these, 25 images were female and 7 were male. Of the teachers, 28 appeared to be white, while 4 appeared to be African American; there were no other visible ethnicities represented. All but one of the teachers was in the center of the picture, surrounded for the most part by children. At another time, we viewed 55 images from Google, but this time we searched for "teacher" alone. Of the teachers that we viewed, 21 were white; 25 were male. All of the male teachers were prominently featured in the middle of the picture or image. Nine of the pictures and/or images feature white, female teachers. One of the female teachers appeared to represent the Muslim faith, but her ethnic identification could not be determined. One female teacher was not centered in the pictures. Five teachers were in nontraditional settings (outside of a classroom or a lab). We found 6 pictures and/or images of students only, usually talking in a small group. Many of the male teachers featured were in very traditional settings—that is, in front of a chalkboard with chalk in hand, in a dress shirt and tie.

How do these results compare to your own results? Do you think the results would be different if we searched for "high school teacher"? Why?

Having considered both your own data and our collected data, write some synthesis statements about the image of "teacher" as represented in the Google search.

Our own synthesis statements and questions are as follows:

The majority of teachers are white; we might theorize that when Western culture thinks of a teacher, it thinks of a white teacher.

Female teachers are less likely to teach at the high school level. Male teachers, because of their dress, appear to be authoritative and more "content" or "business" orientated; female teachers, dressed in softer colors and styles and often placed

continues →

viewing the world through what can be perceived through the senses alone.

Postmodernist thought deconstructs the ideas of the Enlightenment and modernism by rejecting the concept of a unified self and exploring how historical and cultural voices and values work to socially construct the individual. Philosophers such as Ludwig Wittgenstein (1844–1900) described how language is not as a picture but a "box of tools" that forms our image of self. Michel Foucault (1926–1984) further explored how language frames our thinking and thus what and how we observe. The "objective observer" becomes a human-designed myth. Many of these changes in thought are spurred by the realization of physicists that the fixed narratives of "truth" are no longer reliable. "New" science recognizes that new stories must be found—stories that contain not contrite narrative with a fixed plot line, but tales that contain mystery, uncertain outcomes, and connections among characters and events that transcend the modern vision of what is "natural."

Such major shifts have influenced educational research in powerful ways. No longer are the only "experts" those from outside the classroom who observe "objectively" seeking empirical evidence. The narrative stories of teachers and students tell the story of the school in many different, diverse ways, each reflecting a unique and valuable perspective. The influences of class, ethnicity, gender, and learning styles and challenges are seen as windows into understanding school life. School as the "great equalizer" is challenged by

in closer proximity to children, do not appear as authoritative. Perhaps they are perceived as being more concern with the affective?

Male teachers may be pictured more prominently (even though they do not make up 50% of the teaching population) because men who teach are considered differently than women who teach. (Could it be that female teachers are considered to be more "normal" and male teachers more "noble"?)

The public image of "teacher" may be "teacher-directed," "teacher-centered," or "teacher as expert." This is based upon the position of the teacher in the images.

Teachers smile; most of the images included a happy, smiling teacher.

This brief sample of teacher images seems to define "teacher" as one with authority based upon expertise. Thus, students might be defined as needing the teacher's expertise and knowledge. While the teacher is the authority, he is also expected to be cheerful and positive. Since the teacher is the center of the educational experience, success or failure appears to be located at the site of the teacher. Because the majority of teachers are white, it may be that the public image of authority and expertise is centered on white, dominant culture.

Cultural Context Activity: Teacher Gifts and Clothing

This activity may be completed using tools and charts on the companion CD.

We continue to explore images of teachers in Western society in this activity by again gathering images from the Internet. This time, use Google to search for "teacher gifts" and/or "teacher clothing." Remember, this may or may not be your image of a teacher, but you are exploring what society's image of "teacher" might be via public and popular sources.

Instructions

Go online to a search engine of your choice (we used Google), and search for "teacher gifts" and/or "teacher clothing." (If you

continues ➡

such viewpoints; Jonathan Kozol's 30-year work with inner city schools (1985; 1992; 1995; 2001; 2005), for example, demonstrates just the opposite. The factory model of schools and the use of applied behavior sciences are questioned and deconstructed (Giroux, 2003; Goodlad, 2004; Kohn, 1999; Smith, 1998). Students are seen not as a blank slate but as humans constructing reality within a specific cultural and historical place; multiple viewpoints are encouraged in the pursuit of truth. Qualitative research methodology, including action research, and many other forms of "coming to know" reflect these changes in thought.

What we hope to deliberately communicate through this sketch of time and thought is this message: *We do not teach and research in a vacuum.* Our constructed lives, values, beliefs, pedagogies, and methodologies are influenced by a multitude of cultural and historical factors.

When we discuss concepts like *paradigm* and *theory* in education, it is too easy to come to understand these ideas as isolated or separated from those found in art, music, philosophy, or science. When we discuss modernism or postmodernism it is too easy to think in categories, conveying a sense that we have moved from modernism to postmodernism and somehow left behind all the thoughts of a "previous" era. But as Wink (1997) writes, our histories "tend to turn into behaviors that run around behind us and tell stories for all the world to hear" (p. 132). Hargreaves (1994) describes this overlapping of the modern and postmodern era and schooling in this way:

do not have Internet access, you may use the data we collected; see appendix C.)

Select from the list of search results several different retail sites aimed at teachers. Observe the items offered for sale and categorize them using the following descriptors:

the primary colors used

the approximate grade levels of any pictured students

symbols present

slogans present

When you have completed collecting the data, consider these questions:

To what kind of teacher do most of these items seem to be marketed (gender, grade level, and content area)?

What are the recurring themes and symbols that appear to represent a teacher? What are your theories about why these themes and symbols are used?

What might these images suggest about the public image of teachers and, perhaps, education? What is left out of these images (but in your opinion, should be included)?

Do you observe any incongruent themes or images in your search? What might these suggest?

Based upon your responses, write several synthesis statements regarding this data set. Return to the first activity in this section for examples of synthesis statements if you need them.

Activity: Teachers According to Hollywood

This activity may be completed using tools and charts on the companion CD.

One more activity will allow us to triangulate our data, or collect data from three different sources, in our search for a public image of "teacher." Even with three different sources, we will not have a complete picture of dominant Western culture's perception of a teacher, but we will have enough data to raise questions and make tentative synthesis statements.

Movies tell us about our culture—especially movies that are box-office hits and remain popular long enough to be considered "classics." There are hundreds of movies about teachers;

continues ➡

Schools and teachers are being affected more and more by the demands and contingencies of an increasingly complex and fast paced, postmodern world. Yet their response is often inappropriate or ineffective—leaving intact the systems and structures of the present, or retreating to comforting myths of the past. Schools and teachers either cling to bureaucratic solutions of a modernistic kind: more systems, more hierarchies, more laid on change, more of the same. Or they retreat nostalgically to premodern myths of community, consensus and collaboration, where small is beautiful and friendships and allegiance tie teachers and other together in a tight, protected webs of common purpose and belonging. In many respects, schools remain modernistic and in some cases even premodern institutions that are having to operate in a complex postmodern world. As time goes by, this gap between the world of school and the world beyond it is becoming more and more obvious (pp.23-24).

Engaging in the process of action research is a tool one can use to bridge the gap between school and the world outside school. Most important is that educators be aware of these conflicting modes of knowing, of the way paradigms influence not only our own ways of thinking and perceiving but those of others.

Certainly those of us in education, as in any field, represent collections of many systems of thought. The paradigm chart seeks to present not only the collection, but also the overlapping nature of multiple thought-fields. The Venn diagram fades across the Enlightenment, modernism, and postmodernism, but the diagram is all a shade of grey. This is to represent how the Enlightenment is still with us, still influencing who we become as teacher/researchers, just as modern-

some of them are comical, some "made for children," and others marketed as drama. The ones that appear to most pull at our public imagination of what a teacher is are those based upon true life stories. But with movies, fact and fiction become intertwined—we rarely know the "real" story a movie is based upon and those that are fiction are so believable, they seem to become part of our "real" images. In this way, movies influence our way of thinking; they contribute to the images and expectations of education.

Instructions

For this activity, you will once again need to have Internet access. (If you do not have Internet access, you may use the data we collected; see appendix D.)

Using the companion CD or your own Internet browser, locate the following movies. We found all of the movies (and more) by searching amazon.com. Find a picture of the jacket artwork and the promotional description of each movie.

Dangerous Minds (Simpson, Bruckheimer, Rabins, Foster, & Smith, 1995)

Dead Poets Society (Haft, Witt, Thomas, & Weir, 1989)

The Emperor's Club (Abraham, Karsh, & Hoffman, 2002)

Lean on Me (Avildsen, 1989)

Mr. Holland's Opus (Cort, Field, Nolan, & Herek, 1995)

Study the artwork for each movie and read the promotional description carefully. Then, for each movie, answer the following questions:

What key characteristics of successful teachers and/or principals are represented in the data?

How do students appear to be positioned? What kind of students appears to be most "screenworthy"?

What do the data suggest about schools in general?

What in your opinion is left out of these representations?

When we brainstormed possible movies for this activity, we found we could not recall many, if any, movies featuring elementary teachers and children. The few we did remember took place in the early 1900s and featured single women teachers who

continues ➡

ist and postmodernist thought influence who we become as teacher/researchers. For example, in the United States, there is a resurgence of strong belief in empirical research as the only way of knowing, as defined by the federal legislation of the No Child Left Behind Act (2004).

As you click on various icons and travel the distance of thought presented in the paradigm chart on the companion CD, don't think of "leaving something behind"; instead, think of packing your bags and finding them more full as the journey progresses. Finally, this is *just* a chart. Whole books have been written about any one of the icons/subjects presented. (See Linn, 1996; Palmer, 2001; Sharpes, 2002 for further introduction and exploration.) The goal here is to give you a sense of the whole, a sense of the way we are shaped and influenced by our history and our interpretation of that history.

Always be mindful of your own reactions to ideas: with what do you find yourself agreeing, disagreeing, being amused, wanting to know more? Why do you have this reaction? What might your reaction mean in terms of who you are becoming as a teacher/researcher?

ultimately found a husband and presumably left teaching. What other kinds of information about teaching and schools do you think is left out of the Hollywood depictions? Can you find additional data about elementary teachers and children to add to this data? You may also find it interesting to consider additional movies (including those from the comedy genre) to add to this data set.

(◐) Based upon the data collected, create synthesis statements summarizing the public image of the teacher as depicted in Hollywood.

Final Interpretation of Images of School and Society

(◐) Review the data collected throughout this section. Read again responses to questions and synthesis statements. Using this information, conduct a final data interpretation by responding to these questions in your notebook or journal:

What images of teachers are portrayed through the activities you have analyzed?

What paradoxes and tensions appear to exist?

What is a teachers supposed to do (and how should she look)?

What attributes are most important to teachers?

How does the public image distinguish between teachers of different grade levels?

continues ➡

Your Personal Paradigm

Our teaching practice consists of the techniques and tools we use in the classroom. Our practice does not, however, live in isolation. Our classroom practices are grounded in abstract views of knowledge and learning of which we are rarely conscious. We use the term *paradigm* to describe the set of unconscious philosophical assumptions that form the foundation of any body of practice (Kuhn, 1970). We each have within us a personal paradigm that influences our view of the world, what we think about teaching and learning, and—ultimately—the role and purpose of action research as described in this book.

How does your personal paradigm fit into the larger picture? How does your view of teaching and learning reflect central paradigms seen in music, art, science, and philosophy? We invite you to respond to a short, simple survey (figure 1.11) that may help you think about where your views align with two major paradigm movements—modernism and postmodernism—that have had a powerful impact on education.

Self-Study Activity: Personal Paradigm Self-Test

The paradigm self-test may be completed and scored using the companion CD.

Research Worlds, Research Lives: Forms of Action Research

Our personal paradigms influence how we approach life dilemmas, just as our personal paradigms influence the way we approach research. Our purpose, set-

What additional "evidence" would you add to support or oppose the public images represented in the data?

What are your theories regarding these images? Why have they become engrained in the public image of education?

How might these images influence the lives of real teachers, students, and schools?

How do you think these images might influence your own image of teachers, students, and schools?

How do you think such images, representations, and symbols could influence your own process of becoming a teacher?

ting, and needs also influence such decisions. It is little wonder that there are, then, multiple ways to do educational research. Action research is just one way of exploring teaching, learning, and school context. Even within the category of action research there are many definitions and multiple approaches to school-based dilemmas or questions.

Generally, a research approach, just as a teaching approach, depends upon the way the researcher responds to these questions (which ultimately relates to the researcher's paradigm):

➡ FIGURE 1.11: Personal Paradigm Self-Test

For each of the nineteen statements below, consider your level of agreement.
Only check if you strongly agree with the statement.

___1. "Truth" is a relative concept.

___2. "Truth" is absolute either in terms of divine revelation or the accumulated wisdom of the centuries.

___3. The only social constant, or absolute, is change.

___4. The value of an idea can be measured only in terms of its immediate usefulness.

___5. The basic purpose of formal education is to transmit the cultural heritage.

___6. The basic purpose of formal education is to assist in the creation of new culture.

___7. Morality arises from the quality of mutually shared experiences.

___8. The whole is the sum of its parts.

___9. Science is the most powerful way of knowing.

___10. There may be different, but equally valid answers to many questions.

___11. I like art that depicts life realistically, as it actually is.

___12. I like abstract art that is very open to interpretation.

___13. There is much truth to be gained through non-scientific means.

___14. Most of life is a matter of cause and effect.

___15. Most of life cannot be explained by cause and effect.

___16. "Proof" consists of well-reasoned, logical arguments and evidence.

___17. "Proof" is a very tricky concept because there are many equally valid forms of evidence.

___18. Knowledge is mostly discovered in the world outside the mind.

___19. Knowledge is mostly found inside the mind.

See Appendix A to interpret your answers.

What do you believe about the nature of knowledge?

What do you believe about the nature of "reality"?

What beliefs and values do you hold about teaching and learning and schools?

What is the purpose of the educational research? What is to be accomplished and for whom is the research being done?

Influenced by paradigm (or *epistemology*), a researcher chooses a *methodology*, an approach to conducting the research (this is the research design). Paradigm and methodology then drive the choice of methods or techniques used to gather data.

Often, research is generically divided into two groups: *quantitative* and *qualitative*. This somewhat simplistic approach disguises the complexity of choosing a research methodology and methods, but since they are widely used, we will begin this discussion with these two terms.

Quantitative Research

Quantitative research is research that uses numerical data collection techniques, and is generally statistically-based, meaning various computations of numbers are used to prove or disapprove a hypothesis (Coladarci, Cobb, Minium, & Clarke, 2004; Gall, Borg, & Gall, 2003; Gorard, 2001). Quantitative research designs reduce the often complex variables of teaching and learning to objective, numerical measurements. Common quantitative approaches include *correlational*, *causal-comparative*, and *experimental designs* (see tables 1.1, 1.2, and 1.3). The objective positioning of quantitative research enables the researcher to observe and collect data that will further the understanding of what is being studied.

Researchers using quantitative methods in school settings often begin with the idea that certain pedagogies can be proven useful in teaching and learning to all students. Therefore, their methodologies include the use of statistical analysis and rely upon appropriate sample sizes in order to make their work statistically significant. If a teaching approach is found to produce better outcomes in a statistically significant test with population, then it can be generalized that the approach will be successful when teaching most students. Validity and reliability in quantitative research are generally established by (1) the presence of a statistically significant sample population; (2) the appropriate application of statistical analysis; (3) the identification of all critical and influencing variables; and (4) the objectivity of the researcher.

The cultural context section in chapter 4 provides a discussion about statistical analysis in educational research. This section will explain much more about quantitative methods and how to interpret quantitative studies.

As you read through the tables 1.1, 1.2 and 1.3, how did you respond? Be mindful of your reactions. Did you find yourself skimming over the material, or did you find this information intriguing? How would you characterize the tone or feel of these research designs? These reactions may be indications of how this type of research fits your personal paradigm concerning teaching, researching, and learning. From these brief descriptions of possible action research designs, what about them seems useful? What might be dangerous about such designs? How possible would it be to use these designs as a classroom teacher?

➜ TABLE 1.1: Correlational Research

Purpose	Methodology	Validity and Reliability
To investigate the strength of possible relationships among two or more variables in a given population.	Sample population is measured with respect to two or more variables. Statistical analysis of data shows the degree to which variables are related to each other within the population.	Established by calculating correlation coefficient using inferential statistics.

Snapshot Example

Researchers wish to investigate possible links in high school seniors between grade point average and a variety of behaviors. A large population of seniors is asked to fill out a questionnaire in which they self-report the frequency and duration of many behaviors, including watching television, playing video games, doing homework, talking with friends, surfing the Internet, and involvement in extracurricular activities. The survey data is analyzed, and it is reported that a moderately strong correlation was found between extracurricular involvement and grade point average, while a slight negative correlation was found between playing video games and grade point average. No other significant correlations were found. The researchers are careful to point out that no cause-and-effect relationship has been established, and that an experimental research design would be needed to make further claims about grade point averages and behavior.

➜ TABLE 1.2: Causal/Comparative Research

Purpose	Methodology	Validity and Reliability
To explore relationships among specific conditions and a desired outcome in a population.	Sample population is assigned to two or more groups based on one or more criteria of interest. Group members are then measured with respect to one or more variables, and data analyzed to show possible relationships.	Established by using means and standard deviations in the data to calculate the statistical probability that outcomes were different between the groups.

Snapshot Example

Researchers wish to investigate how kindergarten attendance affects academic success in first grade. A large sample of first graders is identified and assigned to two groups for analysis. One group consists of children who attended kindergarten, and the other consists of children who did not attend kindergarten. The academic achievement of all of the first graders is then measured. The data is statistically analyzed to determine if there are significant differences between the two groups. It is determined that achievement was in fact notably higher in the "attended kindergarten" group, and that the difference was significant. It is reported that kindergarten attendance may be an important factor in first grade success, but it is noted that many other variables may play a role as well.

→ TABLE 1.3: Experimental Research

Purpose	Methodology	Validity and Reliability
To determine cause-and-effect relationships among specific conditions and a desired outcome in a population.	Sample population is randomly assigned to treatment and control groups. Group members are then measured with respect to one or more variables, and data analyzed to show relationships.	Established by using means and standard deviations in the data to calculate the statistical probability that outcomes were different between the groups.

Snapshot Example

Researchers wish to determine the effect of a new reading program on the reading ability of third graders. A large sample population of third graders is identified, and each teacher agrees for two weeks to randomly assign half of their class to the new reading program, while half study an alternative, traditional reading program. After the two weeks the groups switch treatments.

A reading assessment is constructed. All students are preassessed on reading level prior to receiving instruction, and are assessed again at the two-week mark, and again at the conclusion of the study. It is found that reading scores on the assessment increase more when students are instructed in the new reading program. It is reported that the new reading program has been scientifically proven to be effective in reading instruction in third graders when compared with traditional instruction.

Qualitative Research

Qualitative research embodies multiple methodologies—narrative, participatory, historical, and feminist inquiries (to name a few)—and therefore defies easy definition (Whitt, 1991). Qualitative research methods generally assume the nature of knowledge as fluid and subjective (as opposed to fixed and objective). Such knowledge is enriched by multiple viewpoints and changes as these viewpoints are used to further construct a knowledge base. Reality is not only known quantitatively, but also constructed by culture, history, and specific settings. While beliefs and values about teaching and learning vary widely among qualitative researchers, there is a sense of respect for the complex and diverse factors influencing schools. Terms like *validity* and *reliability*, which have specific definitions within quantitative research, are often replaced by the term *trustworthiness* (Lincoln & Guba, 1985), or a more recent term such as *goodness* (Arminio & Hultgren, 2002); Richardson (2003) expands the concept of "triangle" with a metaphor of a crystal, noting its multi-facet dimensions. All speak to the act of seeking a variety of voices and perspectives. Qualitative research is generally considered trustworthy if it attends to (1) multiple viewpoints as represented in data sets from multiple sources (referred to as triangulation); (2) "thick description," or research narrative rich with contextual and situational details based upon well-documented raw data; (3) being deliberate and systematic in data collection and interpretation; (4) making one's own biases or position clear; and (5) practicing critical reflection or reflexivity. (See Arminio & Hultgren, 2002; Lather, 1991, 1993; Lincoln & Guba, 2003; Whitt, 1991.

➡ TABLE 1.4: Narrative Inquiry

Purpose	Methodology	Trustworthiness
To explore the experience of schools and schooling as an observer member of the setting and context.	The researcher's goal is to determine a narrative view of the experience that is truthful, informative, and grounded in theory. Data sources include observations, interviews, and artifacts from the field.	Established by triangulation of multiple data sources and inclusion of multiple voices in the resulting narrative.

Snapshot Example

A teacher wishes to better understand the transition between middle school and high school as experienced by her students. She senses that this transition is sometimes traumatic, and desires to increase her understanding in order to better design her instruction, particularly at the beginning of the school year.

She intentionally collects narratives not only of herself through observation and journal keeping, but from students, parents, and administrators through interviews. She reconstructs the stories, collectively retelling the narrative of "coming to high school."

➡ TABLE 1.5: Participatory Inquiry

Purpose	Methodology	Trustworthiness
To collaboratively work to answer a question, solve a dilemma, or improve a situation.	The group gathers data and undertakes outside reading to inform that data. A course of action is then determined. The results are then evaluated using narrative techniques, quantitative analysis, or a combination of the two.	Established by triangulation of multiple data sources and inclusion of multiple voices in the resulting narrative.

Snapshot Example

A group of elementary school teachers has, over the last several years, become dissatisfied with the science curriculum. They have observed that the children become increasingly bored with the textbook curriculum as they progress from first through sixth grade. They decide that changes are needed, but what should those changes be? Through outside reading, analysis of the current curriculum, and dialogue among the group, it is decided that more inquiry methods should be implemented, and that a year-end science fair might heighten interest in science for the students and their families. As the changes are implemented, the group continues to collect data and to meet. During the following summer, a report is compiled and presented to the school board detailing the results of their changes, suggesting that other district schools adopt similar adjustments to the standard curriculum.

→ TABLE 1.6: Critical Inquiry

Purpose	Methodology	Trustworthiness
To address a social, economic, and/or political concern rooted in a form of injustice.	The teacher/researcher focuses on implementing an educational practice that he believes will make schools more equitable and just. Results are documented using narrative and/or quantitative techniques.	Established by triangulation of multiple data sources and inclusion of multiple voices in the resulting narrative.

Snapshot Example

A teacher is in a school that has recently undergone realignment due to redistricting. The school has as a result experienced an influx of new students, resulting in a much more ethnically diverse population. The teacher realizes that the curriculum doesn't reflect multicultural values or voices. He sets about devising a plan to implement multicultural components in his reading program. He will plan, implement, and assess the results in terms of vision, politics, and ethical responsibility. He will share his results with colleagues and the broader population in an effort to bring change to others.

Examine three different qualitative approaches common in action research in tables 1.4, 1.5 and 1.6.

As you did after reading about quantitative research, consider these questions: As you read through the above charts, how did you respond? Again, be mindful of your responses. Did you find yourself skimming over the material, or did you find this information intriguing? How would you characterize the tone or feel of these research designs? Your response may inform you about your own values and beliefs concerning teaching, researching, and learning.

The above charts are a thumbnail sketch of some qualitative research designs. From this brief description, what might be useful about such designs? What might be dangerous about such designs? How possible would it be to use these designs as a classroom teacher?

One term used in both quantitative and qualitative methods is *power*. In both forms of research, *power* means the measure of a design's ability to detect important patterns and differences that exist within the data. In other words, is the design capable of getting to the real heart of the research question? (And in qualitative research, this means recognizing that the question may have changed.) The point of differentiating between qualitative and quantitative methods is not to make an either/or distinction. Instead, making this distinction encourages a both/and approach to making action research as "powerful" as possible by seeking multiple ways of viewing research questions.

Action research is often categorized as a qualitative methodology, even though gathering quantitative data may be included as a data collection method. Why? Perhaps the answer lies in the purpose of action research: improving one's own teaching practice as well as student outcomes and, more holistically, life in schools. Generally, teacher/researchers view teaching and learning as a dynamic process that can be informed, modified, and altered through intentional planning, data collection, analysis, and self-reflection. The process of action research is the process of cocreating meaning with students and often other members of the school and community resulting in action. School communities are recognized by teacher/researchers as being complex; thus, multiple ways of looking and analyzing issues, situations, and questions require more than statistical analysis alone. These ideas are generally associated with qualitative research design.

 ## Frameworks for Action Research Commonly Used by Preservice Teachers

While the term *action research* is most closely associated with integrating practice and research, there are other forms of school-based methodologies that support the same end goal of improving one's teaching practice. Bullough and Gitlin (2001) categorize these approaches as follows: *methods of exploring self*, *methodologies for exploring school context*, and *integrating methodologies*. These methods include self-study (educational autobiography), ethnography, curriculum analysis, and integrated action. Browse tables 1.7, 1.8, 1.9 and 1.10 for more details about these action research frameworks.

➜ TABLE 1.7: Self-Study

Purpose	Methodology	Trustworthiness
To deliberately trace the process of becoming a teacher.	Analyze values, beliefs, and personal metaphors for teaching. Collect multiple perspectives on practice. Track progress in meeting goals, changing values, beliefs, and personal metaphors.	Established through "thick" reflection and description, multiple viewpoints, data sets that support goals, connection to the stories of others.

Snapshot Example

Loren grew up in rural America and understood personally words like *poverty* and *hunger*. Her desire to become a teacher came from her own belief—based on experience—that education is "the ticket" necessary for abolishing cycles of poverty. Loren reflected on and wrote on her experiences, analyzing critical incidents that led her to teacher education. She devised a schedule and plan for becoming the interactive, project-based teacher she hoped to be. Her research not only tracked her progress in becoming this teacher, but also the changes she made in her conception of school, teacher, and students. Her story, when shared with others, lends a strand to the rich tapestry of felt experiences shared by those who have become teachers.

→ TABLE 1.8: Ethnography

Purpose	Methodology	Trustworthiness
To better understand the issues of students and schooling.	Select representative students to "shadow" during their school day. Interview students and collect artifacts of their lives. Make recommendations for future teaching within the school/community context.	Established through "thick" reflection and description, triangulation in data sets, connection to contextually relevant literature.

Snapshot Example

Aaron planned to teach middle school. His own middle school experience was positive, but he was well aware that this was not the case for all students. He really wanted to get to know his students, especially since the school where he was going to student teach represented diverse ethnic groups. He used an ethnographic study to develop his own personal list of "things to remember about middle school students when I am a licensed teacher." His work, when shared with others, serves to illustrate in a general way the task of becoming a good middle school teacher.

→ TABLE 1.9: Curriculum Analysis

Purpose	Methodology	Trustworthiness
To analyze curriculum, based on the literature in the area, to ascertain strengths and weaknesses to address as a teacher.	A specific area of curriculum is identified, and an analysis rubric is developed and implemented based upon the literature from the area. Recommendations are made for teachers using the curriculum.	Established by triangulation of multiple data sources and inclusion of multiple voices in the resulting narrative.

Snapshot Example

The school where Courtney was student teaching had recently adopted a new reading series that claimed as one of its benefits an increase in elementary children's reading comprehension. Courtney developed a rubric based on what the literature reported were essential characteristics to be included in an elementary reading series. She analyzed the curriculum based on these criteria. She held focus-group discussions with third grade teachers in her team and tracked selected student progress with the curriculum. She discovered specific weaknesses that needed to be mitigated by teacher augmentation of the curriculum, as well as strengths that needed to be emphasized. Courtney's work became a powerful aid when shared with others using the same or similar curriculum.

→ TABLE 1.10: Integrated Action

Purpose	Methodology	Trustworthiness
To specifically try out a teaching method, practice, or approach in order to address a concern or to imporve student learning, attitude, or motivation.	Identify the dilemma or concern. Devise and implement a plan or strategy to address the issue. Collect data to analyze the success of the plan or strategy. Consider what has been learned about teaching and learning.	Established through "thick" description, triangulation of data sets, conclusions grounded in literature concerning the method implemented.

Snapshot Example

The students in Andrea's ninth grade basic math class had been taught the same math facts repeatedly. They simply did not understand the larger concepts behind mathematics. The students seemed to "shut down" whenever they were asked about the process behind getting the right answers to math problems. After doing some reading and discussion with her colleagues and others, Andrea decided to implement "visual math" strategies to teach not just the math facts, but the concepts and processes behind the facts.

By implementing this plan and collecting specific data, Andrea was able to understand where students were having difficulties in learning. This knowledge enabled her to develop her own teaching skills to better facilitate learning for her basic math students. As she shared her experiences with others, she was able to serve as leader in implementing the "visual math" strategy.

Self-study is presented here as an action research framework you may wish to consider. However, for preservice teachers, all of these methodologies represent elements of self-study. They all allow the student teacher to critically reflect on process of becoming a teacher. All of them allow the student teacher to reinvent his/her image of the teacher, and to deeply consider issues of teaching and learning. All of them provide a framework the student teacher can return to as a practicing teacher and use to approach dilemmas, questions, and complexities in the classroom. Ultimately, this is why we are teacher/researchers: to continually engage and delight in the learning process with the goal of improving our own practice, the learning environment for our students, and the greater school community.

As you read through the descriptions of different types of action research, what approach seems most interesting to you? Why do you think you are drawn to this approach? (How does it reflect your paradigm?) What would be useful about this approach in your process of becoming a teacher? What might be left out by this approach? What does your selection of this approach say about your own values and beliefs about teaching and the teacher you want to become? Which of these approaches do you think would best "fit" with your student teaching and/or practicum experience?

Being a Student Teacher/Action Researcher

You were asked earlier in this chapter to reflect upon your images of *teacher* and *researcher*, reconstructing a unified concept of the teacher/researcher. You then developed a definition of action research that integrates the combined role of teacher/researcher into the context of schools and classrooms.

If you are using this book you are likely also involved in another role, that of student. Your beliefs about what it is to be a good student will complicate and potentially enrich your action research project. The goal of the next section is for you to expand your definition of action research to include your role as a student teacher, a guest in a school and classroom.

To continue to develop your definition and understanding of action research, consider separately your image of a student. In your notebook, write quickly some descriptive words or phrases you associate with the term *student*. Recall some critical moments of your experiences as a student. In your notebook, record one to three examples of *yourself* as a student. Include how these examples represent you as a learner, the process of your learning, and the conditions for your learning. Combine your personal experiences as a student with your earlier descriptive words and phrases defining the term *student*. Write one or two sentences defining the overall label *student*.

Review your earlier definitions of *teacher* and *researcher* along with your new definition of *student*. Using this information and your continued thoughts on these terms, complete the chart at table 1.11.

Consider your chart and respond to the following questions:

How are the expectations for each role (teacher, researcher, student) similar?

If these titles are combined for one person, what are some spaces of possible conflict?

If these titles are combined for one person, what are the possibilities?

→ TABLE 1.11: Student Teacher/Researcher

	Key Defining Words	Public Image/Perception	Personal Metaphor
Teacher			
Researcher			
Student			

Assuming simultaneously the roles of student, teacher, and researcher involves substantial negotiations of complex political systems, boundaries of thought and expectation, and perceived notions of "success." It is critical that you consider the tensions embedded in being a student teacher/researcher. From one perspective, you are a student, a learner, someone who is acquiring theory, pedagogy, and image. From the perspective of being a teacher, you might be categorized as the "expert," who "knows the right answer." As researcher, you are asked to be the one who questions, inquires, reflects, and considers possible alternatives. Furthermore, you have your own goals, dreams, and aspirations you want to try on and try out as a teacher. And you are doing this all as a guest in someone else's classroom. You may be asked to "conform" or use teaching strategies or classroom management techniques you find do not "fit" your belief systems. As Britzman (2003) writes, "Marginally situated in two worlds, the student teacher as part student and part teacher has the dual struggle of educating others while being educated" (p. 36).

Integrating the Roles

There is a tacit, taken-for-granted, assumption that experience (as opposed to course work, reflection, and/or theory) teaches one to teach. Most teacher education departments consider the centerpiece of their program to be field experiences. But consider this: If experience is the best (and only) teacher, why do you most likely know someone who has been teaching for 30 years that you consider an ineffective teacher? What hasn't she learned from experience? "Experience" may act more to teach you to conform, fit in, or *be* the existing system; for "experience" depends on what is already known, and not necessarily what might be known or could be known if the taken-for-granted assumptions of schools and schooling were further explored. Ultimately, "Learning to teach—like teaching itself—is always the process of becoming: a time of formation and transformation, of scrutiny into what one is doing, and who one can become" (Britzman, 2003, p. 31).

Your teacher-education lived experience will be a time of transformation (Beijaard, Meijer, & Verloop, 2004; Britzman, 2003; Coldron & Smith; 1999; Gee, 2001; Marsh, 2002; Phillips, 2002; Zembylas, 2003). Your own assumptions, theories, and beliefs may be questioned; indeed, you may wonder at times if you should continue the process of becoming a teacher. For others, the teacher-education program is a time of affirmation and the transformation from student to teacher/researcher is perpetually balanced by rewards of fulfilling one's dream. For most student teacher/researchers, there are times when the context of school and being a student teacher demands that ideals and dreams are set aside. Lacey (1977) refers to this as "strategic compliance."

We agree with Bullough and Gitlin (2001) who write,

Whatever approach is taken, you need to be acutely aware of the process of negotiation itself if you desire to direct it. Beginning teachers must be not only students of teaching but also students of their own development . . . to be such a student requires knowledge of self and of context and knowledge gathered in systematic and ongoing ways about the interaction of self and context. (p. 48)

The process of action research provides such a space in which you may consider deeply who you are becoming as a teacher and why you are becoming that teacher. The cultural context section in the next chapter will better equip you for negotiating the role of student teacher/researcher. It will acquaint you with the culture of the school where you will be teaching/researching.

Critical Considerations for Being a Student Teacher/Action Researcher

To explore the complexities of being student, teacher, and researcher, we next consider the guest status of "student teacher." We then apply the work of Clandinin and Connelly (1994; 1995; 1996; 2000) by considering the concepts of *secret*, *cover*, and *sacred* stories.

Guest Status

As a student teacher, you are a guest in someone else's classroom. As a guest, there are certain procedures, processes, and rules with which you will need to conform. As a guest, you need to be mindful of your mentor-teacher's role as "host" even as you are trying on your own version of what it might mean to be a teacher yourself. As a guest, you are not a permanent member of the classroom. You will leave and the mentor-teacher will continue teaching in the school and district. Mentor-teachers all share space and power in different ways; all mentor-teachers communicate in different styles. Learn to "read" your mentor-teacher and his/her classroom well. This will be important as you conduct your action research project.

Time Constraints

A major influence on your action research project will be in the area of time constraints. Some student teachers are in the classroom for a full school year; others are in the classroom for a much shorter amount of time. In almost all cases, student teachers are involved not only in teaching but in coursework and program projects. Design an action research approach that is appropriate to the amount of time you have in the classroom and is compatible with other obligations.

Context Constraints

Most action research projects are subject to various types of context constraints. These include the student teacher's limited experience as a teacher and a limited knowledge/understanding of the school, district, and/or community where she is placed. Part of the action research process includes acquiring knowledge/understanding in these areas and scrutinizing the influences of the latter on the teaching/learning process. Even in instances where student teachers are familiar with the specific school, district, and/or community where they are student teaching, we often find that the change in roles from parent, instructional aide, or student to teacher requires relearning and deepening assumptions about the context. Activities in this book will help you do this.

Multiple, Uncontrollable Factors

Schools are places of chaos in which continual novelty is generated. Schools and classrooms involve multiple, uncontrollable factors; we argue that this is one of the reasons why they are such intriguing places for learning! For the student teacher/researcher, however, this can be a source of frustration. Plans are disrupted and schedules are changed. As a student teacher/researcher, document these "disruptions" and embrace them as sources of data and grist for reflection and change. Often these seeming distractions are simply life trying to tell us something important. Write in your notebook or journal about how they influence your project. And, constantly be in dialogue with your mentor-teacher. Be honest about your needs. Discuss the process. Be deliberate in your action research plan, but be flexible when circumstances merit modifications.

The Great Aha! The Transformation Factor

Becoming a teacher is a process we hope continues for the life of your career in education. Can one really ever "arrive" and stop learning the intricacies of what it means to be a teacher? We don't think so. Conducting an action research project as a student teacher/researcher can initiate a continuous process of transformation. This may mean that your carefully planned action research project takes an unexpected change when you study the data and find that your original assumptions must be discarded. It may mean that instead of one answer to your question, you have five additional questions and no "real" answer. It may mean that the entire framework for your project is based upon assumptions that have no substantial merit in the context of your teaching. Remember, in action research, the goal is not to *prove* something to be "true" or "untrue." Rather, the goals cluster around discovering yourself as a teacher, improving your own emerging practice as a teacher, and facilitating learning for students. This is a messy process; leave yourself open to this kind of open-ended process of discovery.

Leave yourself open for *transformation.*

Simply learning to adopt the multiple roles required of professional educators can be a catalyst for growth. For our student teachers, transformation occurs while being simultaneously a student, teacher, and researcher and a guest in a student teaching setting. Consider the following stories of student teachers negotiating their new identities.

Inside Track: Secret, Cover, and Sacred Stories

In this section we tell the story of two student teachers as they grapple with the roles of student, teacher, and researcher. Clandinin and Connelly (1994; 1995; 1996; 2000) use a narrative structure to describe the lived experience of teachers. Specifically, they identify three kinds of "stories," or narratives, teachers use: *secret, cover,* and *sacred.* Secret stories are those the teacher lives out within the safety of the classroom. Cover stories are those a teacher might tell to disguise the secret practices within the classroom. Sacred stories are those imposed upon teachers via the district office or state or federal governments. The use of this narrative structure to tell the stories of teachers is useful in highlighting the dilemmas, contradictions, and demands teachers live among and around. Such a structure can also be instructive to preservice teachers, who enter the classroom of a mentor-teacher as both a guest and a student.

Phillips (2001) considers the use of narratives in a case study of two preservice teachers' student teaching in two different schools. Both student teachers were asked to conform and to demonstrate competence in teaching, as told by the schools' sacred story, and both struggled with feeling that the approach to teaching they were asked to assume did not represent the best kind of teaching or teaching that "fit" their style.

One student teacher, however, was able to observe, listen, and ascertain not only the sacred, but also the cover and secret, stories of her school. Even though visual mathematics, for example, was not encouraged (sacred story), she found a closet full of manipulatives (secret story). And although the school had adopted a scripted reading program, she discovered sets of novels in yet another "hidden" space. She began careful conversations with her mentor-teacher concerning these "other" teaching strategies and soon, by using the language of the sacred story (state standards and federal mandated testing), she was able to participate not only in her mentor-teacher's cover story, satisfying the demand of the sacred story, but also the teacher's secret stories by using such mathematic and reading strategies in her teaching. This student teacher learned to negotiate power systems at her school by using the sacred story to adopt desired teaching strategies.

The second student teacher did not learn these skills of negotiation. She was more direct and adamant about her philosophies of teaching and was more open in her disagreement with the host school's approach to teaching science. She was offended at the expectation that she, as a student teacher, had to teach science in a traditional manner when research supported an inquiry approach. As a student teacher she maintained that she should be able to explore multiple points of pedagogy. However, her directness, in this instance, forced her mentor-teacher to speak more firmly the sacred story, perhaps in order to protect her own secret stories.

The experience of these two student teachers cannot be generalized for all student teaching experiences, nor are they told here to say there is a "right" or "wrong" way to enter the classroom as a student teacher. They are told to illustrate the kinds of political landscapes that student teachers may be asked to negotiate. Student teachers often have competing demands: teacher-education program competencies, state and/or federal competencies, district and school expectations, and the mentor-teacher's own expectations of what a "good teacher" might be. These are not always aligned, and often represent different kinds of secret, cover, and sacred stories. Furthermore, student teachers are often asked to demonstrate the more traditional version of the "good teacher" before being allowed to deviate from this image. In other words, they must demonstrate their ability to tell the sacred story.

While such demands can certainly complicate the process of learning to teach, they also represent the systems at play for many in-service teachers. In this way, learning to teach *is* learning to negotiate the political landscapes of schools.

Applying the Three Stories to Action Research

Being cognizant of this concept when conducting research in another's classroom can be critical. The student teacher may, for example, be excited about a certain approach to teaching and may anticipate "trying this out" in the mentor-teacher's classroom. If the mentor-teacher is resistant to the idea, the student teacher may too quickly decide that the mentor-teacher is "traditional." But many other factors may be at play: the sacred story of the school or district may not support such teaching methods; the mentor-teacher may use such methods as a "secret story" but does not feel comfortable having such a story be made public. It could be that the mentor-teacher feels threatened by such methodology for a variety of reasons.

What we are suggesting is that student teachers may need to become students of stories. They may need to listen hard to what is being said around them. What "code" language, if any, is used? How are teachers at the school site negotiating government demands? How are they aligning themselves or resisting such demands? What are the differences in what is said publicly and what is done privately?

There are times when student teachers must be compliant in order to gain admission into the "education club." This can be painful; sometimes, it results in a temporary loss of idealism and hope. However, as teacher educators, we have found that action research is a process that student teachers can use in powerful ways to not only support their idealism, but also to learn to teach in an influential manner. Action research, if carefully negotiated, can be an acceptable space in which to try alternative practices. In many instances, this process is shared with a mentor-teacher who equally delights in such learning and supports the student teacher during the difficult times of becoming a teacher.

In your role as student teacher/researchers, we encourage you to enter the classroom as story collectors. Perhaps this is the first critical trait of all excellent teacher/researchers: the ability to hear in multiple layers the stories administrators, teachers, and students tell of their lives. Expect such stories to be contradictory—even as your own stories may be replete with such contradictions. And know that in the retelling of such stories we bring new questions into our lives that keep us intrigued with the teaching/learning process, even as such retellings help us to make sense of our lived experiences.

 Reconstruction: What I Understand Now About Action Research

Throughout this first chapter you have engaged in multiple ways of considering who you are right now as a student entering professional education, and who you might be asked to be as a student teacher. You've also considered what action research is and how action research might for you be part of this process.

Here we've asked you to integrate your concepts of *teacher*, *researcher*, and *student* to create a more unified concept of *student teacher/researcher*. This is a critical moment in your journey since we join a long succession of educators who believe that *to teach is to do research and to do research is to teach*. This concept of *teacher/researcher* owes a rich history to such professionals as social psychologist Kurt Lewin (1948). While Lewin did not intend for his work to be used necessarily in education, his series of four cycling steps (*planning, acting, reflecting, and observing*) became useful to teacher research. Stephen Corey (1953) introduced the term *action research* to education, believing if teachers conducted their own research it would be more meaningful to them. Scholars and teachers such as Lawrence Stenhouse (1975; 1980; see also

Rudduck & Hopkins, 1985) continued to encouraged teachers to see themselves as researchers and thus evaluate their own practice. Carr and Kemmis's *Becoming Critical: Education, Knowledge, and Action Research* (1986), followed by Kemmis and McTaggart's *The Action Research Planner* (1988), contributed to the rising tide of teachers who assumed the identity of *researcher* in their classrooms. There are many recognizable names in the action research field, such as Cochran-Smith and Lytle (1993), Ellliot (1991), McNiff, Lomax, and Whitehouse (2003), Noffke and Stevenson (1995), Schon (1990), and Zeichner and Gore (1995). All have contributed in demonstrating the positive influence of action research as professional development for both in-service and preservice teachers and as a powerful vehicle for altering the status quo of schools. Many others have since added to this rich tradition, including theorists, philosophers, educational researchers, and a host of classroom teacher/researchers, making the community of action researchers lively, diverse, and international (Kemmis & McTaggart, 2003; Zeichner, 2001).

There are some general themes across the various kinds of action research (participatory research, critical action research, classroom action research, and action learning, among others). These themes include the belief that research should involve teachers *inside* the classroom rather than solely by specialists from *outside* the classroom; therefore, teacher research is focused on teacher empowerment, giving voice to the experiences of practitioners. Another theme that resonates is that critical reflection doesn't just happen. Critical reflection must be deliberate and result in transformed practice. Action research is often done in collaboration either informally or formally; such collaboration is often a way to make the research more credible. Finally, teaching and research are viewed as involving a continuous cycle or spiral of planning, implementing, and reflecting and/or evaluating (figure 1.12):

➡ FIGURE 1.12: Cycle of Action Research

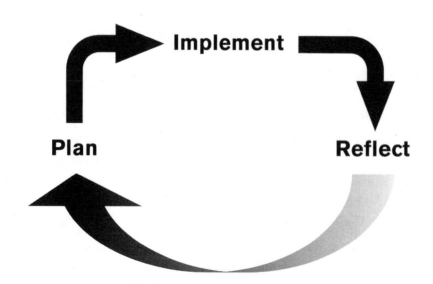

Characteristics of "good teaching," then, involve the refined skills of observation and listening and the ability to place what we see and hear into the social, political, and economic context of both the local and broader school setting; hence the title of this book, *Becoming a Teacher through Action Research: Process, Context, and Self-Study*. For this volume we have selected methodologies and methods from across the field of qualitative/action research (e.g. Clandinin & Connolly, 2000; Kemmis & McTaggart, 2003; Patton, 2002; Reinharz, 1992; Shank, 2002; St. Pierre & Pillow, 2000); we are not presenting here the "right" way or the "only" way to do such research. We have carefully limited and selected strategies we think will be most helpful to you as a student teacher/researcher. We invite you to continue to infuse the concepts of *teacher* and *researcher* as you progress through this text so that you might "own it" and, by taking it into the classroom, join a host of other teacher/researchers actively practicing research to make schools a better place for students. And in the future, we invite you to explore additional paradigms, methodologies, and methods for doing teaching/researching.

 ## Action Research Today: Resources and Websites of the Action Research Community

Before continuing through the action research process, you may want to read, meet, and be further introduced to the action research community. Based upon the introductory material in this section, we also want to pose additional questions for you to consider prior to continuing with the action research process. When you respond to these questions, include assumptions that you've had to think about as you've read this text, concepts with which you agree/disagree, new understandings you are now considering, and directions in action research you think you would like to travel. When considering the last item, include why these directions seem important and appropriate to your situation and in line with your personal paradigm. Save this response. It provides a place you can return to in the future, to mark your own becoming a teacher.

What do you expect to learn from your action research project?
How do you think such learning should look?
What complications and rewards do you anticipate during the action research process?

The following is not an exhaustive list, but a sampler of the resources and websites representative of the action research community. Conduct your own web search, search your university's databases, and use library search engines to find additional resources to fit your interests and needs.

Different Approaches to Action Research and a History of the Action Research Movement

Kemmis, S., & McTaggart, R. (2003). Participatory action research. In H. K. Denzin & Y. S. Lincoln (Eds.), *Strategies of qualitative inquiry* (pp. 336–396). Thousand Oaks, CA: Sage.

Zeichner, K. (2001). Educational action research. In P. Reason & H. Bradbury (Eds.), *Handbook of action research: Participative inquiry and practice* (pp. 273–283). London: Sage.

Zeichner, K. M., & Noffke, S. E. (2001). Practitioner research. In V. Richardson (Ed.), *Handbook of research on teaching* (4th ed., pp. 298–330). Washington D.C.: American Educational Research Association.

Books that Include Chapters or Sections on Action Research Projects Conducted by In-Service Teachers

Armstrong, F., and Moore, M. (Eds.). (2004). Action research for inclusive education: Changing places, changing practices, changing minds. London: RoutledgeFalmer.

Ballenger, C. (Ed.). (2004). Regarding children's words: Teacher research language and literacy. New York: Teachers College Press.

Bisplinghoff, B. S., & Allen, J. (Eds.). (1998). Engaging teachers: Creating teaching/research relationships. Portsmouth, NH: Heinemann.

Burnaford, G., Fischer, J., & Hobson, D. (Eds.). (2001). Teachers doing research: The power of action through inquiry. Mahwah, NJ: Lawrence Erlbaum Associates.

Cochran-Smith, M., & Lytle, S. L. (Eds.). (1993). Inside/outside: Teacher research and knowledge. New York: Teachers College Press.

Meyers, E., & Rust, F. (Eds.). (2003). Taking action with teacher research. Portsmouth, NH: Heinemann.

Mohr, M., Rogers, C., Sanford, B., Nocerino, M., MacLean, M., & Clawson, S. (2004). Teacher research for better schools. New York: Teachers College Press.

Wells, G. (Ed.). (2001). Action, talk, and text: Learning and teaching through inquiry. New York: Teachers College Press.

Action Research Journals

Action Research, published by Sage. Find out more about the publication from the Sage website: <http://arj.sagepub.com/>

Educational Action Research, inspired by CARN, Collaborative Action Research Network, published by Triangle. Read more about the journal from the website: <http://www.triangle.co.uk/ear/>

Online Action Research Communities

Action Research Expeditions: <http://arexpeditions.montana.edu>. A great site edited by Michael Brody from the Montana State University School of Education. Action research papers can be downloaded from this site.

Action Research.Net: <http://www.bath.ac.uk/~edsajw/>. There are lots of resources at this website, sponsored by the University of Bath, including action research theses by teachers, a downloadable form for guiding preservice action research, and many other good discussions and information.

Action Research Network: <http://actionresearch.altec.org/>. An entire online community where researchers and professors of research can meet and interact.

Action Research Special Interest Group, American Educational Research Association: <http://coe.westga.edu/arsig/>. This site includes links to e-journals of action research and the group's newsletter (which often includes interactive discussion pieces).

CARN, Collaborative Action Research Network: <http://www.did.stu.mmu.ac.uk/carn/>. See just how wide the action research network is by perusing the good work of CARN.

Madison, WI Metropolitan School District: <http://madison.k12.wi.us/sod/car/carhomepage.html>. The site includes a good overview of action research and how it is being used in one school district.

Teacher Action Research, sponsored by EdChange Multicultural Pavilion: <http://www.edchange.org/multicultural/tar.html>.

Teachers Network: <http://www.teachersnetwork.org>. An online community "connecting innovative teachers." Snapshot examples of action research projects included at the site.

Teaching Today for Tomorrow: <http://www.7oaks.org/ttt/>. This online journal is "the work of a professional community that values dialogue, plurality and free expression of educational thought." Browsing is easy and there are many inspiring conversations.

Voices from the Field: <http://www.alliance.brown.edu/pubs/voices/index.shtml>. Stories of reform from 1999 to 2002 are included at this site.

Distant Mentors

Jean NcNiff: <http://www.jeanmcniff.com/>. McNiff has long been a leader in action research. Her website includes links to her own work and theses published by practicing teachers.

Jack Whitehead: <http://www.bath.ac.uk/~edsajw/writing.shtml>. Whitehead has worked collaboratively with Jean McNiff for over twenty years. Much of his writing on action research can be downloaded from this webpage.

A Resource Guide

Zeichner, K., & Marion, R. (2001). Practitioner resource guide for action research. Oxford, OH: National Staff Development Council.

CHAPTER 2
DISCOVERING AN AREA OF FOCUS

Introduction and Overview

We research our own issues, meaningful in our current life and practice. We pursue critical questions that resonate with our professional community and have the potential to improve teaching, learning, and life.

You have begun the action research journey by surveying the landscape over which you will travel. You have also done some introspective self-study to become aware of where action research fits into your assumptions, beliefs, and values about teaching, learning, and the world in general. You have glimpsed the action research paradigm and read the "travel journals" of others who have completed the route now set before you.

You are ready to take the first step on your own action research road trip. This step involves determining your destination and goals for the trip, the critical questions you seek to understand on your journey. We use the term *critical question* in place of the usual *research question* because we believe that the focus of your action research plays an essential, even critical role in your process of becoming a teacher. Your critical questions must be meaningful *now*, not in some distant, abstract, or imaginary future. Your critical questions must connect with the larger community of professionals to which you are becoming a member. Most important, your critical questions must have the ability to make teaching, learning, and life in schools better.

This is a tall order, perhaps too tall for people who are simply seeking to become teachers. Some of our students ask, "Why bother? Isn't the work of getting my initial license enough? Isn't my student teaching and coursework enough? Isn't trying to please my mentor-teacher enough?" Most of our students will make very good teachers without the action research project, and when asked, we tell them so. But we hasten to remind our students that we believe that changing schools and making more powerful learning for *all* children is a task that demands more than simply being a very good teacher.

Changing schools demands that teachers have skills, habits, and a framework for looking at the world that comes through doing an action research project. Persevering in the face of burnout and discouragement demands critical self-study and reflective skills, the joy of discovery, and confidence in the pedagogical decisions you make; these are nurtured through the work of action research.

The action research journey may seem long and impossible, and you may wish you could simply read about the journey rather than risk the journey yourself. As you take these first tentative steps toward your goal of becoming a powerful teacher, let your concerns and fears take you to the places you need to go to find a destination that will transform the action research trip from a single place of arrival into a critical project of becoming. This chapter lays out a process for helping you discover your critical questions and area of focus. You may not need to travel through this entire process. If at any time you experience an "Aha!" moment and the area of focus becomes very clear, feel free to skip ahead to the "Formulating a Question" section later in this chapter. If you do this, however, slow down and take a look at the later section, "Building a Research Community: Colleagues, Coursework, and Literature."

 ### Exploring Areas of Interest: Listening to the Self

We research our own issues . . .

The essence of teacher research is the pursuit of one's own issues and concerns. Throughout this and the next few sections, you will have the opportunity to brainstorm possible topics of interest for your action research project. We suggest many different formats, prompts, and techniques for doing this. Not all of our ideas may resonate with you; you should feel free to pick and choose those which seem to be leading you in the right direction. Remember, there is no formula for finding your critical question. You must be willing to follow your intuition and hunches as well as listen to what your setting and practice are saying. We hope our activities help you do this.

Begin by returning to your notes and ideas from the previous chapter and particularly the "Self-Study: Personal Interview" activity. Review some of your core values and beliefs about teaching and learning. As you review these ideas, do any stand out as possible areas of interest for your action research project? Record these and any new ideas you have in your notebook or journal.

What are some political, social, and economic concerns you have that could be related to classroom teaching? What curiosities do you have about teaching and learning? Are there processes, issues, dilemmas you wish you understood better? Are there situations in the classroom with which you are dissatisfied? Do you wonder what happens when certain actions are put into play? What other concerns and/or challenges do you either personally face (or fear) in teaching? What do you want to achieve as a teacher? Who do you want to be as a teacher? What skills, content, and emotional fortitude do you need to become that teacher?

As you look over your responses, try to summarize your thoughts. What do the ideas share? What ideas strike you as worthy of pursuing and at the same time pursuable as you become a teacher? Write down notes about your initial thoughts.

In the next section you will continue to explore and brainstorm action research possibilities by problematizing your practice. You will return to these ideas later to further define your critical question.

Exploring Your School Context: Listening to Your Setting

. . . meaningful in our current life and practice.

For many of our students the most difficult phase in forming a critical question for action research is moving from broad concerns, curiosities, and wonderings to a focused question appropriate for the task at hand. To transform your personal concerns into a relevant question for study requires that you examine your current teaching practice and setting in light of your wonderings. We use the metaphor of *listening* to describe this process, sometimes referred to as *problematizing your practice* (Arhar, Holly, & Kasten, 2001). Learning to listen to your setting is the next step in giving your action research project a powerful life of its own.

Activity: Problematizing Practice Case Studies

Practice problematizing practice by reading through one of the student teacher case studies. We include early childhood, middle school, and high school teachers in this section; choose the one that best fits your interest.

Activity: Problematizing Practice Case Studies

More case studies may be explored on the supplementary CD.

Case Study 1: Early Childhood Education

Today I tried to teach a lesson on sentence fluency. Not so good. I am not sure what happened. The material was prepared, the examples were given, maybe it was the assignment. I asked the students to create a four-sentence poem. I read them some examples, I modeled for them. I had a lot of questions, from all my levels of students. When I collected the papers, a lot had not followed a poem format, at least not one that I recognized. I am not sure if I thought the work was going to be extremely different from the five facts book (we did earlier this week), the two activities are very similar, in some way, identical.

Given the fact that it appeared to me as no one knew what they were doing, the classroom seemed to be on task. Let me say that again: I think they thought they knew what to do; it was just different than I had perceived.

I am not sure if the objectives were met. After collecting the papers I blew the entire lesson and moved right into our reader's workshop. I was so frustrated with myself and the lesson that I just wanted it to be over. I figured that if I tried to have a closure with the students I would just be looking at blank faces. I thought that if I tried to have them answer questions about what good writers do they would mention all the previous points taught and they would miss today's objective. I didn't want to frustrate them or myself anymore.

The strength in today's lesson was the trust that I had from the kids. They so wanted to get it. While I thought it was confusing and the worst thing ever done, the students still stayed as busy as they could and only got out of their seats to ask me questions. I would send them back to their seats and ask for a quiet hand raised, they would comply, and I would work my way to them. They really wanted to do the assignment right.

Today I learned that no matter how good a unit is going, one piece of it will be your weakest link and hopefully you will have gained enough trust from your students so they will remain interested in the rest of the unit. I learned that each lesson requires a lot of thought and planning. I think this one may have been hastily thrown together in order to cover the writing strand. I think there was a better way to teach this point, maybe a different book and assignment. I think that if we had had an activity on the floor that was similar to the Delicious Words (the one we did last week) sentence fluency would be just as understood.

If I could redo this day I would not use *Animals Animals* as the read-aloud [text]. One thing that has been consistent in this unit is the tie from the book to the lesson. I think that this book was a bad choice. I am not sure what choice would have been better. I also would understand the importance of sentence fluency a lot more. I think that I went in today ready to teach sentence fluency and don't have a good grasp on what it is.

For the students I think today's lesson was a flop; for me it was a huge eye-opener. I was so happy with the way things were going that I let my guard down. I thought that every lesson was going to go as well as they had been—wrong. I think that because I thought that, I came in less prepared today, not having given myself as much background on the subject as I had for others.

Case Study 2: Middle School

Today I was frustrated. For the first time I felt as if the kids had taken advantage of my "niceness." I gave them the whole class to work on their personal history projects as the presentations are due next week and Wednesday is grading day, with Thursday and Friday off for Thanksgiving.

The students who were building their presentations on Apple Works or those who needed to scan in pictures went to the computer lab with my mentor-teacher. All others stayed in the classroom with me. This flexibility—because there were two of us—was wonderful, and breaking them into two smaller groups had its appeal by allowing more one-on-one time for students.

However, soon many started to socialize too much and some just put their work away and started goofing around. I asked them to get their work out and help each other if needed. They were allowed to talk quietly as long as they continued to work as several were making posters, etc. When this didn't happen I asked everyone to be quiet and gave them a quick talk about the time I was giving them to work and how we could be doing a lesson instead. And then I gave them about three more minutes to get on task.

When this didn't happen I told them all to be quiet and work. They were shocked that I was unhappy with them. However, two students continued to try to talk and so I gave a citation. It is the first citation I have given and I didn't want to give it. I have done citations before at previous schools, but these kids are good for the most part and I felt that I was being taken advantage of in my goal to give them the ultimate time to work on and finish their projects so they didn't have to do so over the holiday.

Another one almost got a citation for a chair incident but the other boy involved defended him, and though I wasn't sure he was totally innocent I let it go and discussed it with my mentor-teacher, who said I did the right thing. However, he (the student) hopefully now knows that I will not hesitate to use the citation option if I need to.

As tomorrow is grading day, I did grades for the assignments that I was responsible for to give to my mentor-teacher. I carefully planned out everything in advance in our unit, assigning points for the work so that they would equal the total unit amount and be based on the project. But in reality, the family tree seemed to be much harder for some of the students and should have been worth more points than I assigned. I adjusted the work by dropping one map assignment that somewhat duplicated what we did on another, which made something else that wasn't as difficult as the family tree worth almost as much. This seems to be a balancing act.

Case Study 3: High School

Today was my first management and defiance issue. (Background information: today and yesterday half of the students [were observants] in the early childhood development center and the other half were in class; and then they switched.) B. (a student) missed her observation day, as did a few other students. I made the announcement that students needed to remain in their assigned groups and would need to make up the day's work accordingly (either their observation or the class activities). B. decided to go to observe despite my announcement. I hadn't realized this until the end of class; when she came back in I talked with my mentor-teacher about what had happened and then I talked to B. after class. I told her that she needed to make up the time with me in the Family and Consumer Studies office before or after school or during lunch, or that I would write her a referral for defiance because she basically left the classroom without permission. She rolled her eyes and told me that she couldn't today; I said, "Then Monday"; she basically said, "Whatever," and walked off. I have had little encounters with B. before about talking when I was, about not following directions, and about not doing her work, but it was never to this degree of direct defiance. I really don't want this to turn into a Power Struggle.

Use the following questions to problematize the case study or studies of your choice:

What are the student teacher's motives?

What are the student teacher's biases?

What appears to be the problem(s)?

What are some sources to the problem(s)?

What are some different biases and stereotypes reflected in the sources you listed?

How are the student teacher's actions useful and dangerous?

If you are not yet working in a student-teaching placement, skip the next section and return to the activities when you are in your student-teaching setting.

Problematizing Your Own Practice

Of course, the real goal is to problematize *your own* practice. Think of instances from your own student teaching and/or observational experiences. Perhaps you have already begun writing formal observations of your classroom or have compiled a number of written reflections of your own teaching, your mentor-teacher's teaching, or about the classroom setting.

Using whatever data sources you have at your disposal, develop one or more incidents from your student teaching so far. Use formal observations, reflections, and memory to tell a story from your classroom experience. Return to the questions used above in "Problematizing Practice Case Studies." Personalize these questions and analyze your teaching incident.

Listening to Your Setting

In problematizing your own practice, you have spent some time engaged in what we call *listening to your setting*. As teacher/researchers it is critical that we learn to examine our settings—communities, schools, classrooms, and students—closely, with an ear to what direction our settings may be leading us.

What is your setting telling you? Have issues emerged that connect with your own personal concerns and issues in teaching, learning, classrooms, and schools? Take a moment to summarize your process to this point. What potential critical questions does your summary suggest?

Building a Research Community: Colleagues, Coursework, and Literature

We pursue critical questions that resonate with our professional community . . .

Teacher action research is often focused on professional practice in classrooms. As such, it runs the risk of being isolated from the larger community of teachers, scholars, and other stakeholders in the process of teaching and learning. As teachers we must not allow ourselves to become isolated by our own theories, beliefs, and ways of teaching and learning. We believe that powerful action research is created at the intersection of the internal and external, the private and the public, and even the present and the past. In this section you will begin forming this intersection by building around the context of your action research journey a learning relationship with a trusted friend or colleague.

Establishing a Critical Colleague Relationship

Our action research doesn't take place isolated from those around us. Our friends, colleagues, students, adminis-

Cultural Context: Getting to Know Your Classroom Culture

Critical questions for action research can often be found embedded in issues and needs at the school setting where teachers teach and live their professional lives. Frank (1999) writes, "classrooms are particular social settings, mini-cultures in themselves, that are not universal. Events are different in classrooms because teachers and students are different, establishing and creating their own rights and obligations, roles and relationships, and norms and expectations" (p. 7). Knowing the school and classroom culture where you will be student teaching will give you insight into how to make your lessons relevant, what kind of assessments to use, possible action research topics, and what kinds of actions will be valued by the school and classroom community.

To gather data about the classroom where you will be teaching, you will be using both formal and informal techniques. Practice listening well to the language that is allowed (and not allowed) in the classroom by both the teacher and the students, note the behaviors that are affirmed and condoned, and observe the structures for learning most often used and those structures least used.

Classroom Data Collection 1: The Classroom Map

 1. Draw a map of the classroom. Include all physical details, including where desks and/or tables and other furniture is arranged. Note items on the wall and other artifacts that lend ambience to the room. Include computers, sandboxes, rug areas, or libraries. Attend to as many details as you can in your map.

2. Visit with your mentor-teacher about the environmental setup of the room. Ask her/his rationale for arranging the room in such a way. Be curious; avoid being judgmental.

3. Analyze the items on the map by considering the following questions:

How does the classroom represent a "typical" classroom for you?

continues ➡

trators, and extended community all play a role in forming our questions, designing our studies, and interpreting our results. Many of those who influence us as we journey through action research do so in unintentional ways. However, we also meet fellow travelers who accompany us more intentionally as mentors, guides, muses, and—sometimes—critics. These become our *critical colleagues,* coaches and peers who lead us down paths and through thickets through which we would stumble on our own and probably choose to avoid altogether if we could.

McNiff, Lomax, and Whitehead (2003) write the following about the role of critical colleagues in the action research process:

Your critical friends should be willing to discuss your work sympathetically but critically. You and your critical friends choose each other, so you need to negotiate the ground rules of your relationship. They may turn out to be your closest allies, so never take them for granted. As well as expecting support from your friends, you must also be prepared to support them in return. This means being available, even in antisocial hours, offering as well as receiving advice, even if it is painful or unwelcome, and always aiming to praise and support. (pp. 38–39)

Identify a person who can be your critical colleague throughout the action research process. Find someone who you know will be honest and from whom you are willing to accept suggestions. Begin your relationship by reviewing some of your notes in this section; discuss possible areas of interest and critical questions that you think may become your action research project. If your critical colleague isn't nearby, send an e-mail if you can—

What might be missing from this classroom?

What does the environmental setup of the classroom suggest about the teacher's philosophy for teaching and learning? How does it not seem to support the teacher's philosophy for teaching and learning?

How does the environmental setup of the room support the developmental needs of the children or adolescents in this classroom?

How does or doesn't the classroom represent the gender and ethnicity of students in the classroom?

Note where the teacher's desk is: how does this position the teacher?

If there are posted rules, slogans, or inspirational phrases, how might they be categorized? Who and what do they represent?

Write several synthesis statements about what the data might suggest about the classroom culture. Do these synthesis statements suggest possible action research project topics for you? If so, what are they? "Test" these synthesis statements as you continue to be present in the classroom. Revise them as necessary as your insights continue to expand.

Mentor-Teacher Interview

Printable CD Extra: Mentor-Teacher Interview

The suggested questions may be downloaded from the CD.

One of the most important things you can do as a student teacher is to deliberately interview your mentor-teacher about various aspects of the classroom. It is much better to ask rather than to assume through uninformed judgments. Having written this, we realize that mentor-teachers are busy people; they may not have the time to sit down and answer questions over coffee. However, you can have a list of questions ready and ask them throughout the day. Just make sure your mentor/teacher knows that you are doing this and understands the reason you are asking such questions.

Here are some suggested interview questions:

continues →

beginning this relationship deserves care and attention.

Self-Study Activity: Images of the Self

This activity may be completed on the companion CD.

Applying Teacher-Education Course Knowledge

One of the most relevant places where the learning community is fostered is within your teacher-education courses. When considering a research topic, begin by thinking through courses you have taken (or are currently taking) and asking yourself, "How could the knowledge gained in these courses become an action research project?" For example, methods courses provide a plethora of specific teaching and learning strategies. Which of these strategies do you find yourself most curious about? When you learn about some strategies, do you find yourself saying, "I wish I could have learned in this way!" or "I remember a learning experience using a strategy like this and it was so effective!" Other courses like those in human development, practicing diversity, or teaching in an inclusive classroom all provide not only strategies that are potential research topics but also frameworks for critiquing curriculum. Often teacher-education programs include specialty courses in technology, multiple intelligences, or classroom management. If these topics interest you, consider exploring them further, first with your critical colleague, then through connection to distant colleagues.

How is a typical class period and/or day structured?

What kinds of things interfere with this structure?

Are any students regularly pulled out of the classroom? For what reasons?

How is the teacher creating an inclusive classroom for all students?

What routines are established and regularly used?

What does the teacher consider to be some of the most effective teaching-learning strategies for her students?

What are some of the factors the teacher believes most influence her decisions concerning teaching?

What are the rules, policies and/or consequences of the classroom? Why have these been established?

How does the teacher generally believe students, administration, community, and government mandates influence her teaching?

What issues, concerns, or dilemmas does the teacher currently have regarding her practice?

Include other questions that reflect your own areas of interests.

Analyze the data generated from this interview by grouping the data under general categories such as: Teaching and Learning Philosophy; Beliefs About Students; Structures of Classrooms. Revise or create new categories as needed. As you were categorizing the data, did you notice any particular key words or phrases the teacher used more than once during the interview?

Draft synthesis statements from the data you have collected and analyzed. How do these synthesized statements inform you as a student teacher? How do you see yourself "fitting in" to this culture? Did the interview generate any possible action research topics?

Observe

Spend at least 30 minutes observing a class session. Divide a paper into two columns: What the Teacher Said/Did and What the Students Said/Did. Record the phrases and behaviors accordingly. Attempt to do this without using biased or descriptive

continues ➡

Literature Review: Connecting to Distant Colleagues

In addition to a critical colleague, most research projects require reading and review of published work related to the area of study. We conceive of the authors of published work to be our *distant colleagues*. The work of finding our distant colleagues, sometimes called a *literature review* or *theoretical framework*, is vital in grounding the assumptions, results, and conclusions of your research in the broader context of professional inquiry. In this section you will begin this process by allowing distant colleagues through their published work to interact with your process of formulating a critical question.

By now in your academic life you may have performed web searches using tools such as Yahoo! or Google. These Internet search engines are a good place to begin the process of discovery about your area of interest. Using the areas of interests you have brainstormed in this section and with your critical colleague, explore the Internet to see if you can further refine possible topics and discover new ones. (If you are already familiar with Internet searches, you may want to skip ahead to "Testing the Surf: Evaluating Internet Sources.")

Web Searching: Be a Critical Consumer of Internet Information

There are two challenges to finding information on the Internet using search engines: (1) knowing what key words or "search terms" to enter into the search form, and (2) knowing how to critically

phrases. For example, rather than writing, "student sighs as if bored," write, "student sighs." This note taking is described further in Chapter 3: Action Research Design and Methodology.

After note taking, make notes about the observation on the right side of your paper. Pose questions, theorize, jot down additional influences. In this column you might write—opposite of the observation, "student sighs"—"Is the student bored, tired, lacking understanding . . . or just being 16?"

Now analyze the observations for patterns. What language was repeated during the session? How would you categorize "teacher talk" in this classroom? What is acceptable "student talk"? How would you categorize "teacher-student talk"? What kind of student talk was overheard? What might the teacher's behavior (actual physical actions) suggest about his view of "the teacher" and "the student"? What kind of behavior was acceptable for students? Not acceptable for students? Who was engaged most, or least, in the lesson? What does this data suggest about teaching and learning in this classroom?

Synthesize

Review all the data from Cultural Context: Getting to Know Your Classroom Culture. What patterns emerge across these data sets? For example, what language was used by the mentor-teacher across the data sets (the interview and the classroom observation)? What about the physical classroom appears to be consistent with the mentor-teacher's passions, concerns, and interactions with students? How does or doesn't the physical aspects of the classroom support student learning in the observations? What "norms" of the classroom can you identify? What inconsistencies appear to exist?

Deconstruct

Consider how your own assumptions, beliefs, and framework for teaching and learning influence your interpretation of the above data. In what ways do you find yourself intrigued by this classroom culture? In what ways do you find yourself frustrated or challenged by this classroom culture? How is this classroom the way you think education should be? How is it not what you think education should be?

evaluate the information on the websites you find. The next section will help you evaluate the quality of the websites you find. To find search terms, review your notes both from this section and from chapter 1 on becoming a student teacher/researcher. Generate a list of terms. Then, using the instructions below, proceed with your Internet search.

The Internet contains billions of webpages, and you need to find a small number that meet your needs. This is where search engines come to the rescue. From the nascence of the Internet, its engineers and users realized that searchability was the key to making it useful. There are many search engines; our favorite is Google (http://www.google.com).

Search engines work by automatically combing the entire Internet for content and indexing the results in a massive database. When you use a search engine, you enter "key words" or "search leads." The index is then searched, and you are returned a list of webpages that contain your search leads. If things go well, within the first few entries of the list you will find a webpage that contains the information for which you are looking and links to related material.

Challenges to Finding Good Internet Information

Most searches end with either (1) far too many websites to examine, or (2) no websites that have the right information. The search engine itself attempts to solve the first problem by ranking the search results in various ways in an attempt to send you the best pages for a given

Self-Study: Images of Self as Student Teacher/ Researcher

In this activity you will examine yourself as you are becoming a teacher/action researcher within your school setting. Consider these words by Lampert (2000):

For every inquiry into one's own practice, there are many possible stories to tell. For every story that is told, there are many possible meanings to interpret. Stories about practice are not mirrors of experience: like all texts, they are constructed by the author with certain intentions in mind (p. 68).

This activity is designed for you to "hear" some of the stories you are telling about your student/teaching placement and assist you in "locating" that story in your own experience, intentions, and paradigm. Doing so allows you to practice reflexivity in your research. Complete this activity after you have spent some time in your student-teaching position.

While this activity may be completed individually, as with all research, collaboration will add depth through additional perceptions. Use the synthesis statements you write at the end of this activity as a starting point for dialogue with a critical colleague.

Another variation is as follows: Assume the position of interviewer and use the questions to interview a critical colleague. Become the researcher, and based upon the information from the interview, complete the analysis, synthesis, and deconstruction. Return this analysis to your critical colleague: does she agree with your analysis? What does she "see" and "hear" in the interview that you did not? How have your own paradigms influenced the process? Using this variation will better mirror the research process.

Complete the following statements in a phrase or at most a sentence or two. Afterward you will analyze, synthesize, and deconstruct your responses.

Connections

1. My mentor-teacher reminds me of . . .
2. While in my mentor-teacher's classroom, I observed the following incident that reminded me of when I was a student . . .

continues ➡

search. Of course, this doesn't always work, but it helps a great deal.

The second problem can be tricky to solve. You may need to modify your search terms(s) so you get the right webpages. For example, Kevin throws the discus, an Olympic track and field event. When he entered "discus" into the Google search engine, a list of thousands of webpages was generated about a tropical fish people like to raise, known as (you got it) "discus." Now what? Kevin entered "discus throw" and got better results (most people don't throw their fish).

The keys to effective web searching are patience, flexibility, and knowledge about the subject you are searching for. Notice that you need to *have* knowledge to *get* knowledge. The more you know about a given topic the more different search terms you will be able to generate, and the better your searches become. If you are searching in an area that is brand new to you, this process will take patience and flexibility.

Testing the Surf: Evaluating Internet Sources

Suppose you have a generated list of websites that seem to have the information you need. Now you need to evaluate the *quality* of the information you are getting. You may already know that not everything on the Internet is true, trustworthy, or useful. It's time to become a critical consumer of all that information.

Most of the information regarding critical evaluation of Internet resources comes from libraries, which have an important stake in seeing that people become intelligent consumers of informa-

---

3. If I were a student in this classroom, what I would enjoy most is . . .
4. If I were a student in this classroom, what I would not enjoy is . . .
5. If I were a student in this class, how I would honestly respond to the question "What are you learning in school?" is . . . (Note: content or skills are not always what are learned.)

Questions

6. The procedures and/or processes that I question most about this classroom are . . .
7. The strategy I observed being used in this classroom that I'd like to know more about is . . .
8. I find it interesting that my mentor-teacher made this choice. What I would like to ask about this is . . .

Surprises

9. What surprises me most about the student(s) is . . .
10. What surprises me most about this classroom is . . .
11. I just never thought that . . .

Anticipation

12. I can't wait to go back to this classroom because . . .

Fear

13. I am concerned about going back to this classroom because . . .

Analysis, Synthesis, and Deconstruction

You can do this activity alone, but we think it would be more useful to make this a collaborative effort. Interview your critical colleague, using these questions as conversation starters; if you need to wander to make discoveries, feel free to do so!

Connections

Step away from your answers. What do your responses tell you about your assumptions of school, teaching, and learning? What do your responses tell you about how you might define a "good teacher"? How might these assumptions both open up

continues

tion. Libraries also (and rightly so) see the Internet as a tremendous resource, both for the good and for the erroneous. As Smith (1997) writes, you must learn to always be "Testing the Surf." Remember you are choosing to allow the authors of Internet information to influence your critical question, and therefore your process of becoming a teacher. Don't invite distant colleagues who don't prove themselves trustworthy and credible.

Consider the following for Internet resources (Brandt, 2004):

Criteria for Judging Internet Resources

Who is the author?

Is she/he qualified to write this "article"?

What is her/his occupation, position, education, experience?

What are her/his credentials?

Are the facts accurate?

How does this information compare with that in other sources in the field?

Perspective

Does the author have a bias?

Does she/he express a particular point of view?

Is the author affiliated with particular organizations, institutions, associations?

Does the forum in which the information appears have a bias?

Is it directed toward a specific audience? [General public, scholars in a given field, etc.]

Where is the information "published"?

When was it written?

Purpose

To what audience is the author writing?

Is this reflected in the writing style, vocabulary, or tone?

Does the material inform? Explain? Persuade?

---

possibilities and limit learning in your own classroom?

Questions

Is there any pattern to your responses in this section? Is there a general area where questions seem to form? Are some responses more meaningful to you than others? How do these questions—or how could they—relate to the critical question for your action research project?

Surprises, Anticipation, Fear

Analyze these three areas together. How do these responses inform you of your values concerning a "good" education/teacher? What are useful and dangerous about these responses?

Synthesis

In no more than three sentences, describe yourself as a student teacher in your current classroom based upon the data produced in this activity. Is there any information here that might be useful in considering an action research topic and project?

Is there sufficient evidence?

What conclusions are drawn?

Recording Information from Your Searches

As you begin to use your search terms on the Internet, be sure to (1) record information about useful websites you visit, and (2) continually reexamine and modify your search terms. For recording your searches, create a table (see table 2.1). Be sure to use the "favorite" or "bookmark" functions on your Internet browser to store the links to useful websites. Above all, let what you find online speak to you with regard to your critical question. Let your distant colleagues further define your critical question and inspire you to know more. Note the searches and terms that seem the most fruitful as you begin to anticipate your action research project.

Re-Search: Digging Deeper to Find Distant Colleagues

While Internet searches can be fruitful, especially during your initial exploration of a critical question, the voices of our distant colleagues—those who have traveled the roads of our question before us—are found best in published books, journals, and other print media. The authors whose whispers you have uncovered in your Internet searching can be found in full voice by digging deep into the professional literature of education.

You have probably developed a good set of search terms. Now you will apply the terms to searching databases that index the professional literature of education. Your college or university li-

Cultural Context: Analyzing School Documents

To conduct this analysis, you will need to collect documents produced by the school and/or district where you are student teaching. (One official document will work; more than one allows for comparison.) The goal of your analysis is to ascertain what the official stance of the school is toward teaching and learning. This official stance more often than not represents the "sacred story" of the school (return to the previous cultural context side road if necessary). Documents that work well for this analysis include any school publication specifically written for the community, school and/or district such as school handbooks, websites, or newsletters. An interesting extension to this analysis is to collect recently published community newspapers about the school, and/or district and to compare/contrast what is said about the school in the news to the "official documents" of the school.

Analyze the Documents

1. Read through each document carefully. Note specifically any mission statements or school or district goals and objectives. Highlight specific language that addresses the following: academic expectations, behavioral expectations, parent/community expectations, and teacher expectations.

2. Create a chart and categorize the language from the documents into the areas listed above. Add an additional category for words and phrases that seem to "jump out" but don't fit any of the above categories.

3. At the bottom of each chart, summarize what is said in the documents concerning these areas.

Synthesize

1. Synthesize by looking across the categories and summaries you have made from the document study. Interpret what you think is being said about the teaching/learning process. Who are the "ideal" students, teachers, and/or parents as presented

continues ➡

brarian is your best source of information about searching the many education databases (such as the Educational Resources Information Center), and acquiring materials from the vast universe of professional knowledge that exists. Depending on the resources of your institution, you may be able to complete much or all of the search and acquisition process online.

As with Internet searches, it is important and time-saving to record and organize the results of library searches. A common academic format for compiling research information is known as an *annotated bibliography*.

 Activity: Annotated Bibliography

You may use the tool found on the companion CD to create an annotated bibliography, or make your own using the template in table 2.2.

The annotated bibliography will be used again in chapter 3 as you design your research project.

Formulating a Critical Question

. . . and have the potential to improve teaching, learning, and life.

Bring together your thoughts from the beginning of this section, your initial conversations with your critical colleague, and the knowledge gained from your first Internet and library searches to begin drafting your critical question. Consider your general areas of interests and respond to the following prompts that most seem to relate to your emerging critical questions:

What role does/should/might _____ play in the classroom?

How can I _____ as a teacher?

Will this teaching and learning strategy [name your strategy] . . . ?

in these documents? What is the "ideal" school?

2. Consider what this means to you as a student teacher/researcher. Write down possibilities but avoid conclusions.

Deconstruct

1. Consider the assumptions the documents make about students, teachers, parents, and systems for learning. What do the documents assume such groups want to hear? From where might these assumptions come?

2. Deconstruct certain words or phrases that may be commonly used among educators and are used more than once in the documents. For example, the word "excellent" is often used in such documents. "Safety" is another commonly used word. How are these words used? In what context? Are the words specifically defined? How are they defined? What are the multiple possible messages such words convey?

3. Consider your own assumptions in the interpretations you have made. What values and beliefs about education do these represent? For example, if you find yourself support- or disagreeing with statements made, consider why you hold this position and what it says about you as a future teacher/researcher.

Knowing Your Community of Practice

Getting to know your placement, your "community of practice," is about more than just gathering demographic information about the school. Coming to know your community of practice is about listening, interacting, and being aware of how you are listening and interacting. As you review the data and your interpretations, what do you want to remember as a student teacher? How have these activities informed your areas of interest for action research? Does the information open up possibilities for a critical question?

➡ TABLE 2.1: Recording Data from Web Searches

TITLE	URL	
AUTHOR	PERSPECTIVE	PURPOSE
SUMMARY		
SEARCH TERMS USED:		

What happens when . . . ?

How does this [name "this"] . . . ?

I wonder . . .

What are the consequences of . . . ?

What is it like to . . . ?

If this were changed . . . ?

Why does this incongruence . . . ?

Why is . . . ?

Spheres of Influence

Arhar, Holly, and Kasten (2001) suggest that teacher/researchers consider "areas of concern" as a way to conceptualize critical questions. Are the questions too big? Are they too small? Are the questions "doable"? How do our small questions impact the big picture? How do our big-picture concerns impact ourselves as individuals?

Consider a layered depiction of areas of concern, sometimes called "spheres of influence" (see figure 2.1). Note that we have placed *self* in the middle of the figure. We believe that change starts at the level of the teacher-self, the person from whom all other interactions flow outward; yet we also understand these same interactions to be informed by cultural context.

Now travel back through the prompts you completed at the beginning of this section. Label the sphere of influence for each of the prompts. In which spheres of influence does each lie? Do some cut across boundaries? In what way?

➔ TABLE 2.2: Recording Library Search Data

CITATION		
AUTHOR	PERSPECTIVE	PURPOSE
SUMMARY		
SEARCH TERMS USED:		

Good Action Research Questions

What makes a good action research question? We believe that your action research question has the power to create in you a new kind of teacher, energizing and inspiring you to be your best and grow in new areas and ways. You may not have thought about research in these terms before (see table 2.3). Begin to see your action research as a time of excitement, of transformation, and even joy as you become a teacher.

The Evolution of Your Critical Question

Most of our students don't feel like they know nearly enough about their placements, their settings, their classrooms,

➔ FIGURE 2.1: Spheres of Influence

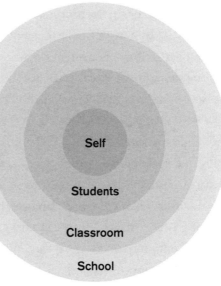

and—most important—themselves as teachers to create a critical question. This is normal. What your action research is asking you to do is to risk a journey in which those questions (think of the meaning of the word *quest*) and many more may be answered or at least better understood. In teacher action research, the questions themselves are fluid. After you formulate your initial critical question, you will return to it for sharpening, modification, and, potentially, a complete rewrite as your project progresses.

We find that many of our students' critical questions undergo a similar process of evolution as they progress through the action research project. Consider the examples of critical question evolution represented in tables 2.4 and 2.5.

➡️ TABLE 2.3: Qualities of a Good Action Research Question

Important to you	Within your sphere of influence
Contains a good idea	Authentic
Focused	Compelling
Supports mission	Benefits students
Informs your work	Is your work—not more work
Has the potential to bring you joy and satisfaction	

Drafting the Question

In chapter 1 we said that all action research studies completed by student teachers have elements of a self-study—all such projects will document your process of becoming a teacher. Therefore, use personal pronouns such as *I* or *my* in your question. Begin drafting your question with, "How can I, as a teacher, . . . ?"

🖊️ Okay—give it a try! Draft a critical question.

Your question may resemble those in the first row of tables 2.4 and 2.5 in that they will need to evolve. Go back and draft your question in two or three forms. Draft one for several areas of interests. Read the question aloud; how does it sound?

We suggest that you begin the process of refining your question right away by reviewing table 2.3. Share your question with a colleague and your mentor-teacher(s). Try it on for a few days and see if you like it. As you observe and work in your classroom, ask yourself, "Is this a meaningful question for me as a student teacher and for this classroom?" Be honest about what your colleagues and your "gut" are telling you: don't fall in love with a first-draft question!

Finally, a reminder: you are not trying to "prove" anything with your critical question. If you find "proving" language—such as, "Will guided reading or sustained silent reading most promote reading comprehension?"—revise your question. Student-teacher action research is attempting to discover something meaningful to you: lessons you can carry with you as a professional educator that will make you a wiser, smarter, more creative, joyful teacher!

After drafting your initial critical question, share it with your critical colleague and your mentor-teacher(s). Continue to allow the question(s) to evolve as you are informed by your setting, coursework, and distant colleagues.

 ## Sharpening Your Critical Question

In chapter 3 you will design an action research study to better understand your critical question. But first let's consider what type of action research approach is best suited to your critical question. Chapter 1: Research Worlds, Research Lives: Forms of Action Research presented an overview of research methodology and designs; you may want to review this section before continuing. Four kinds of action research were presented: *integrated action, self-study, ethnography,* and *curriculum analysis.*

➡ TABLE 2.4: Evolution of a Critical Question: Elementary

What strategies do my first graders prefer in learning mathematics?	First graders are not developmentally ready to articulate their preferences for learning mathematics. Even asking them what they like or dislike may not be particularly trustworthy data. Question for the teacher/researcher: If first graders could articulate a response to this question, what would you hope to discover?
What strategies do my first graders prefer when learning mathematics and how are these strategies developmentally appropriate?	This question is getting closer. It introduces the idea of "developmentally appropriate" strategies. Questions for the action researcher: If first graders choose strategies that are not developmentally appropriate (they choose them because they are colorful, for example) would this really inform your teaching? It seems like you are asking about developmentally appropriate strategies for teaching first graders mathematics. What is it you really want to find out about these?
How can I use developmentally appropriate math assessments in my first grade classroom to guide mathematical instruction?	Now the question is focused. It is within the sphere of influence for the student teacher/researcher; it benefits students and supports the development of the student teacher becoming a teacher; the results will bring the student teacher/researcher satisfaction.

➡ TABLE 2.5: Evolution of a Critical Question: Secondary

How can high school chemistry students learn to study more?	The question is too broad. Questions for the action researcher: How would you define study skills? How do you want your high school students to study? Why do you want them to study more? For what purpose?
Will teaching my high school chemistry students study skills enrich their understanding of the content area?	This is getting closer. The question now includes a purpose for using the study skills. Questions for the action researcher: Study skills is a broad area that has different meanings for different people. What specific study skills to you want to use? What would be most appropriate for your high school chemistry students? What strategies would provide you with data for intervention and supporting student learning?
Will the use of graphic organizers, quick draw chalkboards, and review games increase my high school chemistry students' content knowledge and understanding?	The question is now focused. Specific study skills are identified for use in the classroom. The purpose is clear: to increase students' content knowledge. The student teacher's own practice will be improved through the study.

We used a chart to categorize these kinds of action research (table 2.6), but a better visual may be a Venn diagram of overlapping circles (see figure 2.2):

This diagram demonstrates how elements of integrated action, self-study, ethnography, and curriculum analysis are ultimately pieces of any action research project. To better understand how these approaches overlap, consider the questions posed in figure 2.3 based on an imaginary study involving teaching math, raised by each action research methodology.

In seeking answers to any one of these questions an action researcher analyzes, to some degree or another, the other questions. Choosing the actual approach has more to do with where you will focus your inquiry: on *self*, *students*, *curriculum*, or *ethnographic interactions*.

An Additional Illustration

Note how the question changes in each of the following examples, depending on the focus of the study in table 2.7.

Using your own area of interest, complete the chart in table 2.8 to see how each approach to action research can alter the possible focus of your study. Write a different critical question for each approach using the model given in table 2.3.

Which of the above approaches best gets at your primary area of interest? Take some time to dialogue with critical colleagues, mentor-teacher(s) and instructor(s) to further narrow your action research. Revise your critical question(s) accordingly.

Cultural Context: The Importance of Context for Ramon's Action Research Project

Ramon, a student teacher, is also an artist. As an artist, he wants to learn more about how children develop an artist's identity. He wants to know how children grow in confidence in art as well as what hinders this growth. He often quotes Pablo Picasso, who once said, "All children are artists. The problem is how to remain an artist once he grows up." He envisions an action research project where he teaches art and documents upper elementary children becoming artists and growing their artists' identities.

How would Ramon apply his ideas in different communities, schools, and classrooms? Keeping in mind Ramon's idea for this action research (AR), consider the following settings. How might Ramon's AR project be influenced by each setting? How might it be adapted to better meet the needs of the students in each setting? After each school description, revise Ramon's AR project to better fit the community where he might teach.

Ramon's AR: Setting 1

Mills Elementary School serves students in kindergarten through grade 8 in a rural area consisting of five loosely connected communities; students are bused from a surrounding radius of 60 miles. There is not much ethnic diversity at this school, and most children come from poverty. Ninety-six percent of the students receive a free or reduced-price lunch paid for by a federally funded program. The school lacks adequate funding; students do not come to school with supplies, and teachers must scramble to find basics like pencils, papers, and crayons. Ramon discovers during his interviews that a pressing concern expressed by many teachers at the school is building community among the scattered families. The school also struggles with attendance rates; children are often absent. Furthermore, there is no art instruction at this school.

Considering this context, what suggestions would you give Ramon? Does he need to adapt his AR project? If so, how?

continues ➡

Ramon's AR: Setting 2

Hartford Elementary School serves students in kindergarten through grade 6 and is located in a community experiencing much growth. Not too long ago, the community of Hartford was considered rural, but agribusiness has replaced family owned farms, industry has grown, and the community is now considered to be within a short drive to a major urban area. Once primarily ethnically white, Hartford's elementary school population is now one-third Latino; for most of these children, English is a second language. The school's primary instructional mission this year is to improve overall achievement in reading as recorded on standardized exams. Most of the instructional day is prescribed by set curriculum in reading and mathematics. Other core subjects are taught on an every other day basis; "electives" such as art are taught "when there is time."

Considering this context, what suggestions would you give Ramon? Does he need to adapt his AR project? If so, how?

Ramon's AR: Setting 3

Myton Elementary School serves children in kindergarten through grade 5. It is located in a suburb of an urban area. Children come from mostly middle- to upper-income homes and most are involved in after-school activities such as soccer, dance, and/or music lessons. The parent

continues →

→ TABLE 2.6: Action Research Design Possibilities

Integrated Action	Self-Study	Ethnography	Curriculum Analysis
To specifically try out a teaching method, practice, or approach in order to address a concern or to improve student learning, attitude, or motivation.	To deliberately trace the process of becoming a teacher.	To better understand the issues of students and schooling.	To analyze curriculum, based upon the literature in the area, to ascertain strengths and weaknesses to address as a teacher.

→ FIGURE 2.2: Venn Diagram/Action Research

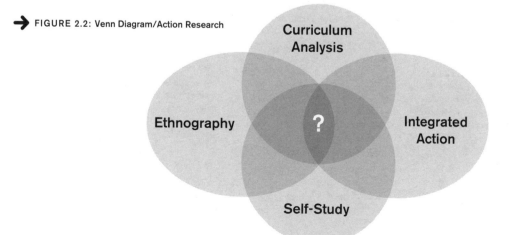

organization is strong and provides additional financial support for programs that might otherwise be cut. They make sure children are able to enjoy yearly field trips to the local science museum and the children's theater. This same organization brings art instruction to the elementary school every Friday with the assistance of a local art organization.

✎ Considering this context, what suggestions would you give Ramon? Does he need to adapt his AR project? If so, how?

Ramon's AR: Setting 4

Rosa Parks Elementary School serves students in preschool through grade 6 in an urban center. The school is ethnically diverse: primarily there are African American children, but there are also Latino, Sudanese, and Hmong. A number of languages and dialects are spoken at the school. The building itself is in the shadow of industry; pollution in the neighborhood is a concern, as the occurrence of asthma has risen dramatically over the last 10 years. Poverty raises many issues for families. Over one-third of the children have a parent incarcerated at a nearby federal prison. School funding is a perpetual problem, as school staff work to meet the multiple needs of children. The staff works to make school a safe place, an oasis for the community, providing after-school programs for children, as well as in adult literacy and English language acquisition. While art is not formally taught, teachers at the school recognize the power of art as a form of expression for children dealing with complex life issues.

✎ Considering this context, what suggestions would you give Ramon? Does he need to adapt his AR project? If so, how?

In all of these scenarios, we believe Ramon could conduct an AR project with a focus in art; however, each situation requires adaptation so that the project actually fits the needs of the children. There are multiple ways Ramon could make these modifications; brainstorm possibilities with your colleagues.

→ FIGURE 2.3: Action Research Designs and Question.

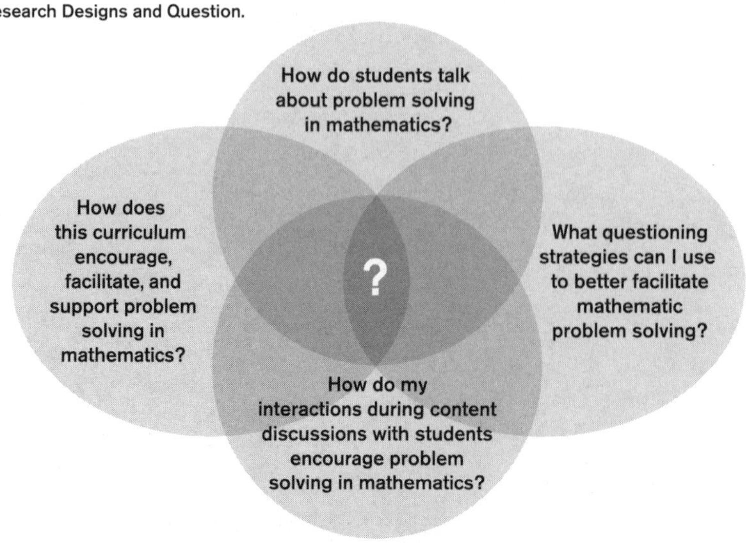

How do students talk about problem solving in mathematics?

How does this curriculum encourage, facilitate, and support problem solving in mathematics?

?

What questioning strategies can I use to better facilitate mathematic problem solving?

How do my interactions during content discussions with students encourage problem solving in mathematics?

➡ TABLE 2.7: Literature Conversations

Integrated Action	Self-Study	Ethnography	Curriculum Analysis
How can I effectively use literature conversation to increase reading comprehension?	How can I improve my questioning strategies to improve the quality of literature conversations and scaffold reading comprehension?	How do the ethnically diverse learners in my classroom talk about literature and how does this inform my assessment of reading comprehension?	In what ways is the adopted reading curriculum effective or not effective in scaffolding and encouraging literature conversations that increase reading comprehension?

➡ TABLE 2.8: Choosing a Research Focus

Area of Interest_____

Integrated Action	Self-Study	Ethnography	Curriculum Analysis

Chapter 3
Action Research Design and Methodology

Science states meanings; art expresses them.... The poetic as distanced from the prosaic, esthetic art as distinct from scientific, expression as distinct from statement, does something different from leading to an experience. It constitutes one. —John Dewey, *Art as Experience*

 Introduction to Data-Collection Methods

One cannot have an action research project without data. Data becomes the evidence of hunches, the confirmation of theory, and the source of paradigm shifts. Data collection is the evidence you will use to respond to your critical question(s) and develop further questions around your research interest. Data will determine the trustworthiness of your project, measuring its depth and defining its usefulness, determining the richness of your experience. Deliberate data collection is the extended eyes, ears, and soul of the teacher; it is the way we come to know our students, change our practice, and grow our teaching identity.

Think of data collection and interpretation as assessment. We know that assessment drives instruction. As teachers, we assess our student knowledge, skills and/or conceptual development in any given area using multiple means so that we can make wise instructional choices. This is the same process in action research: we collect data (forms of assessment) so that we can make wise instructional choices. We circle back to the concept that we are teacher/researchers, and our continual and ongoing research question is, "How can we better facilitate learning for our students?"

What does action research data look like? Consider Lisa, a student teacher examining ways of improving student math achievement by increasing on-task behavior during math time in her first grade classroom. Her mentor-teacher, Mrs. James, collected on- and off-task data while Lisa monitored math time. The students, sitting around rectangular tables, are labeled A–H on the chart. Every three minutes, from 9:00 to 9:15, Mrs. James performed a "sweep" observation of the students, recording whether each was on-task or off-task. The chart she made is shown in figure 3.1.

 **FIGURE 3.1:** Observation Data 1: On-Task/Off-Task Behavior for Students, A–H

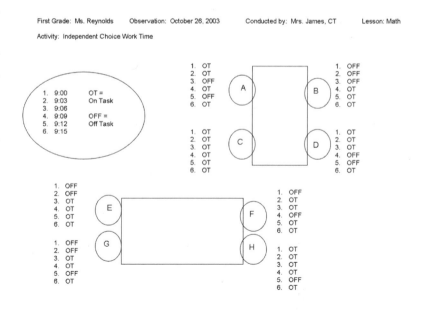

In your notebook or journal, respond to the following questions.

What information does figure 3.1 contain about on-task behavior? What information is provided about student achievement?

Lisa recorded in her notebook the results of math journal entries completed by the children before going outside to recess after the math lesson. Her notes indicated that all six students were successful in learning the math concepts in the lesson. What important information did Lisa's notes contain that the behavior chart did not?

During recess, Lisa and Mrs. James shared their information side-by-side. What questions/issues are brought up by looking at Mrs. James' chart and Lisa's notes together?

FIGURE 3.2: Observation Data 2: On-Task/Off-Task Behavior for Students, A–H

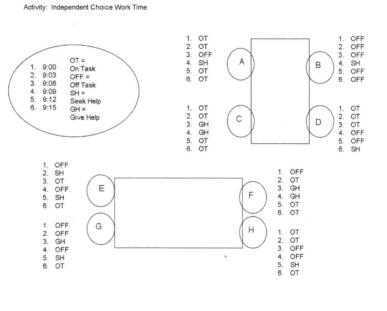

While looking over the chart and notes, Lisa and Mrs. James both saw the same contradiction: If some students were largely off task during the lesson, why didn't this result in those same students not understanding the concept? They realized that more information was needed. (Lisa jotted down a record of this meeting in her notebook.)

Two days later during math time, Mrs. James did another observation session, modified to reflect what was discovered the day before (figure 3.2). What added information is in the second observation chart? How does this information help answer Lisa and Mrs. James' questions?

What other information do you think would be helpful in analyzing Lisa's original question about on-task behavior and math achievement?

In this short example, the observation charts, math journal entries, and Lisa's notes about her meeting with Mrs. James are all different pieces of action research data, providing important information that will help Lisa answer her research question. Other sources of data related to this episode could include Lisa's lesson plans, handouts and other curriculum used, photos of the classroom arrangement, student demographic information such as gender and first language, and so on. In addition, Lisa might interview her students to confirm her hunches. The data-collection methods Lisa is using are associated with qualitative inquiry.

Throughout the rest of this text, we emphasize three broad types of action research data often associated with qualitative inquiry (see chapter 1 for more on being a student teacher/researcher): (1) observations, (2) interviews, and (3) artifacts/documents. When we have collected specific data representing all three types, we are said to have collected a complete *data set*. The purpose of this section is to help you design specific data-collection strategies that will provide a rich data set with which to provide insight and meaning around your critical question.

Why These Data-Collection Strategies?

Qualitative research is a rich and varied field, often contested and resisting standardization (Denzin & Lincoln, 2003a; Lather, 2004; Lincoln & Guba, 2003; Smith, 1993). Lincoln and Denzin (2003b) chronicle the historical field of qualitative research across seven different "moments" or periods since the early 1900s. "Qualitative research means different things in each of these moments," they note (p. 4); each moment is constructed by historical, cultural, economic, and political thought or paradigm.

We have selected specific kinds of methodologies and methods that seem most appropriate for student teacher/action researchers during this moment as viewed through the following theoretical lens or paradigm. In making these choices we:

acknowledge the role of language in constructing and limiting our understanding; therefore, the meanings we construct are partial (Britzman, 2003; Gore, 1993; Lather, 1991; Weedon, 1987)

recognize the powerful influences of culture on ourselves and our interpretations (Butler, 1997; Foucault, 1972; Lather, 1991; Spivak, 1993; Weedon, 1987)

see classrooms as places where meaning (but not always the meaning we intend) is actively constructed (Britzman, 2003; Crotty, 1998; Ellsworth, 1997)

recognize the complexities of these classrooms as the element that brings surprise, joy, and heartache to those of us who teach (Bullough, 1992; Dudley-Marling, 1997; Hargreaves, 1999).

With the above assumptions in mind, reconsider the example with which we opened this section—that of Lisa and her mentor-teacher working to understand on- and off-task behavior. We see in even this short example a layered complexity of meaning, demanding a variety of data-collection strategies as suggested in the qualitative research literature.

Data and Assessment

Action research data collection and instructional assessment share basic principles (table 3.1).

Teachers "do" research every day in their classrooms. When teachers give a test, collect drawings, review student portfolios, listen to children read, evaluate speeches, or review lab reports, they are collecting data. Once the data is interpreted, it will inform them of the effectiveness of their instructional choices and direct them in planning their next teaching steps. Seeing research data collection and instructional assessment as integrated concepts gives meaning and purpose to both. The separation of the two is often more a matter of language, than of concept. We will use the language of research throughout this text, using words like data and data collection, but behind and through these words is the idea of assessment.

→ TABLE 3.1: Shared Principles of Research Data and Instructional Assessment

Data collection and assessment are purpose-driven.	What do I want to find out?
Pairing the research and/or assessment goal with a complimentary data collection and/or assessment strategy is critical.	How does this data collection and/or assessment tool reflect what I want to know? Does the task and/or tool match my overall research/teaching goals?
Both research and assessment data require some kind of criteria and/or standard in order to be evaluated.	How will I interpret the research and/or assessment data? What criteria will I apply? Whose standard and for what purpose will these standards be used?
Research and assessment data can be isolated and useless without interpretation and action.	How will I use the results of the research and/or assessment data?

 ## The Art and Craft of Data Collection

Understanding the relationship between research data and assessment is just part of seeing data collection as both art and craft. There is art and craft in choosing the data-collection strategies, getting the data collected, organizing the data, and interpreting the data.

Here are some general guidelines for the craft of data collection:

be deliberate, even ritualistic in data collection, but, in your deliberateness, be willing to alter the plan as the data informs you

collect generously; organize diligently

collect from multiple and complimentary sources

Remember that data is lifeless without purpose and interpretation; conduct ongoing interpretation, making sure it reflects purpose. (See chapter 4 for more on ongoing data analysis, synthesis, and deconstruction.)

Here are some useful questions for the art of data collection:

Is the data collected meaningful to you? Is it enriching your understanding of teaching and learning?

Is your data gathering manageable as part of everyday teaching?

Does the data provide "Aha!" moments of clarity, help you see something you might have ignored, or confirm a long-held hunch?

Is the data assisting you in constructing meaningful responses to your critical question(s) and/or facilitating needed changes in your critical question(s)?

And finally, some advice; you won't often know what you are looking for until after you've collected it and it is too late to return and gather more data; therefore, collect, interpret, and revise your design—often. (Again, see chapter 4.) Remind yourself as often as necessary that this action research project is not about "proving" something to be true or false: this is about becoming a teacher through action research, about making discoveries in context about teaching and learning processes.

Data-Collection (Assessment) Strategies

In classroom action research, data is collected via three methods: observation, interview, and artifact. A complete data set contains data from each of these three categories. This does not mean that you will have the same amount in each category; depending upon your research question and topic, you may rely more heavily on one kind of data over another. For example, if you are focusing on a single lesson, you may take notes while students are working (observation), have several informal conversations with students (interview), and analyze submitted student work (artifact). On the other hand, you may be gathering information over a more extended time period. The point is that having significant data from each of these categories ensures multiple perspectives and voices and makes your research more trustworthy. (See chapter 4 for information on data analysis and interpretation.)

Observation

To *observe* as a student teacher/researcher is to critically and deliberately watch as a participant in the classroom. The act of observing recognizes that "live action" provides powerful insights for teacher/researchers.

Self-Study: Rethinking Your Action Research Design Through a Cultural Proficiency Lens

Making sense of a situation is always in part an act of self-understanding on the part of the researcher. How one chooses to approach a research situation is shaped by the researcher's subjectivity, his or her place in the web of reality,
—Joe Kincheloe, Teachers as Researchers: Qualitative Inquiry As a Path to Empowerment

In this activity you will evaluate yourself in terms of *cultural proficiency*. Being a culturally proficient educator is critical in any educational setting in which the goal is to teach all students. Culturally proficient teachers know how to create a learning environment in which students of all cultural backgrounds and life histories have a place for powerful learning and growth.

You may have preconceived notions about what cultural proficiency means and how it applies to you and your setting. This activity will help you define cultural proficiency in a way that applies to you, regardless of your setting. Then you will examine and rethink your action research design through a lens of cultural proficiency.

What Does It Mean to Be a "Culturally Proficient" Teacher/Action Researcher?

In your notebook or journal, write out the definition of culturally proficient as you have come to understand it in your teacher-education program. How do you think this definition does or does not apply to you as you become a teacher? What are the specific ways you might be a culturally astute teacher–action researcher?

Your comfort and ease in responding to these two questions may serve to inform you about your evolution as a culturally proficient teacher/action researcher. Evolution is a word that acknowledges that there is no arrival at cultural proficiency—we keep developing, reinventing, and revisiting our paradigm, our pedagogy, and our approaches to solving cultural issues and conflict in our classrooms and lives.

continues

Interview

To *interview* as a student teacher/researcher is to inquire, to ask questions of students, colleagues, supervisors, mentor-teachers, and others connected with your project in order to hear another side, version, or angle of the story. Note that observation data takes on the voice of the observer, while interview data takes on the voice of the person being interviewed. Interview data isn't necessarily always done verbally; surveys are also considered interview data.

Artifacts

An *artifact* is any kind of physical documentation that sheds additional perspective on your research question and topic. Artifacts are pieces of physical evidence, such as student work.

How to Collect Action Research Data

There are many ways of gathering the types of data you will use for your project. Some of these are shown in table 3.2 and further described with examples in appendix E.

Writers have adopted multiple orientations toward the concept of teacher development of cultural proficiency. For example, Howard's (1999) white identity orientation includes "modalities of growth" that illustrate white identity transformations in the areas of thinking, feeling, and acting. He describes a developing and ongoing transformation in thinking, moving from a linear, fear-driven, and autocratic position to a dynamic, self-reflective, holistic mode of thought. Such transformation means moving from a "my way is right" perspective on culture to one that is characteristic of empathy, respect, transparency, and openness to change. He describes a movement from monoculturalism and "treating all students the same" toward a place of advocacy and active learning from other cultures as Eurocentric perspectives are challenged.

Lindsey, Robins, & Terrill (2003) note, "The transformation to cultural proficiency requires time to think, reflect, assess, decide, and change" (p. 40). They focus on the transformation of behaviors. An educator who acts with cultural proficiency would exercise these "essential elements" of cultural proficiency (Self-Study figure 3.1).

This transformation requires deliberate action on each individual's part. It isn't easy to deconstruct what seems "normal" in

continues ➜

Printable CD Extra: Data-Collection Tools

Additional information and templates are available on the companion CD.

➜ **TABLE 3.2: Data-Collection Tools**

Observation	Interview	Artifact
Note taking	Survey	Student work
Anecdotal records	Questionnaire	Videotape
Logs	Attitude rating	Audiotape
Checklists	Formal interview	Photography
Mapping	Informal interview	Portfolios
Shadowing	Focus group	Student self-assessments
	Sociogram	Other school documents
	Multiple intelligence approaches	

SELF-STUDY: FIGURE 3.1

"Essential Elements of Cultural Proficiency" from Lindsey, R. B, Robins, K. N., Terrell, R. D. (2003). *Cultural proficiency: A manual for school leaders* (2nd ed). Thousand Oaks, CA: Corwin Press, Inc.

Assess Culture: *Name the Differences*

- Recognize how your culture affects the culture of others.

- Describe your own culture and the cultural norms of your organization.

- Understand how the culture of your organization affects those with different cultures.

Value Diversity: *Claim your Differences*

- Celebrate and encourage the presence of a variety of people in all activities.

- Recognize differences as diversity rather than as inappropriate responses to the environment.

- Accept that each culture finds some values and behaviors more important than others.

Manage the Dynamics of Difference: *Frame the Conflicts Caused by Differences*

- Learn effective strategies for resolving conflict, particularly among people whose cultural backgrounds and values differ.

- Understand the effect that historic distrust has on present-day interactions.

- Realize that you may misjudge others' actions based on learned expectations.

Adapt to Diversity: *Change to Make a Difference*

- Change the way things are done to acknowledge the differences that are present in the staff, clients, and community.

- Develop skills for intercultural communication.

- Institutionalize cultural interventions for conflicts and confusion caused by the dynamics of difference.

Institutionalize Cultural Knowledge: *Train about Differences*

- Incorporate cultural knowledge into the mainstream of the organization.

- Teach the origins of stereotypes and prejudices

- For staff development and education, integrate into your systems information and skills that enable all to interact effectively in a variety of intercultural situations.

While we have placed these types of data in distinct categories, recognize that there are times when the collection tool may be used for different purposes. An observation, for example, might be done via a videotape recording. A student focus group might be conducted via an audiotape recording. What makes an observation an observation, an interview an interview, and an artifact an artifact, is purpose. Let's return to the definitions:

to observe is to watch, listen in, to use the senses to gather information to interview is to inquire into another's insight

to gather artifacts is to collect physical evidence, such as student work, products, or other records or documents related to your critical question

Data from each of these categories allows you to see your critical question and topic from three distinct perspectives (figure 3.3):

Even with these three distinct perspectives, you will not necessarily see "answers" to your critical question clearly. Our understandings are always partial; we collect multiple perspectives to better piece together our seeing (Ellsworth, 1997; Haraway, 1996; Lather, 1991; Richardson, 2003).

Bringing It All Together: Your Researcher's Notebook

In qualitative research, the process of constructing a rich and varied data set is called triangulation, and it is one of the primary ways we make sure our research is trustworthy. (In chapter 4 we will discuss how to evaluate the trustworthiness of interpretations.) However, even data collected via triangulation can be isolated and taken out of context. One way a teacher/researcher can provide context to data is through a researcher's notebook. A researcher's notebook includes journal entries, sketches, and lesson plans and/or unit overviews, as well as ongoing data analysis. The notebook is also a place to organize contextual information: a list of students in the participating classes, information about those students, school demographics

our way of life. Throughout this text, we've attempted to create a scaffold around your ability to do this through various activities. We have said repeatedly that "context matters." This is because we recognize that none of us can escape being influenced by our personal culture, for culture is "everything you believe and everything you do that enables you to identify with people who are like you and that distinguishes you from people who differ from you. . . . Culture provides parameters for daily living" (Lindsey, Robins, & Terrill, 2003, p. 41).

Viewing Your Research Design Through a Cultural Proficiency Lens

What, then, does all of this have to do with your action research design? At this point, you've most likely successfully drafted the design, so why bring up cultural proficiency now? The answer: We want to be deliberate in taking time to assess our own cultural biases and to be cognizant of how these biases may influence our design. We understand, with Banks (1997), that

[e]ducators communicate their perspectives, values, and attitudes towards ethnic groups to students primarily through unwitting actions and words. Consequently, it is important for educators to examine not only the knowledge that underlies their curriculum and methods but also their own values and perspectives to determine the extent to which they promote equity and justice for all students. (p. 50)

What we learn from writers such as Banks is that we have to be purposeful to affect change. It doesn't just "naturally" happen out of our own good intentions.

FIGURE 3.3: Seeing Your Critical Question from Three Perspectives

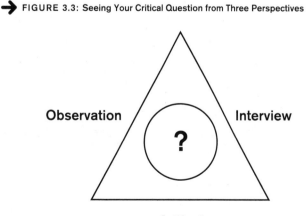

and policies, and other contextual information that may shed light upon the data collected. The researcher's notebook is confidential; it should not be kept in a public place like a classroom. While your researcher's notebook may be partially or even mostly electronic, be very careful about backing up your work and information—you have no research without your data! We suggest that student teacher/researchers take a smaller notebook to class with them to record anecdotal notes; later, place these notes in the researcher's notebook. The researcher's notebook is the mind, heart, and soul of the teacher/researcher chronicling their own reactions to data collected, analytic memos, and interpretation.

For example, Micah conducted a self-study with a focus on how to become a project-based teacher. One of the journal entries she included in her researcher's notebook is at figure 3.4. Micah combined this entry with a lesson plan and note taking/note making completed after watching the same lesson videotaped while she was teaching. This triangulation of data creates both context and trustworthiness. Micah needed both the lesson plan and the videotape, along with her journal entry, to gain a more complete picture of teaching on this particular day.

➜ FIGURE 3.4: Sample Research Notebook Entry

I think the big thing missing from today's lesson was something for the kids to do. I did have one activity from the text that they were to do, but ultimately, there wasn't much engagement happening. For about 30 minutes, I really gave them nothing to do but listen and discuss...surely, this tried their patience. Another folly I made (greater than the former) was to not call Marvin out for his comments. He was being disruptive and mildly rude at times and this should not have been tolerated. But I continued through the lesson, ignoring the conflict and subsequently, had numerous students come up and ask me what we were doing during group work. There seems to be a trend happening here. I do my best to make it perfectly clear what the kids should do and still I get the "huh?" look from several students. In the last two weeks, three of my lessons brought the response, "What are we doing?" from 5-6 students which suggests to me that we have a problem. Either 1) the students are not paying attention or 2) I'm not explaining myself well enough, or 3) someone around them is talking and making it difficult to follow along. Considering there was a bit of chatter happening in the back of class today, I'm inclined to think that chatter was a factor and subsequently, I am not doing my job in insisting and waiting for quiet before instruction.

I am going to watch the video tape in search of insight on this matter. On Tuesday when I watch the tape of my lesson, I will make a point of keeping track of student activity, focusing on the behavior of the students and really honing in on student behavior and conduct. I must fess up to the reality that I tend to avoid points of confrontation and/ or conflict in the classroom and get sort of wrapped in my lesson.... But I need to remember that even small bouts of talking is distracting to students such that they miss the directions. I must keep an eye out for this and hold kids accountable.

I think a couple of strategies that may work to alleviate some of the confusion and repetition on my part is to more readily call on kids (especially if they're talking) to repeat what was said before dismissing students to their task. I really need to start being intentional about this because there is no reason why I should have to repeat directions umpteen times because kids weren't listening. One more thing I must start doing is to prepare overheads with the directions written out so that the kids can read what they are to do as a class and it comes from THEIR lips—not mine. Yes, I think this may be an effective tool that will require a bit of proactive planning on my part.

Understanding Triangulation

Because triangulation is such an important concept in action research, it is worth considering its meaning before proceeding further. We will provide a metaphor for triangulation and a scenario in which triangulation is used, and then allow you space to create your own meaning around this concept.

Printable CD Extra: Practice Data Sets

More examples of triangulated student data sets are available on the companion CD.

Using Triangulation to Find Your Way in the Wilderness

Global position systems (GPSs) have changed the way the authors of this text do our wilderness treks. With a GPS, we can have an accurate way of knowing where we are in the world, latitude, longitude, and altitude. GPS systems rely on triangulation in order to do this. If you are standing in the middle of the wilderness not knowing where to turn next, you can turn on your GPS unit and it will search for satellites positioned in space. You can watch your unit "lock" onto the satellites. The geometry of latitude, longitude, and altitude requires readings from three different observers. In this case, the observers are satellites, and three satellites are required. If you only lock into one satellite, your location cannot be determined. With two satellites you may be able to get a rough idea of where you are but one of the three parameters—

Self-Study: The Action Research Design and Cultural Proficiency

Read through the following example from an action research design. As you read, ask yourself, How does Mark's personal culture matter? How does Mark's cultural identity influence his action research topic, design, and data interpretation?

Mark

Mark is an upper elementary/middle school preservice teacher. His action research question is, Will using homework as an enhancement exercise rather than an extension exercise increase the quality of students' schoolwork and improve their attitude toward homework?

Mark describes his interest in researching homework as follows:

I am interested in researching homework because I think that students often rush through their class work to avoid having homework. I think that allowing ample time for work to be completed during class will increase the quality of the work turned in by the students and improve students' attitudes about homework. After observing the sixth grade students in my class rush through their work in an attempt to finish it, I became curious about studying this. If homework is taken out of the equation—it's already assigned—and students are motivated by turning in quality work instead of finishing quickly, I expect them to perform better. The motivation and expectation should be the same—QUALITY. Furthermore, if homework assignments are geared toward enhancing or enriching lessons rather than extending class work time, I expect that attitudes toward homework will improve and completion rates will increase.

Mark goes on to describe some of his own values:

I grew up in an upper-middle-class neighborhood. As a white male with a secure family background I always had familial support and even pressure to perform academically. I knew that I always could get help from my parents and would get regular reminders from them to complete my homework. While I did not rely on teachers to provide academic motivation, I believe that an important part of good teaching is being able to motivate your students to do their best. A teacher can not be solely responsible for motivating students, but they do play an important

continues ➔

longitude, latitude, or altitude—will be impossible to determine. The unit needs to lock into at least three satellites; when it does, it will give you accurate data to describe your location. However, even with this data, you will need a map; the map gives the GPS data context. The GPS data, with a map, gives you a location.

Work your own way through this metaphor: How is doing research like a trek in the wilderness? How is the triangulation of data like receiving GPS signals from three different satellites? And how is the researcher's journal like the map?

A Teacher Finds Her Way Through the Classroom with Triangulation

In attempting to see if simulations are increasing eighth grade students' understanding and appreciation of current events and issues, Mara collects the following data set:

> She videotapes her students as they role play, within small groups, various people debating the future of a rain forest (observation).

> She provides each small group with a list of questions about the issues raised in the role-playing exercise. Students discuss this within their small groups and the conversation is audiotaped (interview). This conversation is held directly after the role-playing exercise.

> That evening, Mara writes a journal entry in her researcher's notebook about the role-playing exercise. She mentions everything,

role. There are several factors that go into a teacher's motivation of [his] students. One of the most important factors has to be meaningful class work. If students are rushing through work to get it done, the work is obviously not meaningful. There are different things that can be done to give work meaning and one of them is to give the work meaningful class time. If it's important enough to do, it should be important enough to dedicate class time toward doing it. Homework should be meaningful as well. I believe that homework should be dedicated to enhancing a day's lesson or preparing for an upcoming lesson.

Mark describes his own experiences with motivation in the work world and identifies why motivation and expectation are important to him:

It is difficult to remember what my experiences with homework were, especially when I think about sixth grade in 1978–79. However, the following example from my most recent job should give you some idea of why I feel strongly about motivation and expectations being the same. During my last job, before entering my teacher-education program, the salespeople of the company I worked for were expected to close as many deals as possible during the week. Each week—sometimes daily—statistics were posted publicly showing each salesperson's numbers from the previous week. Ironically, sales people weren't paid commission based on sales volume. They were paid based on profit margin. In fact, sales below a certain profit margin were deducted from pay. The salesperson's motivation [was] pay based on profit margin. However, [they were] being asked to produce as much revenue as possible. The motivation and expectation contradict each other. Similarly, students are expected to turn in quality work, but their motivation is finishing quickly, eliminating or limiting homework. Again, the motivation and expectation contradict each other.

In the next segment, Mark talks about his own beliefs about his students and what he assumes about their values:

I think that kids want to do well and want to please other people, like their parents or their teachers. If given ample class time and meaningful homework, I believe that students' work will improve. I also believe that all students have enough time at home to complete the homework [that] they will be assigned. It is my impression that many of the students I am working with have limited parental involvement at home with regards to academics. If I can help create the motivation in my students to turn in quality work by providing them with time to complete assignments and meaningful homework that they are eager to complete on their own,

continues ➡

from funny things she heard, to her worries about management, and to what she would do differently next time. In addition, she includes a copy of her lesson plan. Since her university supervisor conducted an observation during this lesson, she also includes a copy of the supervisor's notes.

The next day, she assigns an essay—"Issues of the Rainforest as I Understand Them"—to the students (artifact). Students have time to draft, revise, and polish the essay over the next week, using multiple resources.

Limitations of Triangulation

Triangulation does have limits, despite suggesting that three views of data provide a complete or whole view of "the" problem and therefore of "the" answer. Richardson (2003) suggests the metaphor of a crystal may be better suited. Crystals come in many shapes and change under varying context. They "grow, change, alter, but are not amorphous" (p. 517). We use triangulation in action research since it is an established concept in qualitative research. However, overlaying the concept of triangulation with the metaphor of a crystal enriches the concept and honors the complexities of teaching and learning.

In your notebook or journal, draw the relationship between the data Mara collected (observations, interview, artifact, researcher's notebook). Show the kinds of insight Mara might expect to gain from this data. How might this data

I expect the quality of their work to improve—their motivation and my expectations will correlate.

Analyzing and Deconstructing the Example

Self-Study Activity: Cultural Proficiency and the Research Design

You can analyze the above example using interactive tools on the companion CD.

Read through the above example one more time to answer the following questions. Using different colors of pen/pencil, underline portions of the text that might answer the questions; color code for the question/evidence in the text. Read for both explicit statements and for the innuendoes of the text.

According to Mark, why is motivation important in and out of school?

Who is responsible for a student's motivation to do well?

Read through the text again and attempt to answer the following questions with evidence from the text. Once again, underline portions of the text that might answer the questions; color code for the question/evidence in the text, reading for both explicit statements and for innuendo.

How might Mark's choice of an action research question reflect his own cultural context?

How might this context influence Mark's data interpretation? For example if students do not do any better with his intervention strategies to improve homework quality, what kinds of conclusions might Mark come to if he does not take into account his own context?

Now, consider the context where Mark is teaching. Here are the details as he provides them:

Walker Elementary School is located 20 miles from a downtown urban area. It is one of the largest suburbs of this city with a population of nearly 80,000 people. Walker Elementary reflects the suburb in that it consists of students representing a wide variety of ethnicities and socioeconomic backgrounds. Forty-three percent of Walker's students

continues ➡

set be enriched by including the perspectives of the students and the mentor-teacher? What other kind of data might be missing from such a data set?

Activity: Triangulation: An Extended Example

An extended example of a complete data set can be found on the companion CD.

Connecting to Your Study

Brainstorm your own action research topic and question using table 3.3. What kinds of data from each category might you collect to best answer your action research question?

How Much Data Is Enough Data?

"How many data sets do I have to collect?" The easy response is this: the more relevant data, the more trustworthy the research. Recall that time constraints, guest status, context constraints, multiple uncontrollable factors, and the transformation factor all influence the action research process (see Chapter 1: Critical Considerations for being a Student Teacher/Action Researcher). The amount of time you are in your placement, your access to the classroom, and how deliberate you are in planning for data collection may all restrict the amount of data you are able to collect.

receive free or reduced [-price] lunch while others are the sons and daughters of a major computer manufacture's managers and executives. Approximately one-third of Walker's students represent a race other than Caucasian. The majority of those are Hispanic.

Twelve of the 29 students (41%) in my classroom represent persons of color. One of the students is on an individual educational program and two of the students are taking English as a second language courses although they both seem functionally fluent in English. Fifteen of the students are male and 14 are female. Only two of the 28 students achieved "exceeded standards" for fifth grade benchmarks on standardized testing.

Overall, I would say that the class is very average academically and the students have a difficult time expressing themselves through writing. They have shown limited vocabularies and poor study habits. On average, less than half of the students will turn in all of their assignments during a given week. With few exceptions, the students seem to accept poor academic work and are apparently more motivated to get work turned in rather than turn in quality work. Is this because the students are trying to avoid homework, or is this because students simply don't care or are not capable of better? I think these students are capable of more and that the quality of their work is related to avoiding homework. This [action research] project will serve to help me answer this question.

continues ➡

➡ **TABLE 3.3: Data Category Brainstorms**

Observation	Interview	Artifact

Ultimately the question, "How many data sets do I need?" may be answered by your action research advisor and/or professor given your individual circumstances. However, it is important that you keep in mind at all times the restrictions on data collection imposed by your position as a student teacher, and that you make these limitations clear in any presentation of your action research.

Is This Enough Data?

Table 3.4 shows a complete list of student teacher Cindy's data sets for her action research project. The focus of Cindy's project was building community among her fifth grade students. Cindy collected data from November through March. She began data collection while a part-time student teacher and continued data collection throughout her full-time student teaching.

Read through the above text again and attempt to answer the following questions with evidence from the text. Once again, underline portions of the text that might answer the questions; color code for the question/evidence in the text, reading for both explicit statements and for innuendo.

How is Mark's background similar and different from that of his students?

How does Mark's background and values influence his description of his students?

How might Mark's background and values blindside the questions he asks? What additional questions might he consider?

In your notebook or journal, explain the connections among Mark's personal context, his choice of action research question, his values and beliefs as evidenced here, and the context of his school. You may find that sketching a diagram or chart is a helpful way of conceptualizing these connections. Demonstrate areas where Mark might want to be particularly wary while conducting his action research project. The introduction of the self- study for chapter 3 and a review of Lindsey, Robins, & Terrill (2003) may provide you with useful information for this activity.

Is this enough data? If this were Cindy's dissertation work for her Ph.D. or if this research was going to be published as "groundbreaking" and be replicated in multiple sites, then the answer is no. However, it was enough data for Cindy to learn critical lessons about becoming a teacher. She learned about how to use data as assessment to drive instruction, and about how to facilitate community among children from diverse backgrounds, language groups, and social classes. Combined with her literature review, she could be fairly certain that what she was learning was consistent with what other researchers have discovered with more in-depth studies taking much more time. While Cindy's study is smaller than a major research study, experience in making these discoveries was personal—her action research project is her story of becoming a teacher; she has personally constructed the resulting insights, meanings, and questions. This action research project provides a place of beginning, a first chapter in Cindy's professional development.

"But wait!" you may be saying; "I don't even have as much time as Cindy!" Don't worry; you can still follow the plan for developing a research design and collecting data in this book, even if you only have time to collect one complete (triangulated) data set. You can still learn about the skills of data collection (assessment) and interpretation. You must, however, recognize and state clearly the limits of your findings or results. In such instances where you are only able to collect a single data set, then focus on what you have learned about the collection of data and interpretation and how you intend to use this in your future teaching career.

➔ **TABLE 3.4: Cindy's Collected Data**

Data Set	Date of Action	Action Implemented	Data Collected
#1	11/7	Conducted a sociogram recording top three students each child would prefer to work with on a class project.	Sociogram identifying stars and isolates within the class
	11/12 through 11/25	Colonization Unit: Students worked in groups on a colonial region project. Cooperating teacher and I observed group interaction during group work time	Artifact 1 (A1): Students listed characteristics of an ideal community A2: Journal entries from group projects Informal interviews with group leads
	12/5	Students drew and described their ideal community	A3: Student pictures and descriptions of ideal communities
#2	1/5	Spanish immersion experience: 30 minutes solid instruction in Spanish with class meeting to follow (no clues were given in English)	Field notes by cooperating teacher Notes taken from student responses in class discussion Student journal reflections: feelings during immersion experience and what they learned about their classmates Researcher's journal entry
#3	1/16	Each team created and named a team mascot, then wrote a description of mascot's diet, hobbies, and a strange thing the mascot could do. The mascot's name became their team name.	Field notes on group interaction Researcher's journal A4: Team mascot posters
#4	1/23	Teams imagined they were teams of famous scientists. They had to draw and describe an invention that would make the world a better place.	A5: Picture/description of team inventions Researcher's journal Field notes on group interaction during teambuilding activity Field notes on group interaction during cooperative science activity Student journals on group inclusion of all members
#5	1/30	Team Word-Creation Game: Two-part experience where students first listed as many words as they could find inside of a phrase, without the help of classmates. Then in the second round they worked as a team to do the same and discovered they did much better working as a team than on their own.	Focus-group interview of a student from each group (tape-recorded) Field notes on group interaction in word-creation game Field notes by university supervisor on group interaction during math problem solving activity Student journals on what they liked best about working in their groups
#6	2/11	Silent Castle Building: Teams had a stack of scratch paper and roll of masking tape and were given 10 minutes to construct a freestanding castle without the aid of any other materials or the use of written or spoken language of any kind.	Researcher's journal Field notes on group interaction by cooperating teacher and myself Notes on group discussion responses Student self-reflections on who they did/didn't work well with and what they could personally do to make their group function better Anecdotal notes on group interaction during M&M math lesson (2/5/04)
#7	2/20	"Take a Good Look" Game: Teams were given one minute to memorize a picture from the overhead projector. Then the picture was taken away and the teams listed as many things as they could remember from the picture.	Student lists of picture observations Field notes by university supervisor on group interaction during game Time interval field notes by university supervisor during math partner work Researcher's journal Time interval field notes by cohort leader on group interaction and inclusion during group work time on math worksheet (2/17/04)
#8	3/3	Star Share: Within individual teams, each student drew a card and shared with his/her group who/what they would be and why, based on the card they drew. (E.g., card says "movie star"; student shares which movie star he/she would be and why)	Student journals on what they've learned about each group member and what did or didn't work in their groups Individual interviews with unofficial group leaders Individual interviews with bilingual students Researcher's journal Interview with cooperating teacher sharing preliminary results of research and seeking her feedback on those results
	3/4	Conducted final sociogram recording top three students each child would prefer to work with on a class project.	Sociogram identifying new stars and isolates within the class.

The Action Research Design

Cultural Context:
The Art and Craft of Negotiation

Printable CD Extras: Action Research Design Templates

Action research design templates can be downloaded from the companion CD.

Now that you have learned about triangulation and data collection, you are ready to begin designing your action research plan. Begin by summarizing the following about your action research project:

The area of focus for my action research project is . . .

Participants in my action research project include . . .

My critical question now reads: . . . .

My action research project can best be described as integrated action research, curriculum analysis, self-study, or ethnography (pick one; doing so will determine what design template you will use. If you have not decided yet, go back to chapter 2 for a review of how to sharpen your critical question).

Once you have these basic questions answered, choose and download one of the Research Design Templates. (The CD-based template will open in your word processing program, and you will able to begin drafting your design. You may also re-create the design format on your own using the included template as a guide.) After completing the tem-plate, discuss your draft plan with a critical colleague and then your university supervisor.

Sometimes our students come back to us and say, "I can't do my action research project; my mentor-teacher doesn't believe in the teaching strategy I want to try." In certain situations, this may be true and the student teacher will need to change the entire topic of her action research (AR) project. However, other times we find the approach the student teacher takes in introducing the AR topics has a great deal to do with how a mentor-teacher responds to the idea.

Here are a few suggestions:

Whenever possible, connect the AR topics to the identified needs of the students, the mission of the school, or concerns your mentor-teacher has shared with you.

Share with the mentor-teacher your own goals for learning. Share your interest, passion, and maybe even your personal story of why this topic is important to you.

Avoid being judgmental and/or "the expert"; in other words, avoid implying a deficit in the classroom that you can somehow "fix" as a student teacher.

Appreciate that even if your mentor-teacher has a different style or approach to teaching, he does have expertise to share with you.

Here are some "lead lines" that our students have found to be successful in negotiating a research topic with a mentor-teacher:

I have an idea for an action research project; what do you think of this? How do you think this might work in your classroom?

I've noticed the last couple of weeks that the students in this class don't seem to _____. I've been learning about _____ in my teacher-education program. What if we . . . ?

My methods teacher introduced this pretty radical idea in class last week. Here's the concept as she explained it. What do you think? I'd love to try this as an action research project!

Most of my school life, I've struggled with _____. I would

continues ➡

Sample Integrated Action Research Design

Figure 3.5 is a sample action research design. How does this design structure Cindy's research? What might be some drawbacks to this design? What are the strengths?

Evaluating Your Own Research Design

Once you have drafted your research design, step away from it and with a critical colleague evaluate the design to make sure it has the potential to answer your critical question(s). Show the design to your mentor-teacher or other important stakeholders and make sure it can be implemented in your setting. Together, discuss issues of triangulation and trustworthiness—does your design seem trustworthy? It is likely that your design will be further evaluated by an instructor or other research mentor; be an active participant in this important process of revising your design.

Finally, remember that your design is still a work in progress. In the process of implementing the project and of conducting ongoing analysis, you may find your data-collection strategies either are not providing the evidence you need to respond to your critical question or that they are not workable in your setting. You may even find your critical question(s) changed, prompting a revision of your design. This is all part of the process: let the data guide you as you go!

really like to assist other students who have this difficulty in school. What approaches have you successfully used?

I am having difficulties coming up with an action research project that is meaningful. When you consider your classroom and your students, do you have any questions that might be meaningful for us both to pursue while I am student teaching here?

Cultural Context: When "New" Information Changes the Design

As a student teacher, it is impossible to know everything about a school community when you enter as a guest for the first time. In some instances, there is very little time between when a student teacher arrives at the school site and begins the action research project. It is particularly important that student teachers keep their senses attuned to the environment to learn information that may change the design or even the question of their research. Read through the two following scenarios and suggest changes in the design based upon the "new" information each student teacher obtains.

Scenario 1: Holly

Holly, a student teacher at a high school, is exploring reasons students are disenfranchised at school. She makes a correlation between students in her classes who are involved in after-school activities and those who are not. She begins to assume that students involved in after-school activities are more motivated than those who are not.

Then, she discovers the fee structure (per student) for various activities and resources at the high school:

$40 for student body

$225 for sports (not to exceed $900 per family)

$125 for dance or cheerleading (per semester)

$95 for any other after-school club (drama, chess, etc.)

continues ➡

➡ FIGURE 3.5: Action Research Design Example

I. Action Research Project Overview

1.　　Critical Question

How can I help to create a cohesive community which encourages meaningful interaction and collaboration between students in an ethnically and socio-economically diverse classroom?

2.　　Setting of the Action Research Project

My action research project will be conducted in a fifth grade classroom of a newer elementary school in a rural community between two larger urban areas. The school is socio-economically diverse and has a 40% Hispanic population, which is reflected in my classroom. There are 30 students in my classroom with various levels of academic interest and ability. The context is very important to this study: I've noted that children in the classroom appear divided by language and gender. These are the two obvious barriers to a cohesive classroom. I have studied Spanish in Guatemala and have an undergraduate degree in Spanish. Having lived "outside my comfort zone," I am comfortable with this context.

3.　　The Story Behind This Action Research Project

This topic plays a major role in how effective the classroom will be throughout the year. Whether the students realize it or not, the classroom is a significant community where they will spend a great deal of time during the next eight months. It would be so good for the classroom to be a positive collaborative environment where the students are learning and growing as a part of a supportive community. But this is limited when the students do not understand they all play an important role in the success of the classroom community. This topic is also important to me because it is highly difficult to teach a classroom full of students who do not work well with their classmates.

Over my career as a student, nearly 17 years, I have participated in some incredible classroom communities which greatly enhanced my educational experience. The cohesion felt in those classrooms was built upon a great deal of respect for the teacher and classmates, an environment of trust and a place where each student was valued for what they could bring to the community. In each of these experiences, the community dynamic was modeled by the teacher in respect for the students and a passion for teaching/learning. My negative classroom experiences were in classrooms where there was not mutual respect for students or the teacher and where the atmosphere was one of mistrust and rivalry rather than cooperation and teamwork.

I believe the foundations of community and cooperation within a classroom begin with the teacher. A good teacher cares for every single individual in her/his classroom, regardless of their scholastic aptitude and social behaviors. In addition, a good teacher looks for the good in every child, sees their potential, builds trust and respect into every student interaction, and believes her/his job as a teacher is to take every child where they are and move them forward; to help every child discover their gifts and abilities and to become all they can be. Good teachers realize the benefits of cooperative learning and give their classes ample opportunities for both individual and group work. This action research project will focus on these teaching practices, with specific emphasis on providing cooperative learning opportunities, as well as teambuilding experiences, in order to build community in the classroom.

As a student teacher, I am limited in my classroom as to how much time and focus can be placed on my research activities (specifically the teambuilding interventions). It is not my classroom and I do not bear the bulk of the responsibility for my students and their progress throughout this year. My cooperating teacher fully supports this action research project and has given some great ideas for teambuilding activities. I continually discuss my ideas with her and we constantly refine our ideas as we interact with the students and observe their peer interactions. In addition, I have never been in a classroom from the beginning of the year until the end. So I have never seen the natural progression of building community in a classroom without the intervention I am proposing in this action research project.

This information all "matters" in ways I probably don't entirely understand, but I do know that my passion to facilitate a cohesive classroom and my strong beliefs in collaboration influence the choice of this topic and the way I will most likely define "success" or "failure" of the project.

4.   Synopsis of Problem

As I watched the students over the first few weeks of school, I noticed how little they interact with one another in a helpful or collaborative way. The students seem to have a difficult time working together in groups. Even though their desks are clustered in groups of four and five to facilitate group interaction, the students do not naturally help each other. We have our bilingual Spanish/English sitting close by our students who speak little/no English to facilitate vocabulary and instructional assistance. But our bilingual students do not give much help to our Spanish only students; and the help they do give is usually a brief and a difficult-to-understand summary of the teacher's instructions.

Our hopes were for the students to help each other and collaborate with each other when they need clarification on assignments. But they seem to be highly dependent on the teachers for support. We see the least amount of collaboration between the Spanish and English speaking students as well as between the male and female students. They do not seem to see each other as valuable resources. We are especially interested in collaboration between the English Language Learners (ELL) and the rest of the class because Spanish speaking students need to be exposed to as much English as possible, both inside and outside the classroom, in order to acquire the language. But the English speakers in our class do not talk, or even try to talk using non-verbal cues, with the Spanish speakers. If only they would interact as a team, helping each other to understand and realizing they are all participants and important contributors to the classroom and to the learning process of the entire class.

5.   Synopsis of Strategy

In my action research project I will apply a variety of community building strategies. My goal is to increase collaboration between students across ethnic, gender, and socio-economic lines emphasizing the strengths and talents each student brings to the classroom community. As a class we will define community and what it means to be a great community, then work toward becoming that community. The teambuilding experiences will be 15–30 minutes in length, focusing on getting students used to their teams and learning how to work with all the team members. The experiences include creating a team mascot, a memory synergy activity, a team story write, a word-creation game, and an imaginative team scientist activity. After the team building experiences, the students will participate in a class project which will challenge them to work together, problem solve, and use the individual talents of each student to be successful.

6.   Timeline

Proposed Date of Action	Action (Strategy, intervention, evaluation, etc. to be implemented)
Week of November 3	Conduct a sociogram.
November 12-25	Work Sample: CT will observe group interaction during group project; Collect artifact #1 from Creating Communities activity (see WS lesson #5); Collect journal entries (artifact #2) from selected students on group work; Conduct informal interviews with group leads; Ongoing observation of collaboration during work time for group brochures; Final assessment of brochures will be partially based on ability to work together collaboratively.
December 5	Collect artifact #3 — pictures and descriptions of ideal communities.

January 5	Conduct Spanish immersion experience: 30 minutes solid instruction in Spanish with class meeting to follow. Write field notes on this experience and collect a written reflection from the students. Collect a questionnaire from each student poling student opinion on collaborative work and community feel of class.
Weeks of January 12 January 19 January 26 February 2 February 9	Weekly teambuilding experience followed by students' journaling the impact of or feelings toward the experience. Take anecdotal records during experiences to record types of interaction. Conduct focus group interviews after week #1 and week #5.
Week of February 17	Carry out class project and collect reflections from students.
January 5-March 4	Weekly observation journals recording changes in interaction and levels of collaborative work and sense of community within the classroom during "normal" nonintervention classroom work.
Week of March 2	Conduct final sociogram and collect final questionnaire from each student.

7.   Common Themes from Literature Review

The teacher: models respect, affirmation, and care to all students; provides opportunities for cooperative learning; promotes feelings in all students of membership in, and responsibility to, the classroom community; does not tolerate an atmosphere of disrespect.

The student: must feel safe and valued in the community; must see her/his place or role in the community to feel ownership and value in the community; must listen attentively to others and be willing to help in her/his strong areas.

English language learners benefit greatly in language acquisition from cooperative learning activities because information is relevant, repetitive, and developmentally appropriate.

A strong sense of classroom community and ability to work collaboratively increases learning in all students, prepares them for life outside of the classroom, and strengthens their character and sense of self-worth.

Students who are able to problem solve in groups and help other students find solutions better understand the solutions themselves and are better equipped for more complex problem solving.

8.   Reference List

Echevarria, J., Vogt, M., & Short, D. (2000). Making Content Comprehensible for English Language Learners: The SIOP Model. Boston: Allyn and Bacon.

Gibbs, J. (2000). Tribes: A New Way of Learning and Being Together. Sausalito: Center Source Systems.

Hubbard, R.S. & Power, B.M. (1993). The Art of Classroom Inquiry: A Handbook for Teacher-Researchers. Portsmouth, NH: Heinemann.

Kagan, L., Kagan, M., & Kagan, S. (1997). Teambuilding. San Clemente, CA: Kagan Cooperative Learning.

Kagan, S. (1995). We Can Talk: Cooperative Learning in the Elementary ESL Classroom. ERIC Languages and Linguistics Digest. Retrieved February 5, 2002, from http://www.cal.org/ericcll/digest/kagan001.html

Lickona, T. (1991). Educating for Character. New York, NY: Bantam Books.

Meece, J. (2002). Child and Adolescent Development for Educators. New York, NY: McGraw-Hill.

Shaw, V. (1992). Communitybuilding in the Classroom. San Clemente, CA: Kagan Cooperative Learning.

II. Methodology: How the Problem will Be Addressed

1.   Data and Documents to Be Collected

Observations:
- Field notes
- Anecdotal record
- Journal
- Checklist
- Shadow study of ELL student

Interviews:
- Informal interview
- Sociogram
- Focus group interview
- Questionnaires (beginning and ending)

Artifacts:
- Samples of student self-reflections
- Digital picture of completed class project
- Samples of student journal entries
- Lists of characteristics of ideal community from Work Sample Lesson #5

2.   Teacher/Researcher Notebook

All documents will be compiled and organized into a research notebook in chronological order. My weekly journals will be interspersed with other observations, interview documentation, and artifacts. I will be reflecting on our major classroom community experiences (noted in the project timeline). Critical analysis points are listed in the timeline and will be added to the notebook. I will perform note taking/note making on informal interviews throughout the community building experiences, which will also be added to the notebook.

3.   Professional and Critical Colleagues and Students

My mentor-teacher is supportive of this action research proposal. She will assist me in observing students and interpreting data results. My critical colleague and I will share our results during regular class meetings and by regularly exchanging analytical memos. Throughout the data collection plan, there are specific places where students will be giving me their insights.

4.   Data and Document Analysis

The sociogram will serve as my baseline data indicating which peers each student would choose to collaborate with for group work. I will use this data as an indicator of my class "stars" or "leaders," the students most frequently chosen by their peers as partners for collaborative work. I will also use the data to help form groups for the different community building activities. At the conclusion of the data-collection period, I will conduct a second sociogram which will be compared to the original sociogram and serve as a point of comparison for increased interaction between students, especially those whose peers did not choose them on the sociogram.

Observations will be conducted by myself, my cooperating teacher, and my university supervisor. Observers will focus on positive teamwork and inclusion, interaction across language, gender, and socio-economic lines, and supportive peer helping behaviors. Attempts will be made to overhear specific interactions between students. I will create a chart to track student behaviors throughout the various observations. At the conclusion of my observations, I will look for patterns on the observation chart which may indicate changes in collaborative behavior and community interaction between students over the course of the research project.

In the focus group interview students will be asked to relate their feelings about classroom cohesion and their willingness to work with different classmates in group activities. Questions will be developed prior to the interview and the focus group will be audio-recorded. A cross section of students will be asked to stay during lunch for this discussion. I will attempt to have the number of girls, boys, English and Spanish speakers proportional to the classroom statistics. After the focus group I will listen to the recording and list responses corresponding to their feelings about our classroom as a community and their willingness to work with their peers. Once all the data is compiled I will look for patterns in the students' responses which may indicate changes in collaborative behavior and community interaction between students over the course of the research project.

Artifacts will be treated much like the observations above. I will create categories of common themes and track student journal entries according to their themes. After the final journal entries are analyzed on the chart, I will look for patterns on the thematic chart which may indicate changes in collaborative behavior and community interaction between students over the course of the research project.

As a whole, all of the data will be analyzed for patterns of change in willingness to work with different classmates, as well as in increased interaction and helpfulness between students of differing language, gender, and socio-economic status. After I have completed all the analysis, I will consider the following questions: What assumptions have I made in interpreting the data? What assumptions have I made about what a cohesive classroom community looks like? Based on my analysis, what other variables of the classroom environment and student behavior may need to be questioned and observed? How does the school system support cohesiveness?

5.   How This Design Deliberately Plans for Trustworthiness

My literature review is not exhaustive, but I believe it does provide a framework for my study. I am beginning to collect data in November, while I am still part time student teaching, to make sure I have as many data sets as possible. I plan to seek multiple perspectives particularly by listening to the voices of my mentor-teacher and my students. I have attempted to outline my own perspectives and biases and will make sure and make the context of my project clear. Finally, I will triangulate my data as much as possible by gathering observations, interviews, and artifacts.

6.   How I Am Gaining Appropriate Permissions

Please see attached the letter I have written for parents of students in my fifth grade class. The letter is written in both Spanish and English and has been approved by the school's principal and my mentor-teacher. Also attached is the Human Subjects Review application which has been approved by my university.

7.   Possible Interruptions, Distractions, and Difficulties

While conducting my action research project, unforeseen difficulties will undoubtedly arise. I expect there will be scheduling issues for the community building experiences as well as the interruptions of shortened school weeks, personal difficulties for individual students, and other unpredictable events. The best way I know how to deal with these problems as they arise is to keep in constant communication with my cooperating teacher and make adjustments to my research timeline as needed. Regardless of the disruptions I must be constant and intentional about my data collection, even documenting the disruptions and the effects they have on the classroom community. I also want to stay open to the idea that changes in my design may be a good thing; that the design may need to be changed to better fit my students.

III. Conclusions and Possibilities

1.   Presentation of Data

Upon the completion of my action research project at the beginning of March, I will bring together my data and synthesize what I have learned. This will be compiled in a written action research report. I will be presenting the data and research notebook at the Action Research Symposium in late April.

2. **What Actions I Expect/Hope to Be the Result of My Action Research Project**

As a result of this action research project, I hope to achieve a cohesive classroom community in my fifth grade classroom, demonstrated by students who respect and value one another and are willing and eager to work collaboratively with any of their classmates. I hope to learn what strategies are effective in creating community in the classroom and understand more deeply how the students think and learn to work with others. In doing so I will be able to adapt my teaching to more quickly and effectively create community in my future classrooms.

 ## Ethical Considerations of Action Research: Gaining Permission

Action researchers must be cognizant of the ethical issues of doing research. This includes gaining permission from participants and the participants' parents if they are going to be included in a research study. While there are strict guidelines for gaining permission from participants in research studies, the kind of action research done by student teachers is categorized somewhat differently, with a relaxing of some of the restrictions.

The genre of action research we have advocated throughout this text is one that is embedded in the teaching and learning process. It represents the cycle of teaching (plan, implement, and assess). The results of such a project should be a teacher with improved understanding and/or skills, and an improved, more just education for students. Because this process is embedded within the teaching and learning process, as a teacher you would not need to gain permission if the research was not formal and you did not plan on making the research public.

Imagine, however, that as a student you found out after the fact that a story was written about you and presented to a group of people you didn't even know. You would have reason to feel like you were deceived. The same is true for participants in the student teacher/researcher's project.

A checklist is given in table 3.5 to determine the level of informed consent (the term researchers give to gaining permission from participants) that may be needed for your project. Answer each of the four questions to determine whether or not you will need to seek permission.

The process of obtaining informed consent, or gaining permission from participants, involves written permission from parents and verbal permission from students. Exact guidelines are determined by the university's informed-consent policy and the policy of the school district in which you are student teaching. We offer these general guidelines:

Check with your university advisor and find out what expectations exist for informed consent; do not begin collecting data until this is known.

Write a letter seeking permission from parents to use data generated by their students in your projects.

The best guideline for gaining permissions is to be open about your study. Discuss it not only with your mentor-teacher, but also with your students. Let them know you are doing this study to become a better teacher. If possible, allow students to assist you in interpreting the data; this will make your work more trustworthy.

The letter sent home to parents to gain written permission should include:

the topic of the project

the objective of the project

strategies that will be implemented

data to be collected

a timeline of the project

how the project will be made public

why videotaping or picture-taking will occur

how confidentiality will be maintained

any potential risk to students, or the absence of risk to students

a return slip to be signed by the parent

Printable CD Extras: Parent Letter Template

You may download a template from the companion CD or use the one in Appendix G.

Make sure the permission letter is approved by your university advisor, mentor-teacher, and the administrator of your school. Check with the school specialist if you are collecting data from those students who may have protected legal status.

Do not use the data from any student where parental permission is not provided.

Confidentiality is the critical issue; make sure you protect all student and school identities by using pseudonyms.

Students who participate in your study should not receive special rewards; nor should your study be in anyway related to student grades.

$50 for the yearbook

$250 for parking

$15–$30 for art, photography, or technology

$10–$20 for foreign-language resources

$15 for life skills studies

$50 for family and consumer science studies

$50 textbook deposit

$12 for the science lab

How might this data provide context for Holly's study? How might it redirect where and how she looks at issues of socioeconomic class, attitudes, motivation, and students being disengaged in school?

Scenario 2: Martin

Martin is not from the small rural community where he is student teaching in a federally funded program specifically for preschool children of migrant families. The town where he is teaching has grown by 1,600 in the last decade to a population of 5,178. Latino immigration/migration has contributed to three-fifths of this growth and now represents 35% of the population. Of this population, many are seasonal agricultural workers, although the community is also growing its nonagricultural employment base. The staff at the preschool has been anxiously awaiting a decision from the city council concerning a land use permit in order to build a new and larger facility.

Martin senses that a number of community tensions play out in daily life between school and community, and somehow he knows that this is important not only to his teaching, but to his action research project on building and maintaining parent involvement in his classroom via parent groups.

Martin attends the city council meeting with his mentor-teacher. The meeting is tense. Opponents focus on a number of issues. Some cite potential traffic congestion. Others question whether a low-income migrant program belongs in a white middle- and upper-class residential neighborhood. Still others question if there is even a need for such a program. Someone states that property values will be diminished if such a center is constructed. Martin's mentor-teacher testifies that the program

continues ➡

→ TABLE 3.5: Guidelines for Gaining Permissions

Question 1: Will your research project be made public? Will it have an audience larger than your professor and your peers? Will it be made into a poster? Will the paper be posted at a website? Will there be a presentation?

YES	NO
You must gain written permission from parents and verbal permission from students. University and/or school district policies may apply; check with your advisor.	If the project is embedded within the teaching-learning project, you may not need to gain permissions. Check with your advisor. Getting permission is always preferred.

Question 2: Does your research project include participants who may be more vulnerable than others or have protected status under law? For example, do you have students in your study who are designated as "learning disabled," or have some other "special" classification? Do you have students who speak English as a second language or do not speak English at all?

YES	NO
Check with your advisor, mentor-teacher, school specialist, and building administrator. Permission is critical. Make sure that any letters sent home can be read and understood by parents.	Please refer to the general guidelines in chapter 3.

Question 3: Is there any possibility the data collected from your research project would be harmful to participants (emotionally, physically)? Remember, the goal of action research is to make the education of and for all students, more just and more equitable.

YES	NO
Rethink and revise your project. The goal of AR is to make education a better place for students. Anything harmful or even potentially harmful should not be included in your project. This includes any opportunities for other students to taunt or tease students, for "put downs," or for any practices that might harm a student's sense of self-worth. Grades should never be tied to participation in action research.	Excellent! Continue to the next question.

Question 4: Do you plan to audiotape, videotape, or take pictures of students? Do you plan to make any of these public during a presentation?

YES	NO
Many times schools have policies surrounding videotaping and/or taking pictures of students, even if they are not going to be made public. Make sure and check with your mentor-teacher. If you plan to include any of the above in a public presentation of any kind, include this in your letter asking for permission. Specific permission must be sought for any images to be placed on a webpage.	Are you sure? Often, audiotapes, videotapes, and/or pictures provide good data for triangulation and placing the data in context.

now serves around 300 "migrant" families, but someone else in the crowd questions the notion of migrant, claiming the definition is too broad. Monitoring the meeting is a federal civil rights officer. A local advocacy group had contacted the federal agency earlier, questioning whether or not the denial of the land use permit was a civil rights issue. One of those testifying is clear in pointing out that this "is not a race or class issue, but a land use decision only." Someone else testifies, "Somebody always has to play the race card and this isn't about race."

The end of the meeting is hardly the end: everyone knows this decision will most likely be settled in the courts. Martin is left wondering how this context is important to his action research design and his research topic on building a supportive parent group and network at the school.

How do you think this context matters? In what ways does this new information influence Martin's action research project?

Self-Study: Analyzing/Deconstructing Your Action Research Design

It is much easier to make the connections between culture and action research when analyzing someone else's work. We are so close to our own sense of culture that we take these daily acts of living and the paradigm behind them for granted. To build a scaffold for your own analysis, work through the following exercises. Keep your action research design draft nearby to mark places where you may want to revise. Specific sections of the BTAR action research design template are referenced in the activity below for revision convenience; if you are not using the BTAR action research design template, work through the questions and relate them to your action research design as you see fit.

Self-Study Activity: Analyzing Your Research Design for Cultural Proficiency

You can use the interactive tools on the CD to evaluate your design.

Begin by considering the setting for your action research project (this is section 1.2 of the BTAR action research design template), giving (1) a brief description of community, school (class, race, mission, values, urban/rural); (2) a brief description of participants; and (3) a brief description of the classroom where the action research project will take place.

How does this context matter to my action research project?

Consider the following questions:

Given your description, do you think the majority of the community would support your action research topic and believe it is useful? Why or why not, or, do you not know? Give a reason for your response.

Given your description, do you think those considered the "minority" of the community would support

continues

your action research topic and believe that it is useful? Why or why not, or do you not know? Give a reason for your response.

How is teaching, learning, and doing research supported or not supported by this context? (This is an important question to consider.)

Examine the community demographics as you have presented them. What do you suppose this community wants from their schools? On what do you base your answer?

What is my comfort level within this community/school context?

In your notebook, create a Venn diagram. Label one circle as "My School Community" and the other circle "Me, as a Teacher/Researcher." Using the demographic and descriptive information from your action research design, explore how you are different and/or the same as the community in which you are teaching. The first time, complete the Venn diagram based upon the dominant population and the second time do it based upon other populations within the school.

Now, review the story behind your action research project (this is section 1.3 of the BTAR action research design template), taking into account the following:

why you are interested in this area

what your own experiences are with this area

how your own values, beliefs, and sense of what "good teaching" is are represented in this action research project

what your biases are

how your position as a student teacher influences the project

How does this information matter to my action research project?

Consider the following questions:

If you met the families of students in your classroom at a social event, what kind of event would most likely be? Would it be (1) a family-sponsored event; (2) a neighborhood block party; (3) a church-sponsored event; (4) an open house at a local art gallery; or (5) a civic event? Would you be comfortable in this setting?

Do you think you could become friends with all or some of the families represented in your classroom if you met them in another setting? Expand on your answer.

Do you believe the majority of the families in your classroom would agree with your description of "good teaching"? Why or why not?

Which families in your classroom would agree with your perception of "poor classroom behavior"? Why?

Use any new information to jot down revision notes for your action research design.

How does the strategic intervention, innovation to be implemented, evaluation to be conducted, and/or other action to be applied in my study, support learning for and by all children and/or adolescents in the classroom?

continues ➔

Consider the following questions:

How does your action research design and specific action support differentiated learning (learning for all students)?

How does your action research design recognize and support diversity?

How does your action research design plan for multiple viewpoints?

How do organizational and/or school systems provide possibilities and barriers to your research?

How does your action research design deal with conflict?

If you are using the BTAR action research design template, use your responses to these questions revise section 1.5: A synopsis of the strategy to be used, the intervention to be tried, the innovation to be implemented, the evaluation to be conducted, or other action to be applied in the study.

How does my design account for cultural proficiency when interpreting data?

Consider the following questions:

Where in the data interpretation might you need to be aware of cultural knowledge when interpreting behaviors and personal interactions? Who might be a good resource for this kind of knowledge if you feel you are lacking in this area?

If there appear to be conflicting results in your data interpretation, how do you plan to resolve and/or represent these conflicts?

What stereotypes and/or prejudices might influence the data interpretation?

What kinds of distrust might exist within the school context that could influence your data interpretation?

What kinds of systems, organization, and/or structures exist that may need to be questioned for their influence upon your data interpretation? What do you assume about these systems, organization, and/or structures?

Having worked through these questions, return to your action research design and read your critical question. How is your critical question reflective of your own cultural context? Do you need to make any revisions here?

Share your revised action research design with your critical colleague as you evaluate your own abilities to be a culturally proficient teacher/action researcher.

Cultural Context: A Tale of One Mentor-Teacher and Two Student Teachers: Context as You

Let's cycle the discussion of cultural context back to you—you are not outside of the school and community context where you student teach and conduct action research. You are a critical element in the direction of the action research project, the way you negotiate and work with your mentor-teacher, and how you perceive the environment around you. You are the "participant observer" (Atkinson & Hammersley, 1994; Patton, 2002); you are the "human instrument" (Lincoln & Guba, 2003). As an active participant in the research study, your own paradigm and resulting attitudes for seeing and doing in the classroom influence the outcome of the study; furthermore, you become part of the population to be "analyzed" in the study (McCotter, 2001; Weiler, 1988).

We recall a tale of one mentor-teacher, Ms. Buckman, and two student teachers, Liz and Jodi. The first student teacher was placed with Ms. Buckman the first half the year; the student teachers were to trade placements the last half of the year. Liz reported:

My mentor-teacher uses a scripted, prepackaged literacy program. I can't implement any of the literacy strategies I've learned in my teacher-education program.

And so, she changed the focus of her action research project.

Midway through the year, Liz went to a different placement. Jodi had implemented literature circles as her action research project in the first half of her placement. After one day in Ms. Buckman's classroom, she reported:

I am so excited! Today I talked with Ms. Buckman about introducing literature circles. She was really supportive. She told me she had wanted to do this but wasn't quite sure how to go about it! I am so fortunate to be able to share with her what I've learned, and to have her expertise about the children and reading instruction to guide the rest of my AR project!

What made the difference? We see how attitude, approach, and a student teacher's comfort level with both the content and the teaching and learning strategy makes a difference in action research projects. Consider yourself as you design, implement, and interpret your action research. You may also want to revisit Chapter 1: Being a Student Teacher/Action Researcher.

CHAPTER 4
DATA ANALYSIS AND
INTERPRETATION

 Introduction and Overview of Data Analysis and Interpretation

You have defined action research (AR), formulated and articulated a critical question (CQ), and designed a well-triangulated and potentially trustworthy AR study. You may be anticipating collecting data, or you may already have one or more data sets. Now what? The next step is to learn the process of analyzing and interpreting your data to answer your CQ. If you are like most of our students, this step seems like moving into a dark, foggy forest of unknowns. Maybe you have never before analyzed or interpreted real, messy data—at least not the kinds of data you are collecting in your AR. You may be unexpectedly haunted at this point by the fact that your data doesn't seem objective or even particularly clear or organized. You may wonder if you have enough data to draw any conclusions from at all.

The purpose of this chapter is to guide you through the process of making sense of your data in a way that not only provides insights into your CQ, but leads to additional questions and perhaps other ways of thinking about your CQ. First, we provide an overview of the interpretation and analysis process. Then, the process is broken down into several important steps. You will understand and write

---

Cultural Context: The Numbers Tell the Story

There is an old story based upon a vaudeville act that both Palmer (2003) and Kohn (1999) use to illustrate the dilemma of data interpretation, particularly when the data to be interpreted has to do with numbers. It is worth retelling here:

A man is walking down the street at night. He comes across another man looking rather frantically for something under a streetlight. The first man asks, "What are you searching for?" The second man replies, "I've lost my watch!" The first man volunteers to help the second man look for the watch. They look everywhere but find nothing. Finally, the first man says, "Certainly, your watch is not here. Are you sure this is where you lost it?" The second man replies, "Oh, no, I didn't lose it here. I lost it farther up the street." Exasperated, the first man exclaims, "Then why are we looking for the watch here?" The second man replies, "Because the light is better here."

Indeed, this is always the danger in data interpretation: We want to look where it is easiest, where there is light, where we aren't forced to look at ourselves. We want to look where the seeing is easy and, we hope, the solutions are easy. This can be true interpreting the informal assessment generated from life in the classroom, as well as when interpreting formal research data.

In Western culture, the light in education often shines brightest on clear, unambiguous data. We seek the bottom line. Numbers are nearly sacred; they are often the final word in a debate. They have the appearance of objectivity and fairness, and therefore wield power and influence. Statistics are used by the dominant culture to sell everything from toothpaste to educational policy. As Kohn (1999) has written:

Any aspect of learning (or life) that resists being reduced to numbers is regarded as vaguely suspicious. By contrast, anything that appears in numerical form seems reassuringly scientific; if the numbers are getting larger over time, we must be making progress. (p. 75)

continues ➡

analytic memos, consult colleagues both critical and distant, and engage in an interpretive process that brings all the voices of your AR project together. We hope you find joy in this journey of discovery.

The strategies described in this book are focused on analyzing and interpreting qualitative data (see chapter 3 on "The Action Research Design" and "Trustworthiness in Data Interpretation" in this chapter).

Interpretation

What does it mean to "interpret"? In your notebook, write a definition of the word *interpret*. Include several examples of the different kinds of interpretation you do in order to make sense of your own life. For example, how do you interpret a "great weekend," a "good deal," or a poem? How does the way you form interpretations reflect on your own values and personal context?

Consider this quote: "Interpretation is an art.... The interpreter must use art, and at best he will be somewhat of a poet" (Tilden, 1977, pp. 26-27). Tilden wrote principles of interpretation to be used by curators of museums to encourage visitors to engage with museum artifacts. He wanted visitors to not simply view museum displays, but to interpret them interactively. How might this same principle apply to the work of interpreting data generated during teaching and learning? Who is the "visitor" to your AR data? What represents the "exhibits"?

We think of data interpretation in action research as a way of making and creating understanding out of the chaos of our practice as teachers. We all auto-

Smith (1998) retells the story of scientific theory in education. He argues that our fascination with statistical analysis and standardized testing in education comes from our desire for control. "Rigorous control," he writes, "was the key element that education adopted from laboratory theory" (p. 55). Experimental research is often referred to as scientific inquiry. Experimental research relies on controlling the conditions, or variables, under which the inquiry is carried out. For experimental research to be valid, all variables must be adequately accounted for.

This means that when experimental research is applied to education, major assumptions must be made about students, parents, culture, class, and communities. Experimental designs "control" or account for such variables through the use of a large sample size. The assumption is also made that the person recording the data and then interpreting the numbers can be detached from the setting, the interpretation, and the students. It assumes the researcher is objective and that the researcher's personal paradigm won't interfere with the interpretation process. Obviously this is a problematic and potentially dangerous aspect of experimental research in education. The assumption of full researcher objectivity is what Haraway (1996) calls a "god trick," the belief in a kind of vision of "seeing everything from nowhere" (p. 253). The same kind of "god trick" can make us ignore what we really need to see and to feel in order to believe we are controlling our reality by being objective.

Control is a sneaky desire. It lures us by promising safety and stability. It can make us believe that what feels chaotic can be ordered and aligned in neat categories. It makes life—especially life in a classroom with 32 very independent, individual human beings—seem desirable and "doable." But the desire for control, partnered with the call for objectivity and the sacredness of the "bottom line," is dangerous in that it can paint a picture of classrooms that is sterile and devoid of the dilemmas, conflicts, joys, and rewards of the lived experience of teaching. The end results of numbers printed across the page can seem more like a spectacle of what is left after the dementors from the Harry Potter children's book series have sucked life out of the living

continues →

matically do interpretation at different levels in our lives as teachers. We make assumptions, judgments, and inferences based upon our students' behavior, dress, and language use. We constantly make informal and ongoing interpretations to create order of our lived experiences. Such interpretations may be useful and dangerous since we often take action or make judgments based upon quick interpretations.

Barriers to Interpretation

In the AR process, interpretation is a more deliberate action. We have a collection of data and we deliberately set about interpreting this data. The data becomes evidence when it is directed toward our question, when it is used with purpose and layered with meaning (Lincoln, 2002). The problem is that the process of interpretation often feels more messy than deliberate.

Furthermore, we often wonder what right or authority we have to make such interpretations. This question can haunt even the most experienced researcher. A lesson from interpretive methodology may allow us to reframe our ideas around interpretation. Tilden's (1977) six principles, written for guiding educators at museums, are also particularly appropriate to interpreting AR data. Consider some of these guidelines from Tilden (1977):

Any interpretation that does not somehow relate to what is being displayed or described to something within the personality or experience of the visitor will be sterile.

Information, as such, is not interpretation. Interpretation is revelation based upon

(e.g., Rowling, 1999). Little wonder that teachers sometimes ignore educational research and standardized tests results and consider them "outside" of their practice as teachers.

Ironically, the field of science best teaches us about how our paradigm for thinking can limit our ability to interpret "scientific rigorous research" from outside our own box of belief (Zukav, 1980). For three centuries, scientific research provided evidence for, and was believed to have proved the classical mechanics of physics. The understanding of the universe constructed by Galileo and Isaac Newton became so accepted that it was considered common sense. Ironically, the most rigorous experiments of the day held clues about the fallibility of classical Newtonian physics, but the received paradigm was so powerful that most scientists couldn't see into their own data. It took Albert Einstein's imploding of classical physics, with his radical theories of relativity, to alter the way we view space and time itself. What Einstein proposed appeared to be nonsense. As Zukav (1980) notes, "The history of scientific thought, if it teaches us anything at all, teaches us the folly of clutching ideas too closely" (p. 251).

In data interpretation, there is always danger that we will find evidence to support that which we want to believe, that which appears to be common sense according to our paradigm, and that which makes us feel less discomfort and more safety. Numbers, in our society, tend to do just this.

But this very thing that makes numbers dangerous also makes numbers useful. If we can understand the limits of objectivity, we can use the principles of objectivity to improve our own practice and educational policy. If we can learn the basics of statistical analysis—putting numbers into proper context—then numbers can be powerful ways of knowing and understanding. To return to the lesson from science: Einstein applied rigorous scientific research *and* imagination to disprove three centuries' worth of physics, just as earlier scientists applied rigorous scientific research *and* imagination to prove their erroneous theories. To simply say, "Numbers are bad," "Don't ever use an objective test," or "Disregard all statistical analysis" would be to miss a

continues ➡

information. But they are entirely different things. However, all interpretation includes information.

The chief aim of interpretation is not instruction, but provocation.

Imagine yourself at a museum. There are scores of displays—but only a few will be meaningful to you. Most likely, the displays that you will label as your "favorites" will be those that resonate with you personally. The same is true in AR data interpretation: the data that will be most meaningful to you will most likely represent a conflict, an uncomfortable space of being or learning, or an unnerving question that relates to where you are in the process of becoming a teacher. This data will move you by affirmation or spur you to transformation. If you find your data is "sterile," then you may want to revisit your question, your method collections, or your motivation for conducting the project. Data has the power to change practice.

In other words, the interpretations you make based on your data are personal, rooted in your individual context and self. This realization may free you from the notion that you aren't qualified to make judgments. Recall that *"Interpretation is revelation based upon information."* *Revelation* is a word shrouded with religious fervor, meaning "an enlightening or astonishing disclosure" (*Merriam-Webster Online Dictionary*, 2005).

Most of all, a revelation is personal. Your AR interpretation may not quite reach the level of "astonishing," but it should be meaningful and significant to you (Eisner, 1998).

powerful way of looking. As discussed in this chapter, multiple viewpoints are what makes research and classroom assessments trustworthy.

In this section, we want to provide a framework for deconstructing numbers in education within a North American cultural context. Entire books are written about this topic, so you will need to look further for an extensive review of statistical analysis in education (see Coladarci, Cobb, Minium, & Clarke, 2004; Gorard, 2001). The goal here, however, is to keep the tension at play between what is dangerous and what is useful, and how teachers can better understand and use the data produced by statistical methodologies. To begin this discussion, here are some broad questions to ask whenever you meet statistical analysis in education.

When considering objective tests, standardized tests, or statistical analysis in educational research, ask:

Are the questions themselves meaningful? What framework for thinking decides which questions are meaningful? Do the questions reflect the context for learning and teaching? Here is a general rule: Know the context and critical questions of the research before quoting the results.

How are key concepts or interventions being defined? Read these definitions carefully; do not assume there is universal agreement on what, for example, "fluency in reading" means.

What other context brings meaning to the numbers? Numbers alone, just like stories alone, always isolate knowledge. While we admit that our knowledge is always partial, we return to the principle of trustworthiness: The more viewpoints entertained, the more trustworthy the data becomes.

Why was this particular methodology chosen? Why was an objective test chosen? Is this the best way to assess the knowledge the researchers were looking for? Why a standardized test? Why statistical analysis? Were these assessments chosen for efficiency or because they are the best way to respond to the questions posed?

Were the methodologies employed valid and reliable? Results printed as numbers don't make the results meaningful in

continues ➡

Interpret to Provoke, Not Instruct

Tilden (1977) suggests that "[t]he chief aim of interpretation is not instruction, but provocation." We like this concept integrated into AR interpretation particularly because it denies "conclusions" or grand statements of "truth." Partial understanding is recognized here; as action researchers we cannot ever know entirely a problem or a solution (Haraway, 1996; Kincheloe, 2003). Data interpretation should incite more questions, more hunches, more places for teacher/researchers to travel next in their professional journey. To *provoke* is to "arouse to a feeling or action" (*Merriam-Webster Online Dictionary*, 2005). Data interpretation should move teacher/researchers to *action*—interpretation simulates change as we reimagine and then restructure our practice based upon data interpretation (Bloom, 2002; Kincheloe, 2003).

and of themselves. How has the researcher accounted for variables? What variables are noted? Are there others that appear missing (and, by implication, ignored)?

What are the limits of knowledge produced by the results? Are these limits acknowledged? Read for what is missing. Read for assumptions. Think about context: What additional information is needed to make the numbers more meaningful and/or the picture more complete? Sometimes we make leaps of faith in data interpretation, from what is actually there to what we want to be there. Do such leaps of faith exist?

There is one more broad principle that we want to apply in our deconstruction and lessons on numbers. This lesson reportedly comes from Albert Einstein's office wall. It is worth posting on every teacher/researcher's wall: Not everything that counts can be counted and not everything that can be counted counts.

The deliberate and formal act of data interpretation in AR mirrors the way effective teachers use interpretation of assessment in daily practice. Those quick interpretations may or may not be particularly trustworthy, but those teachers who allow assessment (not just hunches) to drive their instructional practice are those teachers who are creating spaces for children and adolescents in all contexts, from all contexts, with all kinds of diverse needs, to be successful in learning. Data interpretation is at the heart of learning to teach; this is the means by which teachers tailor instruction for all learners.

Doubting Voices of Data Interpretation

As preservice teachers, there will be a tendency for you to lack confidence in your interpretations. We all surround ourselves with other voices to create trustworthiness in our interpretations and we acknowledge the role of context in the act of interpreting data. Most likely, you will need to refute (more than once!) the "doubting" voice that says, "You don't know enough" (figure 4.1).

Data interpretation in student-teacher action research is "personal meaning making." In the company of friends and colleagues you interpret, assume, ignore, embrace, and question the results of your work. Borrowing again from museum specialists, we learn to be skeptical of orthodoxy, including our own.

None of us really "know enough" when it comes to teaching or researching. Our meaning making is always partial and influenced by our own values and beliefs. Our "conclusions," then,

➜ FIGURE 4.1: Doubting Voices of Data Interpretation

Learn to say NO and keep thinking/writing!

"You haven't proved anything! Your research is a SHAM!"
"Yeah, where are the numbers? This is just what you think!"

Retort:
My research has never been about "proving" anything right, good, wrong, bad, or otherwise.
My research is about my process of becoming a teacher.

"There isn't anything here at all. There is nothing interesting. This is really dumb. This isn't very profound. You should start over." "ppsssst! That's because you are not smart enough"

Retort:
My experience, my learning, is valuable, rich, and worth telling.
There is nothing more profound than the
act of learning to teach.
I will not let this voice de-value these last intense months of my living and learning.

"You are not doing this RIGHT. You are going to FAIL."

Retort from Anne Lamott, Author & Writing Instructor, Bird by Bird *(1994):*
"Perfectionism is the voice of the oppressor, the enemy of the people.
It will keep you cramped and insane your whole life…perfectionism will ruin your writing,
blocking inventiveness and playfulness and life force…
Perfectionism…will only drive you mad." (pp. 28-31)
This isn't about doing it "right." It is about having the courage to explore my own becoming.

"Keep it secret, keep it low: What if 'they' find you out?"

Retort:
All self-reflection requires vulnerability: the fear of "being found out" is embedded
in the belief that I am not good enough. I am.

A Final Retort from T.H. White, The Once and Future King *(1958):*
"Learn why the world wags and what wags it. That is the only thing which the mind
can never exhaust, never alienate, never be tortured by, never fear or distrust,
and never dream of regretting.
Learning is the thing for you." (p. 186)

are tentative and surrounded by self-analysis and reflexivity (Arminio & Hultgren, 2002; Gergen & Gergen, 2003; McCotter, 2001).

Data interpretation is hard work. Despite the feeling that it may be a "leap of faith," some magical ability to gaze into a crystal ball, or simply "touchy-feely," it ultimately requires tenacity to read, think, analyze, synthesize, and deconstruct. Even statistical analyses based strictly on numerical data don't simply speak "truth" on their own. Someone, a subjective person, has to interpret the results. But while all interpretation is subjective, there are methodologies that make interpretation personal without falling into the untrustworthy trap of self-centered babble. In the next section, you will practice and apply some of these methodologies. Remember to stay open; there may be an "astonishing disclosure" sitting right next to you.

Analysis

To *analyze* means to take apart, to break down or dissect (figure 4.2). We divide the data into categories, columns, or other regularized spaces. We separate pieces of the data, making it simpler to study. To analyze is to narrow our gaze; it is pulling in the subjects, problems, and questions with the micro lens of inquiry.

→ FIGURE 4.2: To Analyze/Flower Perspectives

> Key questions for analysis include:
>
> What seems to be happening in this data? What is *not* happening in this data?
>
> What is repeated in this data (words, behaviors, attitudes, occurrences)?
>
> What is surprising, perplexing, disturbing in the data?
>
> What information seems to be missing from the data?

Synthesis

To *synthesize* is the act of putting back together again, of creating wholeness, or integrating pieces to form a sense of harmony or unity. To synthesize the data means pulling away from the parts (analysis) and seeing the data set as a whole. When we synthesize data, we change the lens of inquiry to wide angle and see the data with all of its pieces, as an entire photo (figure 4.3).

Key questions for synthesis include:

What patterns emerge across the landscape of the data?

What is the classroom context for these patterns?

Where are the contradictions, paradoxes, and dilemmas in the data? What does not seem to fit in the landscape?

What are the emotional and intellectual reactions to this data?

What confirms and disaffirms what is thought about the research question?

Deconstruction

To *deconstruct* is to check assumptions, to consider what personal and social context frames our analysis and synthesis. To deconstruct data is to check under, around, behind, and over our conclusions. When we deconstruct data, we put the camera of inquiry down, walk back up the hill, and look behind us to see what view we've been missing (figure 4.4).

Key questions for deconstruction include:

Where have categories of either/or interpretations been made? How can these either/or conclusions be reconstructed using a different lens?

What are the limitations of the analysis and synthesis? What do you not know and what can you *not* know?

What assumptions are being made in the analysis and synthesis? What values and beliefs do these assumptions rely upon?

➜ FIGURE 4.3: To Synthesize/Flower in Context

➜ FIGURE 4.4: To Deconstruct/Peruvian Mountain

What would students, parents, a mentor-teacher, an advisor, or authors in the literature say about the analysis and synthesis?

What is useful and dangerous about the analysis and synthesis?

Context

If you have traveled the "Cultural Context" side roads so far in this book, you have made discoveries of the importance of context in studying our practice as teachers. The cultural, social, and political context of who we are as teacher/researchers creates the lens through which we interpret our data. We like the idea of "situated knowledge" (Haraway, 1996). Situated knowledge means that knowledge (and thus our interpretations of data) is related to specific location, historical and sociopolitical context. Who we are as teacher/researchers matters. Where we've grown up, our ethnic identification, our social class all matter. Our religious beliefs, our values based on gender, our understanding of "good" and "bad" teachers all matter. All of this

→ FIGURE 4.5: Context of Flower

matters when we interpret data. We need to remember our context, and consider who you are in taking this photo (figure 4.5), and we need to ask the question, "Why is this subject/scene one I desire to photograph?"

Key questions in considering context include:

How does the role of the student teacher influence the data and the interpretation of data?

In what ways did the AR project conclude in the way you as the teacher/researcher wanted? How does this reflect your own beliefs/values?

How do the interpretations reflect your beliefs/values of what "good teaching" is, "good students" are, and "good curriculum" should be?

How do the interpretations mirror values and beliefs you hold as a teacher/researcher given your ethnic, gender, and social standings, and other labels that may be used to define you? How are the interpretations limited by these same labels?

How do the interpretations align with the stated school and community values and beliefs where the project was conducted?

Trustworthiness in Data Interpretation

We have stated that the goal of AR is not to "prove" something, but to find insight and meaning in our practice that results in positive changes for ourselves, our students, and the school and communities in which we teach. We have also stated that the meanings we construct are partial, situated in context and place. Given this, how do we create trustworthiness in our research as teachers? What criteria can guide us? The following principles are discussed in the literature of qualitative research and are useful to teacher/researchers. However, the proper establishment of credibility in qualitative research remains the subject of a contested and lively conversation (Denzin & Lincoln, 2003; Lather, 2004; Lincoln & Guba, 2003; Smith, 1993). We have combined principles from qualitative inquiry we think are most useful to student teacher/action researchers and presented them here. While these ideas are presented categorically, they overlap in a more circular fashion, with each criterion embedded within the others. Read the following once as guiding principles for research; read again and see how these qualities represent an exemplary teacher.

Self-Study: The Teacher/Researcher as Strategic Intervention

In the action research design template included in this volume, you are asked to describe a "synopsis of the strategy to be used, the intervention to be tried, the innovation to be implemented, the evaluation to be conducted, or other action to be applied in the study." Such interventions may appear outside of the teacher/researcher but if we recognize that the teacher/researcher is a participant in the study, then we must also see the teacher/researcher as "strategic intervention." You are a strategy; you are the intervention!

To consider the teacher/researcher as "intervention" returns us to earlier questions: "What is good teaching?" "What does a good teacher look like?" The responses to such questions are many and are rooted in cultural and historical settings, promoted by those in authority, and informed by cultural values. The work of Haberman (1991) suggests that what often defines good teaching is more tradition or "ritualistic acts . . . conducted for their intrinsic value rather than to foster learning" (p. 292). Haberman notes that "good teaching" can be identified more by observing students, rather than their teachers.

Consider Haberman's "good teaching" qualities in Self-Study Table 4.1. Compare and contrast your current teaching situation with his list by giving specific examples.

Does your own student teaching or the teaching you are observing qualify as good teaching according to Haberman? Could you list many examples of each characteristic? What are some of the reasons behind your answers? (Think about paradigms, assumptions, and structures of schooling.) Do you find yourself agreeing or disagreeing with this list? How does your reaction relate to your own paradigm for defining "good teaching"?

Haberman also argues that "good teaching" is more likely to occur in affluent schools where higher-order thinking skills are more likely to be encouraged. The pedagogy of poverty involves quite another list of traits. This list is primarily associated with management and control: giving information, directions, and

continues ➡

Theoretical Framework

Place your action research within the company of experts, those "distant colleagues" who have published in the literature (Eisner, 1998; Hubbard & Power, 2003; Johnson, 1997; McCotter, 2001; Patton, 2002). Align your interpretations within this circle to make up for the lack

tests; assigning and reviewing seatwork and homework assignments; and settling conflicts within the classroom. Does this list better describe your current teaching or the teaching you are observing? Why do you think this is true? What drives these pedagogical decisions?

of your own experience, comprehensive data, and/or length of engagement in the project. The

➡ **SELF-STUDY TABLE 4.1:** Haberman's "Good Teaching" Qualities (Haberman, 1991)

Haberman (1991) on "Good Teaching"	My School Site and "Good Teaching"
Whenever students are involved with issues they regard as vital concerns, good teaching is going on.	
Whenever students are involved with explanations of human differences, good teaching is going on.	
Whenever students are being helped to see major concepts, big ideas, and general principles and are not merely engaged in pursuit of isolated facts, good teaching is going on.	
Whenever students are involved in planning what they will be doing, it is likely that good teaching is going on.	
Whenever students are involved with applying ideals such as fairness, equity, or justice to their world, it is likely that good teaching is going on.	
Whenever students are actively involved, it is likely that good teaching in going on.	
Whenever students are directly involved in a real-life experience, it is likely that good teaching is going on.	
Whenever students are actively involved in heterogeneous groups, it is likely that good teaching is going on.	
Whenever students are asked to think about an idea in a way that questions common sense or widely accepted assumption, that relates new ideas to ones learned previously, or that applies an idea to the problems of living, then there is a chance that good teaching is going on.	
Whenever teachers involve students with the technology information access, good teaching is going on.	
Whenever students are involved in reflecting on their own lives and how they have come to believe and feel as they do, good teaching is going on.	

theoretical framework you decide upon guides your research, and your choice of method and methodology, your way of thinking about the data (Arminio & Hultgren, 2002).

Multiple Perspectives

Multiple perspectives are foundational in creating trustworthiness (Gergen & Gergen, 2003). Seeking multiple perspectives, insights, or "voices" provides for layers of interpretation the teacher/researcher could not attain in isolation. Seek and listen to the voices of colleagues, mentor-teachers, participants (students), and advisors, as well as those in the literature. Multiple perspectives are sought through collecting data from multiple sources (a matter of design) and from seeking differing perspectives during analysis (a matter of interpretation). In this way, the teacher/researcher may be seen as a *bricoleur*—a handyman, do-it-yourselfer— or a quiltmaker (Denzin & Lincoln, 2003b; Kincheloe, 2003), using the available tools to piece together meaning.

Describing Context, Relationships, and Methods

Making clear the cultural, social, and political context of the study, as well as the relationship of the researcher to the researched and the methods of the study, is all critical in establishing trustworthiness in action research (Arminio & Hultgren, 2002; Eisner, 1998; Gitlin, 2000; Jarrett & Odoms-Young, 2005; Johnson, 1997; Whitt, 1991; Willig, 2003). Be clear in describing the school context (Chapter 2: Getting to Know Your Classroom Culture). Describe well your position as a student teacher and your growing relationships with your students; take care to be accurate in describing the methods you used in your study.

Self-Reflexivity

When practicing self-reflexivity, "the investigator relinquishes the 'God's-eye view' and reveals his or her work as historically, culturally, and personally situated" (Gergen & Gergen, 2003). Practicing self-reflexivity as a student teacher/action researcher means describing your values and belief systems, what is important to you, your past experiences, what you know, what you think you know, and what you want to know about teaching because "*How* we know is intimately bound up with *what* we know, where we learned it, and what we have experienced" (Lincoln & Denzin, 2003. p. 631; emphasis in the original). This is a kind of self-interrogation, recognizing the role of the teacher/researcher in choosing methodology and methods, curriculum, and making interpretation and evaluation. Self-reflexivity keeps transparent the paradigms, theories, assumptions, judgments, biases, and the transformation of thought throughout the research process. Such reflexivity is yet another piece in constructing qualitative research that is credible (Arminio & Hultgren, 2002; Gergen & Gergen, 2003; Johnson, 1997; Lather, 1991; McCotter, 2001; Moore, 1999).

Moral and Ethical Considerations

As a student teacher/action researcher begin by asking, "Why is this project important to the participants?" The deeper the response is in regard to making teaching and learning practices more just and fair, finding ways to educate all children, and making the school a more caring place of learning, the richer the level of trustworthiness. Action research and teaching is a commitment to ongoing "critical conversations about democracy, race, gender, class, nation, freedom, and community" (Lincoln & Denzin, 2003, p. 612); thus, we recognize that our teaching and research is not isolated to the classroom. Ethical and moral considerations include issues of *representation* (Fine, Weis, Weseen, & Wong, 2003). Is the text that you present "faithful to the context and the individuals it is supposed to represent" (Lincoln & Denzin, 2003, p. 618)? This is a critical question for student teacher/action researcher to consider. Yet another moral and ethical consideration is one of *agency* or *praxis* (Bloom, 2002; Kincheloe, 2003; Lather, 1991). Does the study result in transformation in your own thinking toward being a teacher and your own practice as a teacher? Does the study make a difference in the lives of your students? Could it impact the school or community in a positive way?

Tentative Statements of Conclusion

Self-Study The Student Teacher/Researcher and Classroom Management

The student teachers we work with "get stuck" most often in the action research process because of "classroom management issues." At times we receive this kind of e-mail from students:

I am going to have to change my action research project. As you know, I was going to use "literature circles" as my strategic intervention. I was hoping to see how literature circles might support reading comprehension, but after today, I know this isn't going to work. The students were terrible. Not one group really talked about the novels they are reading. Chaos ruled. My teacher says that this group just can't handle this kind of unstructured learning. I am going to have to do something different. —Leona

Our students, for the most part, agree with Haberman's (1991) list of "good teaching" characteristics. They see themselves as teachers who are student-centered. They resist notions of "teaching straight from the text." They move into the classroom with a vision of students actively "owning" and guiding the learning; they anxiously wait the day they can "take over" and implement authentic assessments, group work, and relate content to students' interests and lives. When the day finally comes, their experience may resemble Leona's experience. So what happened? Is it true that some students "just can't handle" student-directed learning? Are some students "not ready"? Do some students need a teacher to tell them what to do in order to stay on task?

Research is about telling stories that are partial; we do not tell an "entire story" (Elam, 1994). As teacher/action researchers, our "conclusions" are tentative because we recognize our partial knowledge; we can never know all of the "truth" of our stories (Haraway, 1996; Lather, 1993; Lincoln & Guba, 2003). In the retelling of our experiences, we resist grand narratives or statements. As student teacher/action researchers, your retellings are located in your limited experience and engagement with students and school communities. This meaning making is hopefully significant and powerful for you; it is enough that it is your story of becoming a teacher. You should not feel compelled to make it more or less.

Pamela's Story: How Paradigm Matters

Trustworthiness, because it involves self-reflexivity, can be very difficult. We know a story about a student teacher named Pamela who was asked by school district officials to investigate a new reading program being field tested in her school. Pamela excitedly consented to study the reading program, and we encouraged her to create her AR project around this topic, which she did. It was clear from the beginning that the school district was very enthusiastic about the new reading program, and was hoping Pamela's study would add some weight to their impending decision to implement the program districtwide.

Pamela completed a thorough literature review, seeking out faculty who were expert in literacy programs and who advised her of the powerful and dangerous aspects of the new reading program. She collected a reasonably rich data set, adding participant voices and multiple perspectives. She was clear about the context of her study (English language learners) and engaged with the students, parents, and reading program for eight months during her student teaching.

Of the four students Pamela tracked closely through the eight months, three displayed a pattern in which their Lexile reading scores improved somewhat initially, but then declined to previous levels. The students reported in interviews that the program was "boring."

Pamela expressed some concern and puzzlement about these negative results, and provided additional data about each student to attempt to explain her findings. However, she was ultimately unable to provide a trustworthy interpretation, writing the following in her results section:

Out of everything that I have been observing and learning from these students, the most important improvement has been their increased confidence. I know that even for those students that I didn't follow closely their own self-confidence has increased in their ability to read. For me to be able to state that with no question in my mind, I can say, "This program is successful!"

Pamela was unable (understandably, given her position as student teacher and the context of her study) to be completely self-reflexive about what her data was saying. She was unable to let go of her preconceived ideas about what the study was "supposed" to show or prove. Letting go of our "private universe" of ideas about our AR question is the hardest part of data interpretation. We refer to this passage by Elliot Eisner (2002):

Our inclination to control and predict is, at a practical level, understandable, but it also exacts a price; we tend to do the things we know how to predict and control. Opening oneself to the uncertain is not a pervasive quality of our current educational environment. I believe that it needs to be among the values we cherish. Uncertainty needs to have its proper place in the kinds of schools we create. (p. 11)

A Final Word: The Importance of Getting the Data

Student teaching is overwhelming: there are units to plan, lessons to adjust, assessments to be evaluated. There are so many expectations, so many "performances," and so many criteria to be demonstrated. So we circle back again to this critical piece of advice: *There is no research without data.*

You must be deliberate in planning and collecting data. You must be deliberate about ongoing data analysis. You must practice direct communication with your mentor-teacher and your advisor.

Ongoing Data Analysis, Synthesis, and Deconstruction

What do you see, how do you react, when you see figure 4.6 and its caption? Jot your quick responses in your notebook.

→ FIGURE 4.6: Arctic National Wildlife Refuge. ©Subhankar Banarjee.

The way you responded to the title of the photo reveals something about your own values and belief systems. Your response may classify you as "environmentalist," "pragmatist," "spiritual," "capitalist," or any number of other labels with which you may identify. Depending upon your viewpoint of the terms *arctic* and *wilderness*, you probably trust some voices on this topic more than others. This illustrates, in yet another way, why *paradigm matters*.

Listen to these conflicting voices on this topic in figure 4.7. Each of the speakers "sees" the photo differently: some as a way of life, others as economic wealth, some as national security, and others as a place to be preserved, a sanctuary. Whatever your opinions, you are more likely to listen to those you agree with. You will build your arguments using their expertise. The same phenomenon occurs in action research. You have a hunch about a dilemma or question in the classroom. As you build your literature review, you will tend to listen to those voices that most likely align with your own values. Again, this is why paradigm matters, why you must deconstruct what frames your own ways of thinking, and practice active reflexivity.

While finding agreeable company is comfortable and supportive, being a classroom teacher requires listening to more voices than just those of the people with which we agree. Most of the time, solving problems in the classroom requires listening to everyone. How astute are you at this skill? Developing multiple ways of looking and listening increases the trustworthiness of our AR work and our practice as teachers. In this section, we explore ways of looking—ways of listening—to build trustworthiness in our interpretations.

One of the ways we implement multiple perspectives and ways of knowing is through ongoing data analysis, synthesis, and deconstruction. Rather than waiting until all data is collected, action researchers conduct ongoing analysis during the data-collection process. Some reasons for doing this are:

To modify the AR design; through ongoing analysis, action researchers may realize the data they are collecting doesn't adequately address the question, and in these cases,

→ FIGURE 4.7: Voices

Alaska's Arctic National Wildlife Refuge is the crown jewel of America's National Wildlife Refuge System. Tucked away in the state's remote northeast corner, this 19.6-million-acre wildlife sanctuary is an awe-inspiring natural wonder: a sweeping expanse of tundra studded with marshes and lagoons and laced with rivers dramatically situated between the rugged foothills of the Brooks Range and the wide, icy waters of the Beaufort Sea.

—Defenders of Wildlife (www.defenders.org/wildlife/arctic/overview.html)

Drilling in the ANWR will not threaten that natural preserve and will increase U.S. energy independence. Studies by the U.S. Geological Survey (USGS) estimate that drilling in ANWR could yield up to 16 billion barrels of oil--an amount roughly equal to 30 years of oil imports from Saudi Arabia.

—The Heritage Foundation (Coon, 2001)

The Arctic Refuge is a place of living grandeur, one throbbing with life, an Arctic legacy of world importance that we must treat with respect and restraint. Its presence honors the past, assures the Native peoples, especially the Gwich'in of Alaska and Canada their subsistence and cultural identity, and makes a bequest to the future. Few people will ever visit this remote place. But one need not see a grizzly or a throng of caribou or fog-shrouded peaks rising above nameless valleys to benefit from their presence. Wilderness values are too precious to permit them to succumb to special interests. One must question what is ethically and esthetically correct, and not just what is economically and politically expedient.

—George B. Schaller (2003, p.68)

The Inupiat people believe that this highly prospective area represents our nation's best hope for significant new deposits of a critical strategic resource. We believe that delays in development deprive us of the economic benefits from our lands.

—Jacob Adams, Chairman & President,
Arctic Slope Regional Cooperation
(June 1995)

NOW THEREFORE BE IT RESOLVED:
That the Tanana Chiefs Conference Board of Directors urges the U.S. Congress and President to recognize the rights of our Gwich'in people to continue to live their way of life by prohibiting development in the calving and post-calving grounds of the Porcupine Caribou Herd; and

BE IT FURTHER RESOLVED:
That to 1002 area of the Arctic National Wildlife Refuge be made Wilderness to achieve this end.

—Tanana Chiefs Conference Board of Directors
Resolution # 90-2: March 1990
Mitch Demientieff, Secretary-Treasurer

data-collection methods need to be modified.

To recheck and possibly modify the critical question; through ongoing analysis, action researchers may discover the question, itself, has changed.

To change the course of practice; ongoing analysis can show us as teachers that some of our practices, choices, or decisions are not the best for our students, and this may be the best reason to do ongoing analysis—to alter the course of our teaching to make our classrooms better places for learning.

Ongoing Analysis: The Analytic Memo

Jane was student teaching and conducting her AR project in a seventh grade low-academic-level math class located in a rural community. Her AR critical question was, "Will teaching math concepts to my seventh grade students with tactile presentations/activities have a positive effect on their learning?" Jane confirmed through a learning-style inventory that most of her students were kinesthetic learners, yet most of the instruction in the classroom consisted of visual and verbal modalities for learning (lecture from the overhead and individual book work). Jane hoped that through the implementation of kinesthetic teaching and learning structures her students might become mathematical problem solvers who might actually enjoy math.

SS 4.3: Creating a Scaffold for Learning

You may have decided that the "best practices" taught in your teacher-education program are not "real world" teaching strategies. After a hard day of teaching you may find yourself saying something like, "These kids just can't work with manipulatives, be trusted with a science lab, or be allowed to work with anything that has the potential to bounce." These frustrations, all of which and more we have heard from our students (and experienced ourselves) stem from the dissonance between our beliefs about teaching and what happens in our practice. Whitehead (1989) calls this experiencing living contradiction; such contradictions encourage us to ask revised questions, seek additional voices, and rethink our teaching.

When this happens, revisit your personal paradigm and consider how you define words like authority and respect. Where do your definitions come from? Who taught you these meanings? Consider again how both your own paradigms of the "good teacher" and the "good student" and the context of your student teaching affect your teaching. Finally, think about the differences between teacher-directed learning and student-centered learning. How are these differences experienced by students?

Most often, we find student teachers enthusiastically embrace student-centered teaching; for this we are thankful. However, if students in their classes are more accustomed to a "pedagogy of poverty," then an abrupt change to student-centered learning can be uncomfortable. When expectations for what is "normal" in a classroom are violated, even if for reasons of higher order thinking, fairness, and/or compassion, discomfort, resistance, and even open rebellion may be the result. Therefore, successful change requires care, thought, patience, and intentional support. In short, change requires a scaffold.

Consider this example. Suppose students have learned that being successful at school means completing the worksheet in a timely manner and getting the right answers. When confronted with an inquiry-based lesson in which they are asked to risk posing wrong answers, what will be the result? The lesson may not

continues ➡

In a formal analytical memo, she analyzes her first data set. This data set, collected over a two-week-period, includes:

Observations from four 70-minute lessons, including one lesson covering prime numbers with tiles and another using Microsoft Excel software to teach divisibility rules.

Two interviews: one a learning style inventory and the other an activity preference survey.

Artifacts or student work from the lesson using tiles, the spread sheets from the Excel software project, and a three-dimensional poster project demonstrating math concepts learned.

Informal analysis in her researcher's journal of each of the lessons she taught.

Find Jane's memo, along with our responses in italics, in figure 4.8.

How does this memo demonstrate a teacher/researcher analyzing, synthesizing, and deconstructing data? Return to the introduction of this section and read again the critical questions to guide analysis, synthesis, and deconstruction if need be. You may also want to review the Cultural Context sections in chapter 3. In what ways does Jane analyze, synthesize, and deconstruct this data set? How does she or doesn't she address context? Respond to Jane as a critical colleague by writing questions that would further her analysis, synthesis, deconstruction, and attention to context.

Having read and considered Jane's memo, you can, we hope, begin to more fully understand the purpose of ongoing

"work." Or if students are used to having all lab material supplied for them, they may be baffled that you ask them to think of a way and find the supplies on their own to conduct an experiment. If they are used to being given a study guide to memorize in review for the test, they may be confused about why you are asking them to construct their own study guide; they may see this as a waste of time, or even worse, they may think you are trying to trick them. If students have learned that "doing school" is an individual pursuit, a competition, with the best person landing the A grade, then they may not be enthusiastic about a cooperative learning assignment where they are paired with students they do not respect.

Picture a scaffold with ascending steps (Self-Study figure 4.1). If you are asking students to leap from teacher-directed learning to student-centered learning without the intermediate steps, you may be inviting a teaching-learning crash, as students fail in making the jump. This doesn't mean that the strategy you've tried "doesn't work" with a certain group of students; it does mean that you may need to intervene as the teacher and provide scaffolding for students, facilitating their learning and their thinking to higher cognitive and interpersonal levels. This may also mean providing scaffolding for their attitudes of respect for one another, for diverse opinion, and multiple viewpoints around conflict.

Don't totally reject a certain teaching strategy, and possibly your action research project, if you find yourself struggling with these kinds of issues. Rather, consult with your mentor-teacher, university advisor, critical and distant colleagues. What steps do you need to take to scaffold the learning for your students? How do you need to reframe the project to move both students and yourself towards the kind of student-centered learning you desire? What structural changes do you need to make in the classroom? What teaching skills do you need to modify, improve, and/or reframe in order to make this happen? What are your students really telling you? Listen to context; examine your own assumptions.

Work with Self-Study table 4.2 to begin your analysis of what might need to occur in your classroom if you are experiencing this kind of challenge. Be specific with your examples.

continues

analysis. Ongoing analysis should occur on a regular basis throughout your data collection period. We recommend a formal analysis after every complete data set is collected.

Informal Ongoing Analysis

Informal analysis occurs in your researcher's journal, where you think aloud about what is happening in your classroom: the responses of students, the results of data collection, informal observations and comments by students and other professionals in the classroom, critical incidents, how students demonstrated (or didn't demonstrate) their learning on assessments and/or any other stories of your practice.

One more word on ongoing analysis: *All action research is, in one form or another, a self-study.* As you reflect on your data, *you* are learning, *you* are changing, *you* are getting better at what you do as a teacher, and *your own* assumptions are being challenged. As McNiff (1988) has written, "I join in the game. I win and I lose; I live and I learn" (p. 52). You are a participant in this AR process; you are developing your own "living theory" (Whitehead, 1993).

Alternatives for Organizing, Writing, and "Doing" Ongoing Analysis

There are times when a teacher/researcher organizes the data she has collected and finds herself staring at the data, waiting, desiring, hoping that it will get up and dance. Instead, it remains fixed to the flat surface of the page. She knows "something is there," but that something seems illusive and remains out of sight

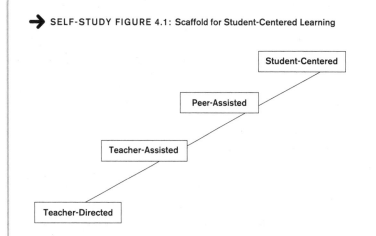

→ SELF-STUDY FIGURE 4.1: Scaffold for Student-Centered Learning

Collect data on the outcome of your plan; conduct analysis. Record your own thoughts in your researcher's notebook. Be deliberate and tenacious in your strategic intervention. Is this starting to sound familiar? Yes, this is the action research process! This kind of action/self study research is the kind of research where action and evaluation occurs simultaneously with students and colleagues within context (Hamilton, 2005); therefore, the research invites and embraces change. You may find that your critical question is modified some to include, "How can I intervene and build scaffolding for student learning when using literature circles to increase reading comprehension?"

This book is all about process, not arrival. Engage in the process of critical analysis. Don't be "stuck" by either/or choices based upon hard days of teaching (trust us—we all have them). Rather, use what feels like "failure" to rethink teaching and learning. Listen hard to your students; face what you want to ignore. (Maybe your own paradigm needs a corrective widening!) Be creative in coming at "the problem" from more than one way. Allow learning to happen.

Heidegger (1972) has written,

Teaching is more difficult than learning because what teaching calls for is this: to let learn. The real teacher, in fact, lets nothing else be learned than—learning. . . . The teacher is ahead of his apprentices in this alone, that he has still far more to learn than they—he has to learn to let them learn. (p. 15)

And to this, Greene (2001) adds that "the teacher has to learn what it is to learn to let others learn" (p. 83). And so we embrace contradictions, dilemmas, and challenges to do the work of such learning.

➡ SELF-STUDY TABLE 4.2: Problem Solving: Constructing a Scaffold

List How the Problem Looks, Sounds, and Feels.	List How You Think the Classroom Should Look, Sound, and Feel.	Brainstorm on Why You Think This Gap Exists (and What You Are Basing This Upon).	List the Steps You Can Implement. How Will You Evaluate Your Success?

➡ FIGURE 4.8: Jane's Analytic Memo with Response

DATE: November 23
TO: Donna
RE: Data Set One   Hillside Middle School   7th Grade
FROM: Jane

I administered a learning style inventory to my seventh grade math students. Almost half of my students scored the highest in the kinesthetic modality. Even more convincing, eighty-six percent of the students scored either their highest or second highest score in the kinesthetic modality. With these results, I am more convinced how necessary it is to provide opportunities for students to learn through kinesthetic activities and presentations.

Yes, it looks like the learning styles inventory did confirm your hunches about the way your students learn. Given that these students have all been labeled "low achievers" in math, it does make one wonder if they are really "low achievers" or if they simply haven't received teaching in a way that makes mathematics make sense.

When I looked at my topic that I was to teach for my curriculum unit, the greatest challenge to me was, "How am I going to make this information meaningful?" My students have learned this material before with no or little retention. I wanted to really effect change in their learning and thinking. Since my critical question is, "Will teaching math concepts to my seventh grade students with tactile presentations/activities have a positive effect on their learning?" I decided that through the inclusions of these types of activities, I could facilitate my students' learning in a meaningful way.

The observations that I made during the different activities did tell me that the students were engaged. At times, there were a few students off-task, but with more direction, these students usually got back on task. My cooperating teacher remarked how engaged the students were during the Visual Math lesson.

Yes, looking at your observation charts, there is a high level of engagements. How did you define "engagement" during the observations? Did your CT do observations as well? Getting your CT's viewpoint is critical—keep this up!

As part of my action research, I gave a survey two weeks after I completed my teaching unit to have students evaluate what activities helped facilitate learning for them. I was a little surprised by the results. One-third of my students indicated that they did not feel that the Visual Math lesson teaching factors, prime and composite numbers had helped them learn the math concept.

Did you expect them to enjoy, even have fun, doing this activity?

Reflecting on why this may be true for them when it seemed to directly contradict the observations and the related work demonstrating their understanding, I think one reason may be the uncomfortable feeling one has when they are in that disequilibrium stage of moving from not understanding to a stage of understanding. This lesson required students to construct for themselves an understanding about prime and composite numbers. The students had to build configurations out of tiles. A few of the students felt uneasy with this task, as they had not worked with this type of manipulative before.

What theorists are informing your own emerging theory? What personal experiences with math inform this emerging theory?

All of my students understood when we were finished with the lesson why the number one is not prime. Their work clearly demonstrates this. I feel this is a tremendous accomplishment. I did not just tell them this concept. They experienced it, and, the evidence suggests, they learned it.

Yes, this appears true! Do you have plans to re-visit this concept to see if it "sticks"?

The other activity that received the most negative feedback was the computer assignment. During this activity, students were to manipulate an Excel program and derive for themselves (with a buddy) divisibility rules. Students felt that this was a hard assignment. One student (female) felt the activity made her feel badly, because she "did not get it right and everyone makes me feel bad."

Were you able to follow-up with this comment? Did someone make her feel badly? Or are you assuming what made her feel badly was the difficulty of the task?

The assignment was difficult, because students were required to think about division instead of being given a list of rules as in the book. The observations of this activity tell me that students were engaged. The artifacts such as the quiz and the 3-D poster show me that student concept achievement was high. I feel that having physically manipulated the numbers, the students have an experience to hang their knowledge on and will retain this information better than if they had just memorized the facts out of the book.

Again, the assessments seem to confirm your assertion: students did learn through the Excel activity. Does it bother you that students do not seem to be "having fun" during these activities? Why and how?

One of the questions I asked on the survey that I gave was "Did I lecture enough?"

Interesting question to ask: what was your motivation behind this?

Most of the students that I have in this class have not been very successful with the "lecture and then do homework" approach to learning mathematics. However there are a couple of students in this class that have been successful learning through this method. One of these students, even though she did well on tests and quizzes and turned in a wonderful 3-D project, felt that I did not lecture enough. One of my questions I have is about the quality of her learning. Did she learn better conceptually through the activities we did than she would have if I had only lectured and she had completed work out of the text? Is her conceptual understanding higher than it would be if she were to simply hear a lecture and then do the math?

Good questions. Do you think some learners can "get it" by lecture and worksheets? How might such a comment also reflect what we know about how females are socialized? In other words, think about the fact that girls, traditionally, do not manipulate toys like boys. Could this also be a "comfort zone" issue?

My hunch is that anytime you are constructing the information for yourself rather than having a person just tell you the information, your conceptual understanding will be higher.

Yes—again, consider what theorists and personal experiences inform your emerging theory.

The activities that I planned at times were painful for my students as the activities caused them to stretch themselves and construct knowledge for themselves. The students at times were quick to give up and needed frequent modeling of how to think critically for themselves and to keep at the task at hand. I think with more practice, my students would get better and better at thinking for themselves. It feels like they have been conditioned to sit and listen and wait for the bell of clarification to go off in their heads as the teacher lectures. With these students they have become too accustomed for the bell not to go off and they have accepted just not getting a concept. Instead, they need practice at grappling with a concept and manipulating it until they can personally make the concept meaningful.

You may be on to something here. Yes, your students will get better at using the strategies of manipulatives--this is a learned art. But here is another question, "Will you get better as a teacher in organizing, facilitating, and teaching through manipulatives as well?" You mentioned this is your first time teaching in this way: how might your own acquiring of skills effect student learning?

I thought students would jump at the chance to use manipulatives, especially the computer. However, the complexity of what was asked made the manipulatives seem less like playing and more like hard learning. I hope to continue this type of teaching with activities for conceptual learning. This type of teaching provides a satisfaction so different than just standing at the front and lecturing with the overhead.

How you write that you thought students would "jump at the chance to use manipulatives" says something about you—your own beliefs systems. Does the fact that they did not jump alter your thinking? How?

I am thinking of different levels of satisfaction. I get satisfaction from going for a quick ride on my bike, a 10- miler around the wetland area where I ride. But I get another level of satisfaction from doing a 100-mile day. Your students are learning the satisfaction (as you are) of doing the 100-mile day in learning mathematics—it takes a lot more training, work, and thinking, but the end result is much more satisfying than the quick 10-mile turnaround!

beyond the corner. In these instances, an alternative approach to get the analytical juices flowing may be in order.

We have included a few examples of prewriting activities to help you as you engage in ongoing analysis and analytic memo writing (figures 4.9, 4.10, and 4.11). We've borrowed and adapted two strategies from Elbow (1998) and another from Rico (2000) that we find helpful. Use these strategies not only to do formal ongoing analysis, but also informal analysis about any classroom incident that may eventually become part of the AR study (figures 4.9, 4.10, and 4.11).

A More Structured Analytic Memo-Writing Process

"Wait!" some of you are saying, "I don't draw, doodle, or cluster. I don't think in metaphors or symbols. I need something sequential." Some of us need a more linear, sequential structure to provide scaffolding for data analysis. If this is true for your way of learning, we've created a template based upon the key questions presented in the introduction to this section to use for data analysis (figure 4.12).

Resisting Conclusions: Going with the Questions, the Dilemmas, the Conflict

Be patient towards all that is unsolved in your heart and try to love the questions themselves like locked rooms and like books that are written in a very foreign tongue. Do not now seek the answers, which cannot be given to you because you could not live them. And the point is, live everything, live the questions now.
—Rainer Maria Rilke, *Letters to a Young Poet*

The power of asking questions is that questions keep things moving. Conclusive statements shut down the conversation and therefore the possibilities. Consider these statements:

The student is lazy and unmotivated.

The students are not developmentally ready.

The material is too difficult.

The curriculum doesn't allow for that.

This teaching strategy just doesn't work with my kids.

Each statement may hold some truth and help represent a dilemma. But if statements like this are allowed to stand alone, without debate, or turned into a question, they close down the possibilities of exploring potentially erroneous assumptions, finding solutions, or seeking other voices or perceptions.

During ongoing analysis, resist making conclusive statements. Instead, pose questions that will further your exploration of your critical question. Freewrite and let the questions flow; for example:

I want to call this student lazy and unmotivated. After all, this was a great lesson in my opinion. Am I personally offended because he/she didn't think it was a great lesson? Is it just easy to say a student is lazy and unmotivated? Why would a student be lazy and unmotivated? What do I mean about these terms? What about this lesson (content and strategy) appeals more to me than to the student? Am I trying to be the entertainer of the year or am I trying to teach? What's the difference? Is there a real learning problem here or was it just a bad day?

The same principle can be applied to dilemmas and conflicts. For example, a student may seem excited about the assignment and be very involved in class, but never turn in his homework. Don't dismiss this; *study it*; believe there is something to be learned from this situation. Look not only at the individual and the specific setting, but also at school structures, social and cultural considerations, and other influences that might broaden the inquiry.

Furthermore, conflicts often represent painful, if not rich, places of learning. Classroom management issues often represent such places of conflict. Again, don't ignore these instances. Ask hard questions like:

Why does this situation make me feel like I will never be a teacher?

Why don't I like this student? As the teacher, I thought I was supposed to like, even love each student? What's wrong with me?

Why do I feel so hopeless?

Why do I need control?

What structures or processes may be in place that makes management "impossible" for both me and the student?

Kessler (2000) offers a process of creativity that may be helpful for action researchers in engaging with questions, dilemmas, and conflicts. Stages, as she warns, are rarely as sequential as they appear on paper. These steps, however, may be useful in ongoing analysis and creatively thinking out of a teaching dilemma (figure 4.13).

Getting Stuck/Getting Out: Seeking Other Voices

When you get stuck in the AR process, seek other voices—those of critical colleagues, mentor-teachers, students, parents, professors, and the literature. After seeking other voices, patterns of advice will most likely emerge. Begin creating a plan of action (adjusting the research design, teaching strategies, assessment/data collection) based upon the advice of these voices.

Changing Courses: Using Ongoing Analysis to Redirect and/or Refine the AR Study

Ongoing analysis often requires that the teacher/researcher modify or outright change the way data are being collected or even rewrite the critical question. Table 4.1 describes common situations our students encounter and the kinds of response we provide them.

➡ FIGURE 4.9: The Loop Writing Process

Peter Elbow describes loop writing as a voyage—you leave on the journey, make discoveries along the way, and then return. Only when you return, the place where you started is changed. Consider a teaching incident: a management struggle, a project that did or didn't go well, how well students did or didn't learn, etc. Reflect on data that doesn't seem to connect with other data or what you believe is really happening in the classroom. Or, after studying a complete data set, mull the details around by loop writing.

The Voyage Out

Use any one of the following strategies to "leave the port" and travel with your data:

- Dialogues. This is a good way to promote multiple viewpoints of the incident or data set. Write a dialogue between two or three students discussing the lesson or the classroom incident. Write another dialogue between a student telling her mom or dad about the lesson. Write another dialogue between an author who has published on your action research topic and yourself concerning your data set. You can write dialogues between any number of participants, both those present in the classroom and those who may not be present but could have an interest, and thus consider multiple ways of looking at your topic.

- Narrative Thinking. If you are confused about the subject, write the story of your thinking. "When I first planned to teach this lesson, I thought … and then … this happened … and I thought that …"

- Story. Use a story format. Drop the formality of "memo writing" and begin with a story line, "It was a regular day in room 234 when the student teacher decided it was time for a change …" Sometimes, it is useful to write in third person, putting yourself outside of the situation to see it a little more clearly.

- Scenes. Write in "scenes." Focus on individual moments and write them as vignettes by stopping the action and focusing in on the moment. Don't necessarily write these in chronological order—write as they come to mind when you recall the lesson, incident, or data set.

The Voyage Home—Or Looping Back to Where You Began

- Read what you have written.

- Take notes in the margins; use a highlighter.

- Write back to yourself in the attempt to create coherence out of this draft writing.

- Return to the guiding questions in the introduction to data analysis and attempt to answer them based upon your draft writing.

Adapted from:

Elbow, P. (1998). *Writing with power: Techniques for mastering the writing process* (2nd ed.). New York: Oxford University Press.

➡ FIGURE 4.10: Open-Ended Writing Process

- Write for 15–20 minutes without stopping. Put down as fast as you can all the thoughts, feelings, facts you happen to have about the topic. Write fast. Don't think, "Oh, now I need to analyze, synthesize, deconstruct and consider context." Rather, just pour words onto a page about the incident, data, or question you have.

- Release your writing—let it go where it goes.

- Pause. Find the center or focus or main point in what you wrote. Write it down in a single synthesizing sentence.

- From this single synthesized sentence, let loose with a new round of writing. Use that focusing sentence for a new burst of nonstop writing. Don't try to consciously connect the sections of writing and, again, resist thinking, "Okay, it is time to analyze the data."

- Keep alternating this cycle until you feel you've gotten to that "something" that you knew was there in the data, knew you wanted to see in the incident, or possible ways to re-frame a dilemma.

- Now, draft a memo addressing your action research data.

Adapted from:

Elbow, P. (1998). *Writing with power: Techniques for mastering the writing process* (2nd ed.). New York: Oxford University Press.

Activity: Changing Courses-Video Vignette

The companion CD includes a video vignette collected from one student regarding how her AR project changed during ongoing analysis.

A Story of Change: No Science Here

Kelly believes in science education. She found it disturbing to read how many girls lose interest in science in middle school, primarily due to socialization that "science isn't girl stuff." In response to these concerns, she designed an AR project geared primarily for fifth grade girls at her school. Her idea was to instill such a love of science through project- and inquiry-based strategies that the girls would be excited about continuing in science through middle school. While the units would be taught to both boys and girls, Kelly had read the literature about how to make sure girls were more completely included in science instruction. She even planned a "field trip" to the sixth grade science classrooms in the middle school so the girls, especially, would feel like science leaders when they transitioned to the middle school.

The first of several planned science units went well. Assessments demonstrated that all students had learned the intended content and concepts, and the attitude assessments also demonstrated that the girls had responded positively to "being scientists." But after that, things changed: Kelly wasn't teaching science anymore. She asked her mentor-teacher about the delayed science units and at first the mentor-teacher assured her that she would get to teach the additional planned science units. But the teaching time never came. Kelly finally scheduled an

➡ FIGURE 4.11: Drawing, Mapping, and Graphing Your Thoughts

"The end of one turn of the spiral becomes the beginning of another … We are designed for possibility."
—Gabriele Rico

Gabriele Rico, author of *Writing the Natural Way: Using Right-Brain Techniques to Release Your Expressive Powers* (2000), reminds us that we don't have to begin with words. Rico wrote her dissertation about the technique of clustering when teaching students about writing, and although she wanted to write a book on what she discovered, the words wouldn't come. Rico reportedly sat down on the floor with a big sheet of butcher paper and began her very own cluster. With "natural writing" in the center of the cluster, she covered the paper with associations. Seeing this kind of "big picture" gave her the words she needed. She color-coded the words into the 12 chapters of what would become *Writing the Natural Way*. She went on to create a cluster for each of the chapters followed by one-paragraph descriptions and a one-page book proposal. She did this in one day, sent the book proposal off, and, three days later, she had a book contract. ("Writing that Works: 2000 issues notes." Retrieved July 9, 2005 from http://www.writingthatworks/ issuenotes/2000-authors/rico.html.).

That's a testimonial!

We have used clustering throughout this textbook and we encourage its use here in doing on-going data analysis. The theory behind clustering is deceptively simple: Your right, creative brain knows something your left, logical brain doesn't know. Clustering allows the right brain to "talk" and in the process of doing so, you can make creative and important discoveries. If you are not familiar with clustering, here are some simple steps to follow in using it for on-going data analysis:

* Use a blank piece of paper (the authors of this text like butcher paper and markers but blank 8½ x 11 and a pen or pencil will do).

* Write your question, critical incident, a summary word of your data set, or some other word phrase that represents your data in the center of the page.

* Let your brain wander! Don't try to be deliberate about getting to an "answer." Do word associations with the center phrase, branching out to other clusters, and branching, yet again. Let your brain spiral in and around and over itself. Continue doing this for as long as you can.

* Stop and take time to look at the entire cluster. What patterns do you see? What is repeated? Is there a single name, thought, concept, idea or question that seems to persist? If so, you may want to cluster again.

* Respond to your own cluster by answering these questions:

1. I am surprised …

2. I have discovered …

3. I wonder …

* Return to the task of writing the on-going analytical memo now that you have "the words."

If you would like to know more about Gabriele Rico's work, with additional instruction on clustering, you can find this information at http://www.gabrielerico.com/main/aboutgabrielerico.htm (retrieved July 9, 2005).

→ FIGURE 4.12: Structured Template for Ongoing Analysis

1. Divide your data by type (observation, interview, artifact, researcher's journal, other). Read through your data; make notes in the margins. *Analyze* your data by responding to the following questions. Use the data in your responses. Do this for the data from each type.

- What seems to be happening in this data?

- What is *not* happening in this data?

- What is repeated in this data (words, behaviors, attitudes, occurrences)?

- What is surprising, perplexing, disturbing in the data?

- What information seems to be missing from the data?

2. When you complete this for each data type, *synthesize* your data by considering the following questions. Again, jot down responses. Use the data in your responses.

- What patterns emerge across the landscape of the data?

- What is the classroom context for these patterns?

- Where are the contradictions, paradoxes, and dilemmas in the data? (What does not seem to fit in the landscape?)

- What are the emotional and intellectual reactions to this data?

- What confirms and disaffirms what is thought about the research question?

3. Next, *deconstruct* this data set by responding to the following questions. Again, use data in your response. Also, include your hunches.

- Where have categories of either/or interpretations been made? How can these either/or conclusions be reconstructed using a different lens?

- What are the limitations of the analysis and synthesis? (What do you not know and what can you not know?)

- What assumptions are being made in the analysis and synthesis? What values and beliefs do these assumptions rely upon?

- What would students, parents, a cooperating teacher, an advisor, or authors in the literature say about the analysis and synthesis?

4. Now, *consider context*. Respond to the following questions about your data set.

Use data in your response.

- How does the role of student/teacher influence the data and the interpretation of data?

- In what ways did the action research project conclude in the way you as the teacher/researcher wanted? How does this reflect your own beliefs/values?

- How do the interpretations reflect your beliefs/values of what "good" teaching is, "good students" are, and "good" curriculum should be?

- How do the interpretations mirror values and beliefs you hold as a teacher-researcher given your ethnic, gender, and social standings? How are the interpretations limited by these same labels?

- How do the interpretations align with the stated school and community values and beliefs where the project was conducted?

continues

5.   Finally, look back over all of your notes. Take special notes of areas that seem repetitive in your responses across the above categories.

•   Do you need to change your data-collection methods to better answer your critical question? What changes need to be made?

•   Does the critical question still seem pertinent, relevant? Or does this data change your perception and thus the focus of your research?

•   What practices in your teaching do you need to change based upon this data?

6.   Talk over these last three items with your critical colleague, mentor teacher and/or instructor. Strategize and implement the next stages of your research.

➔ FIGURE 4.13: Kessler's Process of Creativity

Preparation: Focus on the problem. Apply rational and linear approaches to gather all the information possible. Work through your data. Read it again and again. Write in your journal. Read it again and again.

Incubation: Let go of the problem. "Sleep on it." Allow the brain to consider other possibilities. Talk about the problem with others.

Illumination or Inspiration: This is the "breakthrough" or "Aha" moment in which a new idea, concept, or direction comes into view, helping you to resolve or understand the dilemma, question, or conflict in a different way.

Verification: Refine the inspiration or the idea. Use the advice from the literature, your mentor teacher, critical colleagues, and instructor. Return to preparation. Cycle back on the plan and re-create this. See where this leads you in your teaching practice now.

---

appointment with her mentor-teacher to discuss the problem. Why wasn't science being included in the curriculum? Would she be able to teach the planned science curriculum, which was also her AR project?

The mentor-teacher explained the dilemma: the district was no longer focusing on science in the fifth grade. Science was not on the list of state-mandated exams for fifth graders. Therefore, the district had decided that science should be set aside to allow more time to get students ready for the exams. The mentor-teacher didn't like this decision and initially thought she would allow Kelly the time to teach the science units, but this was becoming impossible. There would be no more science in fifth grade, unless there was time after the exams were taken late in the spring. By that time, Kelly would no longer be a student teacher in the classroom.

Kelly was aghast at the decision to drop science. She was also seemingly without an AR project. After regrouping and talking more with her mentor-teacher and her professor, she redirected her inquiry, asking how state-mandated exams influenced curriculum and teaching practices in her classroom. The result of her project impacted decisions at her school; it also provided Kelly with lessons about the political landscape of teaching.

Most of the time, AR projects don't change this dramatically, but circumstances do require this kind of flexibility and probing of causes. Use ongoing analysis and the use of questions to continue to refine and redirect your own project as needed.

Printable CD Extra: Practice Data Sets

We have included, in appendix H, one short data set with which you can practice ongoing analysis.

Additional practice data sets can be found on the companion CD.

Words of Encouragement

Most of our students struggle with being confident about their ongoing analysis. Doubt can haunt the process. You will likely have moments of feeling like a novice, not an expert; a teacher, not a teacher/researcher; and most of all biased, not objective. Learn to say "no" to these self-criticisms.

Remember this wisdom from Gardner (1993):

[M]ost researchers remain open to the possibility of surprises or of new discoveries: after all, if one knew exactly what one expected to find, then the journey would hardly be worth the undertaking.... A degree of asynchrony is delectable. (p. 384)

Organizing Data for Ongoing Analysis

Confidentiality

As you collect and analyze data, it is critical that you attend to issues of confidentiality. These issues include:

Keeping student assessments confidential.

Leaving personal reflections (the researcher's notebook) in a nonpublic place.

Maintaining and keeping data analysis confidential and in a nonpublic place.

Using pseudonyms or other devices to maintain school and student identity confidential.

If confidentiality is breached, it is often because of careless organization: a journal is left open on a teacher's desk, student work is left by a copy machine, data analysis is on the bottom of a pile of student work that is later distributed to students. Be deliberate in organization. Know the place and time for sharing information and for keeping it to yourself. Make it a priority to protect student confidentiality.

→ **TABLE 4.1: Changing Courses**

This data set doesn't really answer my CQ!	Evaluate the data you have. What is missing? Change your design to collect the data that will help you better understand your question.
This data is good but in collecting it, I've discovered some completely different information about my classroom. My critical question doesn't really seem to fit anymore.	Based upon the data, what do you think your questions should be? Revise your critical question. It is fluid—like your study. Document in your notebook or journal the changes you make and the critical incidents that have precipitated the changes.
I am drowning in data! I can't keep up with analyzing it all!	Consider collecting data on a smaller group of students. For example, choose five students who are representative of the entire class, and collect data on those students only.
The teaching strategy I am using as the basis of my action research doesn't appear to be working at all! What do I do?	Rethink your assumptions: What are you assuming about yourself, your students, the context of this classroom? Review Chapter 3: When New Information Changes the Design . Check with critical others: your mentor-teacher, your critical colleague, your instructor. Review Chapter 4: Teacher/researcher as Strategic Intervention for information about constructing a scaffold for learning. Change strategies if you believe you can better serve students in a different way, but figure out first how the data informs the way you do change the teaching strategy.
I began with these assumptions about teaching and learning in my classroom, but now that I've analyzed this first data set, I see where I had it wrong. Now what?	Great! This is all part of the action research process. Document the changes in your notebook or journal, then check with your mentor-teacher, critical colleague, and instructor and make the changes you need to in the design and/or the critical question.

Deliberate Acts of Organization:
The Alternative to Data Scatter

These are the primary ways our students have organized their data. Some use a single system, others a combination:

Notebook: a large three-ring binder works best.

Crates: hanging files work well in crates.

File boxes: hanging files also work well in file boxes and can easily be transported. An additional advantage (we are told): when tipped over, the files do not tumble into disarray!

Electronic files; use a scanner or digital camera for student artifacts. Create a special folder with files for all other data.

Here are some of the ways our students arrange their notebooks, crates, file boxes, and/or other organizational structures:

Chronologically: all data are combined together according to the chronological order of teaching experiences and other settings in which data were collected.

In data sets: data are organized by complete data set. For example, a lesson plan is kept with corresponding observational data and student work. The analytical memo is placed with this data.

By data type: all observation/interview data is organized together. All student work is kept in another place, and lesson plans in another, and so on.

Work with whatever seems logical to you, but make sure you are deliberate about keeping your data organized. Make sure you date and label everything, and keep like data types together. Those teacher/researchers who do not attend to issues of confidentiality and organization can find themselves mired in distracting and sometimes harmful professional and personal circumstances. So while it may seem mundane, be deliberate in these areas!

 Data Interpretation

Ongoing data analysis is the term we use to refer to the process of analyzing, synthesizing, and deconstructing data as it is gathered throughout the AR process.

 Cultural Context: A Quick Guide to Reading Empirical Research

One of the hardest parts of understanding empirical, scientific research is the technical language used. While many empirical studies are very powerful and worthwhile for study by educators, their usefulness is sometimes cloaked in a morass of terminology, statistical tables, and graphs. Worse, it is often difficult to distinguish bad empirical research from good because both use the same mathematical language and employ words like "significant" in precise ways that require careful reading and deconstruction.

Finally, the objective nature of empirical research is such that it tends to minimize and mask the biases and intentions of the researchers. However, these biases and intentions exist in empirical studies, and in our opinion, play an important role in all phases of empirical research, from inception to design to interpretation of results. Empirical studies all too often leave to the reader the critical task of determining researcher biases and intentions and the role they may have played.

To begin to experience these useful and dangerous elements of empirical scientific educational research, imagine the following dialogue:

Q: What do you mean by empirical research?

A: By empirical research we mean research that relies exclusively on new, direct, and observable evidence, or data, as the basis for conclusions and interpretations. Technically, this definition could encompass almost all of what we would reasonably call research. After all, most research relies to some degree on data. In practice, though, empirical research attempts to reduce or eliminate subjectivity by relying as exclusively as possible on objective and (ideally) quantifiable evidence or measurements, rather than on the opinions, biases, or intentions of the researcher.

Q: How is empirical research different from experimental research?

A: Experimental research, as a subset of empirical research, does two things. First, it attempts to establish cause-

continues ➡

We apply the term *data interpretation* to refer to the final interpretation a teacher/researcher brings to the whole of the data collected. At this point in the process, the teacher/researcher has crate(s), file box(es), and/or notebook(s) of organized data. Ongoing data analysis has guided the process of action research, but what happens now? How does the teacher/researcher make sense of all this data? Where does one begin the task of data interpretation?

The General Steps of Data Interpretation

Here we outline the general steps of the data interpretation process. Note, however, that the notion of "steps" can be deceptive. Steps can make a process look simple, linear, and even rigid when in fact they require critical thought and fluidity on the part of the researcher. These steps are meant to be useful in providing a scaffold for the data interpretation process as presented here. This is not *the* way, but *one* way of approaching data-interpretation that has been useful to many preservice teacher/researchers. There are other ways to undertake data interpretation; perhaps you will invent your own process. However you arrive at the end of data interpretation, the goal is still the same: making meaning of the data.

The six steps of the data-interpretation process are generally as follows (see figure 4.14):

1. Getting started: Revisiting, reflecting, and rereading collected data and ongoing analysis.

2. Create mind maps, timelines, and/or charts, generating categories.

and-effect relationships among variables. It does this by carefully designing an experimental test whose results permits the researcher to reasonably claim the existence of a cause-and-effect relationship. Second, it limits its data to strictly quantifiable measurements, so as to permit a rigorous, unambiguous, and mathematical analysis of results.

Q: Can you give me an example?

A: Sure. Suppose you wanted to know whether a certain form of instruction, such as using math manipulatives, results in an increase in the ability to solve math problems. You could design an experiment to test whether there is a cause-and effect-relationship between using math manipulatives (proposed cause) and problem-solving ability (desired effect).

Q: So I would start using math manipulatives in my classroom and measure its effects on problem-solving ability through testing students before and after instruction?

A: Yes, but that is only part of the story. Suppose overall problem-solving ability among your students went up after you started using manipulatives. Are there any other possible reasons they might have improved in problem solving?

Q: I suppose so. What if my science unit on inventions somehow helped them do better on their math? Or maybe the gains were caused instead by the worksheet-driven part of the math curriculum. How could I be sure that it was the manipulatives that caused the gains in learning?

A: This is where having an experimental design becomes important. In order to establish the cause-and-effect link between manipulatives and problem-solving, you need both a *treatment group* and a *control group*. Think of how we test a new drug: the treatment group receives the drug, and the control group gets a placebo. The results obtained in the treatment group are compared to those in the control group. If the treatment group results differ from the control group, then we can be more sure it was due to the treatment.

Q: Can you talk about this using our example?

A: Sure. Your class—the group being taught with math manipulatives—is the treatment group. The control group would get taught math without manipulatives. But it's a little more com-

continues →

3. Expand your interpretation by adding raw data.

4. Apply layers of interpretation by adding the perspectives of others.

5. Return to the questions and apply them to your interpretation.

6. Draft synthesis statements, summarizing what you know.

In the next section we will provide scaffolds for data interpretation. It may be helpful to read this section and then choose the scaffold that best fits your way of learning and knowing. This section is interactive, and assumes that you have organized your data and completed ongoing data analysis.

 ## Scaffolds for Data Interpretation

Approach data interpretation with anticipation, a sense of curiosity, and an openness to possibilities outside of your current paradigm for thinking. Be deliberate about setting aside space and time to do data interpretation. Don't attempt to do all of your data interpretation in one evening or one setting. Allow "think breaks" between the times you work on interpretation to make connections and create space for those "Aha!" moments. If necessary, seek support and feedback from your critical colleagues.

Activity: Mind Maps, Timelines, and Charts

These scaffolds may be created using interactive tools found on the companion CD.

plicated than that. There are all the other variables to consider: age, gender, and mixture of ability levels, especially in math. The control group would need to be very similar to your class in these ways. Also, the control group would need to be taught in the same way as your class in all the other subjects *except* math, where no manipulatives would be used until the experiment was finished. In this way, the treatment—math manipulatives—is isolated as the only factor that could plausibly have caused differences between the groups in learning.

Q: Hmm. But how would I get a control group? It seems like it would be hard to find a class of kids just like mine, taught just the same as mine, by a teacher similar to myself.

A: It's even a bit worse than that. Strictly speaking, experimental research requires random assignment of subjects to treatments. Ideally, this would mean randomly assigning students (subjects) to treatment and control classrooms or groups within a single classroom. Often this is infeasible, so researchers use other means such as seeking out and matching groups that already exist; in other words, you would literally find a classroom like yours in a different school and use it as a control group! Other quasi-experimental designs (termed such because they don't use random assignment) seek to measure student improvement over time, so that differences in initial ability between treatment and control groups don't matter as much. Unfortunately, the construction of control groups is an area in which researcher bias can play a crucial role in biasing the outcome of an educational experiment. One point to remember is that no experiment, at least in educational research, is perfect. The point in experimental research is to create a situation in which statistically significant differences between the treatment and the control groups can be reasonably attributed to the treatment.

Q: Statistical significance—I hear this term a lot. What does it mean?

A: Let's suppose that in our example your class's average score on problem solving after using manipulatives for several weeks is somewhat higher than that of the control group. Assuming you are comfortable with the validity of the control group, would you then feel comfortable reporting to the school

continues ➡

Getting Started: Mind Maps, Timelines, and Charts

Our students report that getting started with data interpretation can be the hardest part of action research. We agree. The initial step in interpreting is to simply *play* with the data, interacting with it in a dynamic, fluid way. This can be uncomfortable. That said, the longer we simply explore the data without any preconceived answers or conclusions in mind the more powerful the interpretation process.

We suggest three options as ways to get started with interpretation. For any option, start with butcher or poster paper, a large white board, or even a graphic thinking tool such as the popular computer program *Inspiration*. While these activities may seem rather out of place in formal research, we have found that such creative approaches to interpretation are very useful:

1. Create a mind map (diagram). Start by writing your CQ in the middle of the work space. Branch off from your CQ using lines, arrows, and shapes to represent what you have learned about your research project and what questions you still have.

2. Create a timeline of your study. If you did this study as a student teacher, start the timeline with your initial entrance into the classroom, even if you were not collecting data at that time. Add just the dates of important "landmarks" during your learning-to-teach and data-collection phases. Add to the timeline

board that manipulatives worked better than nonmanipulative-based teaching?

Q: Not necessarily. I think I see what you mean. If the scores were drastically different I would be pretty sure the treatment worked. But for a small difference I wouldn't be so sure. Maybe if we both retook the test again the results would be reversed. Maybe the other class just had a bad day. On the other hand, if practically all of my students did better than practically all of the control students, even if by a lesser amount, then I would be pretty sure there was a difference. But if the difference was small, it may not be worth reporting. I'm guessing that statistical analysis comes into play here.

A: Correct. Using statistical tests, we can do two things. First, statistics such as mean and median summarize numerically the difference between the treatment and control groups. Second, and most important, statistics are used to analyze the two groups of scores so as to determine whether they are actually different due to the treatment, or different simply due to uncontrollable, "random" effects. If the difference is deemed as random, then the two groups actually have the same "true" score. The mathematical procedure used to make this determination is called an ANOVA—analysis of variance. The formulas used in an ANOVA discern from the distribution of the scores in both groups how sure we are they statistically different. The probability score (called a p-score) is reported as a number between 0 and 1. A p-score of 0 means there is 0 probability that the difference between scores is due to chance; we can be 100% sure it was the treatment. A p-score of 1 means that we are utterly unsure of how to explain the difference. Most of the time the p-score is somewhere in the middle.

Q: How sure is sure enough?

A: Traditionally, educational researchers use $p < .05$ as the cutoff for confidence in a result. This translates to 95% confidence. When we achieve 95% confidence, we use the term "statistically significant" to describe the result.

Q: Are statistically significant results hard to achieve?

A: They can be, especially for effects (differences) that are small or even medium. Unless the treatment makes a very

continues →

when you collected data. Add specific incidents connected with data collection, such as, "Taught lesson using computer simulations." Add any other specific incidents that occurred during the data-collection period. Include even those incidents that may not seem related. Complete the context for your study by adding memorable incidents from your entire student-teaching period. You may want to include emotions as well as actions.

3. Create a chart showing what you knew about your research project, what you have learned about your research project, and questions you still have about your project. Leave a lot of blank space on your chart to work with later. This option may work if you tend to be a linear/sequential thinker (table 4.2).

Expanding Your Interpretation

The goal now is to expand the representation you have developed to answer the question, "How do I know this new information?" This is a critical step in the process, one in which you find data to support your intuition and hunches. This step should result in a greatly enhanced mind map, timeline, or chart.

Add data to the mind map, timeline, and/or chart that supports what you have learned. Draw connections, invent codes or symbols that help represent your thoughts as they are forming. Be creative.

sizable difference, the result of an experiment involving two classrooms of 30 students each is unlikely to be statistically significant.

Q: So how do we create significant results?

A: The most common way is to increase the sample size. The underlying mathematics of the ANOVA is such that the greater the sample size (referred to as n), the greater the experiment's power to identify smaller differences as statistically significant. If the experiment includes 10,000 students, even a very small effect may be deemed significant while a much larger effect among 50 students may be deemed not significant. So in experimental research, the greater the n the better. There are other ways to increase an experiment's power, such as using different statistical procedures to attempt to control other variables not taken into account in forming the control group, or creating

continues ➡

➡ FIGURE 4.14: Data Interpretation in Action Research Projects

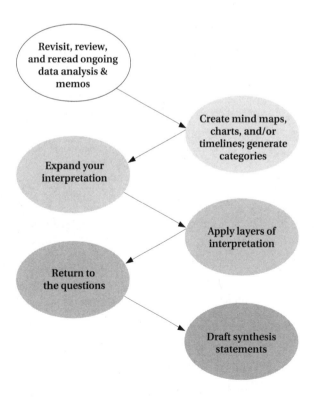

➜ TABLE 4.2: Forming Initial Categories

What I thought I knew about my research topics/question	What I now know about my research topic/question.	What I still wonder about my research topic/question

Use student voices in your work. Code (mark in a meaningful color or symbol) places of conflict, discontinuity, or uncomfortable self-spaces of learning, "Aha!" moments, places of affirmation concerning your research topic, and places that raise further questions about your research topic. Highlight the data and/or incidents that represent the most learning. These often represent further points of conflicts, discontinuity, or uncomfortable self-spaces. You may find that some

conclusions and areas are not well supported by data. This may mean that this area either needs further data collection, or may need to be dropped as a focus.

Applying Interpretative Layers

Interpretative layers are the different layers of meaning we apply to our data. Each layer of interpretation allows the teacher/researcher to see the data from another angle (figure 4.15). The voice representing each layer affirms, denies, or leaves in question a hunch, belief, or assumption. The layers reflect macro and micro ways of seeing, exposing cracks or even whole patterns that may have been overlooked. As you layer your interpretation, add ideas to your map, timeline, or chart.

Imagine altering a photo using digital technology. It's fun play. The subject of the photo stays the same, but the way it is seen is changed by applying alternative filters, shades of color, and brush strokes. Sometimes these tools alter the original picture in such a way as to bring out details or features that were previously unseen. Layers of interpretation create a similar sense of collected meaning.

so-called composite variables that more closely target the desired effect. Sometimes the statistical tests used to achieve significance are quite complex and create a dilemma for the reader in interpreting the procedures properly. You must bear in mind that the researcher's goal is to achieve significance, even for potentially very small effects, so sometimes very complex measures are taken to squeeze every last ounce of power out of an experiment.

Q: That doesn't seem quite right. Let's say you manage to achieve significance for a small effect. Shouldn't a small but significant difference mean less than a potentially large but insignificant difference?

A: Absolutely. When reading studies, one must look not only at the statistical significance, but practical significance as well. Experimental research studies sometimes focus exclusively on statistical significance, leaving issues of practical significance to the reader. It's up to you to decide whether the results of research have practical significance or usefulness. That's why you have to become literate in all forms of research likely to affect your teaching practice.

In the next Cultural Context section you will read through an empirical research study with the above dialogue in mind. Remember that the ultimate goal is to determine the "truth" of the research through our own paradigmatic lens, and to critically assess what the research means and does not mean in our own practical perspective.

Layering gives research what is termed "thick description" (Geertz, 1973; Patton, 2002), weaving trustworthiness into the research project. Not all of the layers described may be appropriate for your study; choose those that will bring the most meaning into your work. Even after doing this, the meaning will be partial and incomplete. You may find that rather than arriving at one place, you have arrived at various places of interpretation. You may find more questions than answers or solutions. What is most critical is that you make significant discoveries for yourself in your journey of becoming a teacher.

Interpretative Layer 1: Different Perspective(s)

Seek another perspective on your data by sharing your analytic memos or other synthesis statements with your critical colleague, mentor-teacher, student teaching supervisor, university instructor, and/or another specialist in the area. Parents of students you are working with, for example, can give a critical missing perspective. Not all voices may be necessary; choose those that will reflect an important new light on the study.

Here's an example: Reed's study involved implementing a plan to create a scaffold for emergent and struggling readers. When it came time to conduct his final data interpretation, he asked his mentor-teacher to read through his preliminary statements about each student. The mentor-teacher offered a personal view of each student's achievement. The reading specialist also proved to have valuable insights, especially in helping Reed to identify potential learning disabilities and to see how the intersection of learning to read and learning English played out in each student situation. Reed also interviewed parents to see what improvements they saw in their child's reading. His university instructor provided another important piece: insights on how Reed's own learning to teach contributed to the overall study.

Cultural Context: A Primer in Reading Empirical Research

In this section you will be guided through reading, analyzing, and deconstructing a sample article (Gningue, 2003) representing "typical" quantitative research in educating. Of course, no research is truly "typical"; there are literally hundreds of possible experimental designs. The proper interpretation of many designs requires specialized knowledge in statistics and therefore lies outside the scope of this book. Every study has its own strengths and weaknesses. The intent of this exercise is for you to develop a critical stance toward all forms of research, including those that involve quantitative analysis.

We present and annotate from the article selected sections of text, as well as the ANOVA analysis. With each selection, you will be prompted to return to some of the questions suggested earlier in this section.

Reading the Abstract

Most research articles include an abstract, a self-contained summary of the purpose, methods, and findings of a research project. Consider the abstract of our sample article (Gningue, 2003, p. 207):

This article describes two professional development experiences for middle and high school mathematics teachers: one long term, the other, short term. The training of the long-term group took place over an entire semester, in a 15-week, 45-hour graduate course, at an urban institution in New York City, that accented the use of computing technologies, especially the "TI83 Plus" graphing calculator and the

continues →

Interpretative Layer 2: Participant Voice(s)

In qualitative research, this layer of interpretation is often termed a *member check*. In collecting this layer of meaning, you return to the participants in the study— most likely, your students. Employ any method of interview that works best for your AR situation. A whole-class discussion, focus groups, surveys, or written responses all work well. Do this by using your synthesis statements and asking the participants to respond to them. This may be one of the most important layers of interpretation you can add to your study. In doing a member check, you are asking the people closest to the study, "Do you see what I see in this data?"

Interpretative Layer 3: Expert Consultation

Return to the literature and consider your data interpretation in the light of experts. How does the literature support your emerging theories or synthesis statements? Are there gaps, discontinuities, or disagreements between what you are discovering and what the literature says? Revisit your distant colleagues and theorize together about these issues.

Interpretative Layer 4: Placing the Research in Context

Step away from your research study. Consider your research in the context of your student-teaching/practicum/teacher-education program experience. How do critical incidents that may seem at first to be unrelated influence your data interpretation? How is your data interpretation limited? How have your own developing abilities as a teacher influenced the study? Are there issues, conflicts, and details unique to this class/school/community that may influence the way you interpret the data? How are your own beliefs, assumptions, and views of education shading the way you view the data?

"Geometers Sketchpad," to enhance the teaching of mathematics in secondary schools. The training of the short-term group took place in a series of three workshops totaling 7 hours, with teachers from the institution's Professional Development School, using essentially the same kind of technology tools. Attitude changes about the use of technology, obtained through a 16-item pre- and post-survey given to both groups, are presented. Comments from teachers' written reports and reflections about their beliefs in the effectiveness of using technology in the mathematics classroom are included as well. Professional development in computing technologies can be effective in changing teacher's attitudes and beliefs if implemented through a long-term, sustained, and coherent form of training that provides teachers with opportunities for active learning in the use of relevant technology tools in general.

Answer the following questions in your notebook or journal and make additional comments:

What is the researcher's critical question? Is this a "good" critical question? (Refer back to chapter 2 if necessary.)

What intervention is being studied? In other words, what is being tried?

What is the context of the study? In what ways has the researcher been successful and unsuccessful at employing the

continues ➡

➡ FIGURE 4.15: Interpretative Layers

Different Perspectives

Participant Voices

Expert Consultation

Placing the Research in Context

Looping the Interpretation

Step away from your mind map/timeline/chart. Consider the following questions:

> Where is there consistency between the layers of interpretation?

> Where is there discontinuity between the layers of interpretation?

> Freewrite about the above or scribble notes on your mind map, timeline, chart. Deconstruct your assumptions. Raise questions. Respond again to the question, "What do I now know about my research question/topic that I did not know before?"

Returning to the Questions

If you are working with a chart, return to your chart column "What I still wonder about my research topic/question." Add to this column now that you have applied interpretative layers to your data. If you are working with a mind map or

"control group" concept? How large are the groups being studied? What affect will this have on the results of the research?

What is the main source of numerical data for this research?

What other data will be used to bring additional meaning to the numbers?

Reading the Methods

Consider now details about the study teachers and context (see Cultural Context table 4.1):

This study uses a repeated measures design. This means that the survey was used in a pretest/posttest format with two groups, one receiving the treatment of interest (long-term professional development) and one receiving (in this case) an alternative treatment (short-term professional development).

Answer the following question in your notebook or journal and make additional comments:

In what ways are these groups well matched, meaning that comparisons between them will be valid? In what ways are they not well matched?

continues →

→ **CULTURAL CONTEXT TABLE 4.1: Research Participant Descriptions and Context**

"Long-Term" Participants	"Short-Term" Participants
(n = 12) included four female and eight male teachers . . . who were students in the Master's of Mathematics Education program. . . . The investigator chose this course for the study because it was redesigned to meet the request of students in the Master's program for more implementation of technology. Participation was voluntary. They were informed that lack of participation would have no influence on course grade.	(n = 11) included six female and five male teachers . . . none of these teachers had used technology to teach mathematics concepts. The technology training of the PDS teachers took place because one of the year's main PDS goals was to increase mathematics teachers' awareness of technology-based curricula . . . the [decision was made] to use the only two citywide Professional Development Days available that year, to conduct three workshops to train them on how to use computing technologies to enhance the curriculum . . . not much computing technology was available at the PDS site.

Source: Gningue, 2003, pp. 211–212.

timeline, ask the question, "What do I still wonder about my research topic/question?" Expand your mind map or timeline with these thoughts, additional questions, and/or partial understandings you have about your research topic.

Ask yourself, "How do these additional questions represent limitations of my study? How do these additional questions represent my own biases and/or assumptions? How do these additional questions represent continued areas where I want to explore?"

Drafting Synthesis Statements

Identify from your work what seem to be the major themes—we use the term *categories*—of your study. Create a table listing your categories (table 4.3). Draft synthesis statements for each category. Each synthesis statement should be very succinct yet include what you learned, how you know what you learned, and what other voices say about what you learned.

Alternative Scaffolds and Variations on these Scaffolds

You may find other ways to record your draft thinking, categorizing, theorizing, and grouping. For example, you may want to draw your interpretations or use more word associations. You may find that these scaffolds are not necessarily helpful. Use whatever method you can to make meaning of your data.

Check with your critical colleague after interpreting your data. Once you've done this, you are ready to more completely fill in the interpretation with supporting data and more formally frame the meaning, knowledge, and/or discoveries of your AR project.

Reading the Numbers

Cultural Context Activity: Analysis of ANOVA Tables

For those readers who need more background in this area, this activity on the companion CD includes interactive ANOVA tables with enhanced definition of terms.

We now show and explain two examples of ANOVA tables from the sample study (Gningue, 2003, pp. 215–216), one analyzing item 1 of the attitude survey, showing a significant difference between pre- and posttest scores for the "course" group, and another analyzing item 2, showing no significant pre- and posttest differences (see Cultural Context table 4.1).

Answer the following questions in your notebook or journal and make additional comments:

On item 2, it appears that there was a noticeable "mean difference" (MD) between pre- and posttest results for the "course" group, but the difference was not judged "statistically significant." How do you interpret this?

Suppose the researcher wished to further study item 2. How could she redesign the study so as to increase the chances of finding a significant difference between pre- and posttest scores?

Reading and Deconstructing the Results

In total, the above study found that a "favorable shift" in the course group only occurred statistically for two items, 1 and 14 (Gningue, 2003, p. 219). Four other items (2, 3, 4, and 15) showed positive changes in the means that were not judged statistically significant.

Read the author's interpretation (Gningue, 2003, pp. 218–219) and consider the comments that follow, making comments of your own in your notebook or journal:

[Course Group:] What may explain the course's positive outcomes may be the length and extent to which concepts were studied. It took teachers 15 consecutive weeks to learn, practice, reflect, and be tested on the different activities involving the "TI83 Plus" graphing calculator and Geometers Sketchpad.

[PDS Group:] [T]he training seemed to have no effects on its participants' views about the use of technology. . . . Such results were

continues ➡

→ CULTURAL CONTEXT TABLE 4.2: ANOVA Tables

Item 1. Calculators Should Only Be Used to Check Work
(0 = strongly disagree, 4 = strongly agree)

Group[1]	Test[2]	Rank[3] 0 1 2 3 4	Mean[4]	SD[5]	MD[6]	t[7]	p[8]
Course (n = 12)	Pretest	1 3 2 4 2	2.25	1.29			
	Posttest	6 5 0 1 0	0.67	.89	1.58	3.50	.027*
PDS (n = 11)	Pretest	3 3 2 3 0	1.45	1.21			
	Posttest	1 8 0 1 1	1.36	1.12	0.1	.166	.871

Item 2. A Graphing Calculator Can Be Used as a Tool to Solve Problems that I Could Not Solve Before
(0 = strongly disagree, 4 = strongly agree)

Group	Test	Rank 0 1 2 3 4	Mean	SD	MD	t	p
Course (n = 12)	Pretest	2 2 2 4 2	2.17	1.40			
	Posttest	0 3 0 6 3	2.75	1.14	-0.58	-1.17	.267
PDS (n = 11)	Pretest	1 0 3 4 3	2.73	1.19			
	Posttest	1 1 2 3 4	2.73	1.35	0	0	1.00

*p < .05[1]

Source: Gningue, 2003, pp. 215–216.)

(Footnotes)

1   Group: Denotes the two experimental groups. The "course" group received long-term training, and the "PDS" group received short-term training.

2   Test: The analysis compares pre- and posttest scores.

3   Rank: Raw data from the Likert scale–type instrument. Numbers indicate how many participants ranked the item at each level.

4   Mean: Average ranking among group members.

5   SD: "Standard deviation" is a measurement of the variability in the data. SD indicates for the reader how much the rankings tended to vary among participants. The higher the SD the greater the variability, or "spread," in the data. In interpreting data, the SD must be viewed alongside the possible range of data. If the SD is small or large compared to the range, this means that the spread of data within groups is small or large. The pretest SD was 1.29 compared to a mean of 5, meaning that there was substantial variability among the participants in how they responded (note that there was no consensus in the rankings for this item). The posttest SD was .89. There was somewhat greater consensus among participants on the posttest.

6   MD: "Mean difference" is the average difference between pre- and posttest results for the participants in each group. For the "course" group, the difference was 1.58; for the "PDS" group the difference was 0.1.

7   t: The "t-score" is a statistic that gives a measurement of the statistical difference between the pre- and posttest for each group. The t is based on the pre-and posttest means, SD, and n, the number of participants. The higher the t-score the greater the statistical difference between the pre- and posttest scores.

8   p: t-scores are converted to "p-scores," a measure of the probability that the pre- and posttest scores are in fact different statistically. In this case, the "course" group comparison yielded a p-score of .027, meaning that we can be 97.3% certain statistically (1-p converted to a percentage) that difference in the pre- and posttest scores are different for reasons other than chance. This exceeds the generally accepted threshold of 95% confidence, so the difference in scores is deemed "significant." On the other hand, the "PDS" group comparison yielded a p-score of .871, indicating a confidence of only 13%, far below the threshold. We must conclude that the difference in scores for the PDS group is likely due to chance.

---

1   p < .05: This indicates for the reader which comparisons indicate statistically significant differences at the 95% confidence threshold.

Evaluating the Trustworthiness of Your Interpretations: A Checklist

Even after our students complete their data interpretation (sometimes working through the process several times), they are still haunted by a doubting voice that says, "You have no right to say these things; you're not being objective; this only means something to *you*." Beyond simply repeating our previous retorts of such voices found earlier in this section, we now suggest a checklist of criteria to help you evaluate the level for trustworthiness in your interpretations. Evaluate your interpretations of each criterion in your notebook. (Note: this checklist assumes that your research design was built on a trustworthy foundation formed by triangulated data collection as described in chapter 3.)

Activity: Checking for Trustworthiness

The companion CD includes an interactive version of this evaluation checklist.

Trustworthiness Checklist

_____*Criteria 1: Trustworthy interpretations represent multiple perspectives and are thickly layered.* Sufficient, rich data of multiple types (observation, interview, and artifact) and sources (teacher/researcher, students, mentor-teacher, etc.) support the interpretation. There is evidence of layering shown through the inclusion of outside voices such as those of critical colleagues and the research literature.

not surprising since the length and the extent to which the concepts presented to PDS teachers were very short, and their experiences with technology limited because of time constraints.

Summarize the Author's Interpretation of the Results

Deconstruction means to suggest possible alternatives to the author's interpretations of the study. Before looking at additional data from the study, take a moment to brainstorm possible alternatives to the author's interpretations as noted above.

The study's author includes some additional data in the form of participant comments and reflections. Consider these comments made by two of the workshop (control group) participants in regards to learning how to use the calculators in their classroom (Gningue, 2003, p. 221):

This is fine information, but I wonder why we are spending time on stuff we don't have, and I can't see when we'll have this stuff. We need to focus on attainable goals and situations. I suggest we get trained on how to do things with little or no technology, because that's where we are. (John, PDS teacher)

Good crash course, but the material relevant to 6th grade curriculum was not reviewed. (Christine, PDS teacher)

The author interprets these comments by noting:

Indeed, the workshops did not provide teachers with time to develop a plan for using suggested materials and methods in their classrooms. A long, sustained, and more coherent form of training would have provided more opportunities for active learning, and could lead more PDS teachers to report more favorably about their use of technology. (p. 221)

Answer the following questions in your notebook or journal and make additional comments:

Based on the above participant data, what alternative interpretations could you suggest?

What are the strengths of this study? What are the weaknesses?

How does the readers' stance (personal interests, beliefs, biases, and paradigm) affect the reading of this study? How could different readers draw very different conclusions about the study, and how would these different conclusions be grounded in different paradigms?

continues ➡

_____Criteria 2: Trustworthy interpretations include articulated description of context, relationships, and methods. The data interpretation is cognizant of the context of the study and how this context may influence the study; it recognizes relationships and how these relationships affect interpretations. It is clear how and why the study was conducted.

_____Criteria 3: Trustworthy interpretations practice self-reflexivity There is careful attention given to your own role as student teacher/researcher in the data interpretation; your own values, beliefs, and biases are recognized to the extent possible in the interpretations.

_____Criteria 4: Trustworthy interpretations arise from extensive exploration and analysis of the data. The data analysis included analytic memos, deep examination of the data, and a thorough approach to finding patterns and creating themes. There is evidence you have spent time considering the data in such a way that honors all the participants of the study.

_____Criteria 5: Trustworthy interpretations acknowledge their own limitations. The interpretation shows a clear understanding of limitations such as the guest status of the researcher in the classroom, researcher biases, and time constraints.

 Cultural Context: Research and Educational Policy in the Classroom

Recently we received an e-mail from a former student now teaching fifth grade. Adam has been using a variety of methods for teaching reading, including the use of heterogeneously (mixed-ability) grouped literature circles. In fact, in the three years he has been at his school, he has trained other teachers in his fifth grade team to use literature circles, and through action research, they have demonstrated the benefits of this strategy. Even the district reading coordinator has become involved in the project, supporting training in all elementary schools. That's why Adam was surprised to receive an e-mail from the coordinator stating, "We need to stop using heterogeneous[ly] grouped literature circles. All the research now supports reading instruction at grade level only with use of controlled reading sources." That's when Adam wrote to us. "Is this really what all the research is saying?" he asked. "It depends," we replied, "on what research you are reading. All the federally funded research will demonstrate that homogeneous grouping at reading levels is the best kind of reading instruction."

How can we know the results of research on reading that hasn't even been completed yet? To answer this question involves a mini-lesson in how research can become public policy in the United States. The National Reading Panel (NRP) was established in the United States in 1997 to review research on effective reading instruction. Of the 15 people on this commission, only one was an elementary school teacher. In this review, no studies documenting research on English language learners (non-English speakers) were reviewed in the phonics section of the report. The NRP reported positive results for five of six instructional strategies, but they never claimed these were "essential components" of reading (Yatvin, 2003).

Yet, Reading First (Title 1B), an initiative of the No Child Left Behind Act (NCLB), requires that all funded research and programs in the area of reading conform to these "five essential components of reading," even though the original research never established these criteria as "essential," nor did it take into account English language learners.

continues ➡

➜ TABLE 4.3: Synthesis Categories

Category			
Synthesis Statement			

_____*Criteria 6: Trustworthy interpretations are tentative.* The interpretation avoids broad generalities, leaves issues open, suggests further questions, and admits partial understandings influenced by your own values, belief systems, and biases.

_____*Criteria 7: Trustworthy interpretations result in meaningful action.* Your interpretations represent meaningful and insightful ways for you to improve your practice in some way and contribute to making education a little more rich, caring, just, and/or tolerant for students.

Simmons and Kame'enui (2003) is often used in evaluating reading curriculum and Reading First government grants; it is organized around the "five essential components of reading": phonemic awareness, phonics, fluency, vocabulary, and comprehension. This hypothesized model (not proven in the NRP report) assumes a sequenced, building-block approach to teaching reading. Such an approach often favors homogeneous, same-ability grouping.

As a result of this government policy, research on reading funded by the federal government must be based on instructional strategies demonstrating possibility through randomly controlled experimental studies. Such reading research must adhere to the federal government's theoretical acceptance of reading as step-by-step process. Furthermore, research in the area of phonemic awareness, fluency, vocabulary, and comprehension as defined by the NCLB conforms to large random-controlled trial studies and statistical analysis, whereas research into other reading models requires painstaking and detailed analyses over time, which are much less likely to conform to the government's definition of research.

The link between educational policy and educational research will influence you and your teaching. Many of the curriculum schools choose will be based upon "research."

That's why, as a teacher, ignoring this kind of talk is a disservice to yourself and your students. In addition to using the guidelines provided in this section for learning to read research, we adhere to this wise counsel from Pearson (2004), who writes, "The road from research to policy is fraught with many

continues ➜

dangers—potholes, blind corners, road hogs, and detours that can frustrate even the most thoughtful traveler" (p. 238). He then offers these suggestions:

Beware of "headline" research. Often times, "research" as reported in the media is contrary, and sometimes, has not received "peer review" required within the academic community. Don't just believe the research you read about in a brief two-column newspaper report—find the original study if you are really interested and read it carefully before accepting the results or quoting any study as "truth."

Remember: Opportunists select the research they use! Politicians, policy-makers, text book publishers, district coordinators, university professors, and teachers often quote only the research that supports a program or curriculum which fits their personal paradigm. For a balanced view, read from both sides of any fence!

Sometimes, what we want to believe becomes "evidence." It is easy for all of us in education and those outside education to "slip over the line" as Pearson says, and "privilege ideology and belief over evidence." At the time of this writing, for example, experimental research design is the privileged voice of research. These kinds of studies can be useful; however, disregarding all other voices and ways of doing research exclusively is very dangerous. Sometimes, we just don't know, and in such instances, we must "fess up to the fact and make it clear that we are basing policy on values, beliefs, and hunches" (Pearson, 2004, p. 238).

What Can I Do As a Teacher?

By this time, you may be feeling a bit overwhelmed and even discouraged. After all, what can a classroom teacher do in the face of such authoritative "research" that may result in mandated instruction you do not believe is best for your students? What can

you do if you find yourself part of a "random" group of professionals? How do you respond to claims that "this is what research supports"? We offer these suggestions:

Read research yourself. Teachers become "victims" of policy-makers when they do not know the research or they are only reciting what they read in the morning's newspaper. Read all kinds of research: even research with which you may disagree. Find a few good sources and read often. Learn to read abstracts and conclusions since your time will be short.

Learn to ask, "What research?" All of us in education seem to be guilty of overusing the phrase "this is research-based" without really knowing the source of the "research." Once you find the actual source of research on which policy is based you can begin to evaluate and critique its claims.

Cultivate a basic understanding of statistical analysis. Consider such books as Kranzler (2003) as a starting point if you find such analysis intimidating.

Find other professionals who are committed to hearing the many voices of educational resource. Don't just become a voice that complains, "This is bad." Become the active voice of an informed professional. Find local groups and/or affiliates of national groups of committed professionals. Join national organizations in your content, grade, and/or interest areas and attend conferences. This will provide for you a means of keeping abreast of the many changes and pathways of policy that will affect your classroom teaching.

Perfect and do your own action research. We remember when teachers took back classroom research through action research and changed the course of educational policy; it can happen again! Learn how to make your research trustworthy. Work collaboratively with other teachers. One way to avoid feeling helpless and overwhelmed is action in the company of colleagues.

CHAPTER 5
TELLING THE STORY OF YOUR ACTION RESEARCH

 Telling Your Story

No journey carries one far unless, as it extends into the world around us, it goes an equal distance into the world within. —Lillian Smith, *The Journey*

You now have a story to tell.

You've learned something important about teaching and learning. You have constructed meaning that makes the act of educating students more just, compassionate, and meaningful. You have (we hope) done a thorough job of analysis and interpretation, creating rich meaning from your raw data, just as the artisan twirls raw wool and dye into multicolored strands of yarn.

How will you share your story? How will you weave the multicolored yarn of your data interpretation into a tapestry that tells others of the mood, the patterns, the interconnections, and the "warp and woof" of your journey? Having reflected inwardly on the data, how will you extend the meaning outward, toward your colleagues in education?

"Going public" is an essential part of action research for three reasons. First, the process of going public is the process of articulating the actual learning that has happened, bringing together in one coherent whole both the journey and the destination. Second, sharing energizes professional educators—we love exchanging and brainstorming ideas, learning from each other as we read and experience (though vicariously) each other's travels. Third, sharing is celebration—there is great joy and satisfaction in sharing meaningful discoveries.

How you go public and share your research project will most likely be prescribed to some degree by the requirements of your teacher-education program. You may be required to write a formal paper, present a portfolio, create a poster or brochure for public display, or show other compiled evidence of your work. You may have the flexibility to use alternative means to go public, such as artistic representations or even performance. In this chapter we outline several of these possibilities. Use whatever specific information applies to your project and requirements.

If you are like many of our students, you may be leery of the process of putting your journey to words. Academic papers and projects you have done in the past may have seemed like dry, academic exercises lacking in personality and creativity. Action research, even written as formal academic work, must be anything but dry and impersonal. It is critical, no matter what the presentation mode you use, that your work reflect a blend of personal and professional tone and style, and that it is interesting, engaging, and yes, even captivating to the reader. This process takes some time and effort; we can give you general guidelines for developing your personal/professional style and voice.

In this section, the side roads of cultural context and self-analysis merge with the main road of action research (AR). This is symbolic in that at this stage of your AR journey all "roads" merge as you complete the project and travel on to your next place as a professional educator. It is practical since any public presentation is a combination of the cultural context of academics and your personal style and expression.

Finally, throughout this section, there are specific suggestions, outlines, checkboxes, and other guides for going public. Don't let the seemingly straightforward guides limit your imagination. Eisner (2002) writes, "Imagination is no mere ornament; nor is art. Together they can liberate us from our indurated habits" (p. 10). As you go public with your action research story, let the process of creating be influenced by both imagination and art. What have you learned in the AR process that has opened up possibilities you might otherwise not have imagined about schooling? How have you changed? What emotions have you felt during the course of doing action research? How will you represent these? Don't consider data interpretation "done" as you begin to design your presentation; stay open to surprises even as you arrange, organize, and represent your work in its "final" stage. Your research may come together on a deeper level even while in the final stages of work. After all, as the poet William Stafford writes, "You can't tell when strange things with meaning will happen" (1993, http://www.newsfromnowhere.com/stafford/wspoem04.html, accessed June 4, 2005).

How Should Action Research Sound? The Cultural Context of Academic Work

When you hear the word *academic*, what do you think of? Just for fun, and harkening back to an early activity in this book, brainstorm a list of adjectives you might associate with *academic*.

Read through your list of words: Do you see yourself? Our students tend to think of both starched white collars and slumped-over disorderly tweeds mumbling in dim light when they consider the idea of an academic. It is time to face the fact that as one who has deliberately designed, implemented, and interpreted an AR project, *you* are an academic! You may need to revise your images if they don't fit you.

There are a number of myths surrounding the act of being academic. One seems to be that such work is rarely practical. This myth contrasts with your AR project. While it is surrounded by the voices of experts, it is grounded practically in the classroom, it is *research* in *action*, concerning practical dilemmas and questions. Another myth is that academic work is rarely personal. Your AR project, again by contrast, represents personal meaning making and places *you* at the center of the work.

A final misconception may be that academic work all "sounds the same," and is "devoid of voice." Listen to the voice and style in each of the following selections from well-known researchers, taken from opening paragraphs of published works:

The problem of this essay is that I need to do some fieldwork but don't know where to go. For quite some time now I have been stalled in an ethnography—stopped, stuck, dead in the water. And since I am convinced that the technology called the essay can take me places I have been unable to imagine, I have decided to attempt a nomadic journey, to, in fact, travel in the thinking that writing produces in search of the field. (St. Pierre, 1997, p. 365)

In 1969, I was a junior at the University of Wisconsin and a member of Students for a Democratic Society (SDS), an organization formed to protest the war in Vietnam. Many of my activities as a member of SDS revolved around recruitment—talking to other students and getting them to come to rallies and be active in the demonstrations against the war. . . . After a simple recounting of some facts about napalm, brutality, and lives lost, the recruit was often on board. However, one group of students seemed to respond differently to my sales pitch; they were the art students. Their response was often that their politics were taken up in the art studio, not on the streets. I did not understand or accept this response. My response was one of anger at what I regarded as their conservatism and lack of activism. (Gitlin, 2005, p. 15)

People have gotten killed
And I really don't want anyone to suffer or die
But despite my sorrow and guilt I can't help but think
"First World blood is so much more expensive than Third World
blood."

My legs are trembling and so are my hands grasping the paper with the scribbled poems. I am very conscious of the fact that my jeans and shirt are not appropriate apparel for the evening. I surreptitiously try to display my *Allah* medallion more prominently, but my fingers refuse to cooperate. (Chaudhry, 2002, pp. 96–97)

These pieces were all published in either prominent educational research journals or collections of research works. The authors use *personal* (and thus their *political*) engaging voices, enticing the reader into the work to follow. "Academic" presentations can be personal, convincing, and inspirational, a living celebration of learning.

That said, the cultural context of higher education, the "academy," often does privilege certain kinds of research and presentation style more than others. Strictly rationalized patterns of thought sometimes carry more weight in academe. Modernist roots of thought mesh well with our "increasingly technicized cognitive culture" (Eisner, 2002, p. 8). Not surprisingly, statistical analysis and an objective, stereotypically scientific voice in presentation are privileged in much educational research, especially in the United States (see Chapter 4: The Numbers Tell the Story).

For example, many of us were taught to use the third-person voice in academic writing, avoiding the personal pronoun *I*. Consider the following opening passage, which uses a more traditional academic voice:

Over the past 20 years, our understanding of reading acquisition and reading disabilities (RD) has increased dramatically. This understanding has been informed by the ongoing consolidation of a substantial scientific knowledge base in beginning reading, consisting of converging, multidisciplinary research evidence (Adams, 1990; National Reading Panel, 2000; National Research Council, 1998). One of the most salient and compelling conclusions to emerge from this knowledge base is the vital and cumulative consequences of establishing or failing to establish beginning reading skills in the early grades (Cunningham & Stanovich, 1998; Stanovich, 1986). (Coyne, Kame'enui, Simmons, & Harn, 2004, p. 90)

As readers and listeners, we expect to hear or read certain kinds of styles in certain kinds of contexts. When attending a lecture series on world affairs, for example, one most likely does not expect to hear a presentation that is slapstick in nature or uses a great deal of slang; if attending a variety show highlighting local talent, however, one might expect just about anything! Cultural norms determine what is "acceptable" and "appropriate" in a given situation. Negotiating research methodology, voice, and style within the academic culture is an ongoing evolution. We provide some guidelines; you will need to do some work to find what is appropriate in your own setting.

Guidelines for Going Public with Your Action Research

As a preservice teacher presenting action research, expect to negotiate the tension between being professional and personal; you may think that somehow the two cannot go together. Preservice teachers should consider some general guidelines when presenting action research. For instance, it is appropriate to share:

> personal struggles of becoming a teacher during the AR project (how much is shared depends on how these struggles influence the actual process and results)

> conflicts that influence the AR process and results

> moments of chaos and joy, and "mistakes," as they relate to the AR process and results

It is not appropriate to share:

> personal stories that may be harmful to other people by exposing issues, moments, or questions they have not given you permission to share

> negative incidents that reflect anger you have not yet worked through

> judgments based upon your own value system and not data

The merging of the professional and the personal has to do with *how* you share them. For example, here are two different ways a preservice teacher might write about her relationship with her mentor-teacher as it relates to her AR project:

I did not agree with my mentor-teacher, who apparently did not think it was important to take the extra time to do the preparation for the *Jeopardy* review game for the students in her fifth period class. Her class didn't do nearly as well on the final exam as my class, and I attribute this to my mentor-teacher's lack of commitment in preparing the review game.

The *Jeopardy* review game was successful; students did do well on the final exam and it appears this was a positive factor in these results. It did take me a great deal of time to prepare the game. My mentor-teacher and I discussed this: was it worth the gains in student learning to fall behind in other areas of my own work? How does a teacher find balance in making such decisions?

The second example not only uses different wording, but implies a different approach to this common preservice teacher dilemma. The first example reflects an attitude of judging, the second an attitude of questioning. Note that the second paragraph does not mention that students in her mentor-teacher's class did not do as well on the exam. Why? The AR project was not being conducted in the other classroom. There could be a number of other reasons that students in that class period did not do as well on the exam, besides the absence of the *Jeopardy* review game. However, the writer does mention the important question about use of time. This discussion is critical to the AR project and to future teaching plans the preservice teacher might design. Attention to this kind of detail makes the presentation of your work not only both professional and personal, it also makes it ethical.

Additional Guidelines

Other general kinds of guidelines for academic work that the cultural context of the academy requires are as follows:

Research writing should be very clear in identifying *who, what, where, when, how,* and *why.* None of this should be left open to readers' interpretations.

Credit should be given where credit is due. In other words, cite sources when directly quoting or referring to someone else's ideas.

Be explicit about limitations. This is particularly important to preservice AR projects where the limitations include critical variables like the amount of time spent collecting data and the amount of data.

Maintain confidentiality. Use pseudonyms for all proper pronouns.

Be tentative in pronouncing grand narratives or making sweeping conclusive statements. For preservice teachers and their AR projects, this means using language like, "The data suggest . . . ," "The data appear to . . . ," "This is also supported in the literature, as well as in . . . ," or "In my experience in this classroom . . ."

Any AR presenters should also be mindful of the following:

Purpose: What is the heart and soul of what you want to share? Spend your time and energies here.

Audience: For whom are you presenting? How much do they know about the context of your study and of your student teaching experience? Present for the appropriate audience.

Limitations: What time, physical and/or other cultural boundaries exists that will determine how you present your AR project? (For example, how much time do you have for a presentation? Are electrical plug-ins available for use of technology?)

Developing Personal and Professional Style and Voice

Style

Style in writing is not something glib—oh, yeah, she has style. It means becoming more and more present, settling deeper and deeper inside the layers of ourselves and then speaking, knowing what we write echoes all of us; all of who we are is backing our writing. —Natalie Goldberg, *Wild Mind: Living the Writer's Life*

In the epigraph, Goldberg is speaking of writing style, but she might well be describing the process of creating art, a presentation board, or the choice of font for a title page. *Style* as we use it here is about who you are and who you have become as a teacher. Style is how you represent the "layers" of yourself as a teacher in going public with your action research.

Most of our "style" comes from the context in which we live our lives; this has been a theme throughout this text in the "Cultural Context" side roads. Most of us wish our style as teachers to be "professional." Our vision of "professional" behavior, attire, and presentation is based upon the intersections of class, gender, ethnicity, and other cultural values, all embedded in the place where we learn these "professional" traits. In the context of going public with your AR project, you need to think about how professionalism is defined by your university culture. While there are some general kinds of norms that the academy (in a general sense) tends to privilege, every university, school within the university, and teacher-education program has its own rendition of professional. Reading the culturally privileged norms—the often unspoken codes—can be important in any professional educational setting. Once you know them you can decide whether to conform, how much to conform, or whether to choose your own way.

For example, you may propose to present your AR project as an interpretative dance. You believe this is "acceptable" since the syllabus indicates you may use "alternative forms of representation." However, as you proceed with your plans, you are asked to "complement" your dance with more and more traditional pieces of writing. In such an instance, you may be experiencing a "cultural code" that does not accept "dance" as "professional" or "appropriate" for university work.

There are many looks that may be considered *professional*—the term does not imply a "cookie cutter" look, set of actions, or language. There is room for individuality. If necessary, negotiate and nudge the systems of "tradition" to find your own way.

So what do you consider your "personal style"? If your teacher-education instructor asks you to look "professional" for an event, how does that translate into behavior for you? What are the professional expectations for dress at the school where you student teach? How does the culture of the community where the school is situated influence this? Use figure 5.1 to map out what the terms professional and personal mean to you.

Voice

Being professional is more than looks alone. Seen more deeply, professional identity is about *voice*. What *voice* should you use when going public with your personal AR journey? *Voice* is a term we use in writing, but again, it can apply to all kinds of presentation. Everyone, Fletcher (1993) tells us, has an inner voice: "The writer may not know exactly what the inner voice represents (uncon-

FIGURE 5.1: Venn Diagram: Personal and Professional

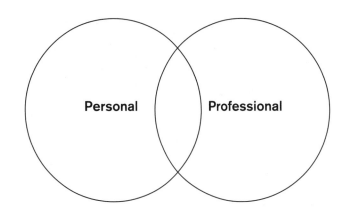

scious? Superego? Spirit?) but the writer does know one thing: the inner voice is spokesperson for the inner life" (p. 68). What is the "inner life" of your experience telling you about your AR journey? Let your inner voice interpret the discoveries you have made in your journey. What specific moments come to mind, what student faces appear in your memory? What dialogue from the classroom do you hear? These are the lived moments in the classroom, the collected data that represents a story—*your* story. Going public with your story requires personal style and voice, overlaid with a professional framework, giving your presentation richness and reality reflective of life in the classroom.

Assuming you've been through the data interpretation phase and are contemplating going public with your action research at this time, pause for a moment and reflect on your "findings" or "results." List these and then brainstorm words, colors, metaphors that best represent these results. How can you both personally and professionally represent these in the voice projected in your final presentation? How will this look, sound, and be interpreted by others?

Some Guiding Thoughts on Going Public

Strive to be genuine and sincere in presenting your AR project. It is enough that you have journeyed through this process of learning to teach. Do not try to represent more or less than your own personal story of becoming a teacher. Seek to honor the students and the other professionals who have assisted you along the way. Circle back and answer these questions: "Why teaching?" "What kind of teaching?" "Who have I become?" And enjoy this final phase: it represents a great deal of effort and learning on your part. Celebrate this by designing a meaningful final presentation for both you and your colleagues.

 Moving from Data Interpretation to Public Presentation

Listen to the past, future, and present right where you are. Listen with your whole body, not only with your ears, but with your hands, your face, and the back of your neck —Natalie Goldberg, *Wild Mind: Living the Writer's Life*

Listening is critical in getting started in the actual process of planning your AR presentation. In front of you, you have clusters, charts, categories, a timeline, and/or scribbles from your data interpretation. Now what? Listen. Follow Goldberg's advice by allowing your hands to scribble (and your head to follow), your feet to dance the rhythm of your story, by remembering moments of learning so rich that the hair on the back of your neck stands up. Listen to that data and the interpretation you have done. Return to the activity in the above section and use some of these memories as starting points.

Additionally, use the data-interpretation tools to make the transition from interpretation to presentation. The act of organizing your thoughts about data interpretation for a presentation allows you to better articulate what you have learned.

Examples

Laurel used a series of clusters in completing data interpretation. As a result, she had three clusters centering on study skills she had introduced and used in the chemistry classroom: perspectives (students, her mentor-teacher, and her own) of the usefulness of each of these study skills, what the actual data said that supported or contradicted these perspectives, and a final cluster with unanswered questions. Laurel decided to organize her story according to each study skill she had tried during her action research. She created a new cluster by putting "study skills" in the center; she then made subcircles of "wall graffiti," "warm-up questions," "concept test cards," "chalkboard strategy," and "review games" (the study skills she implemented). Around this she organized the lessons learned; the perspectives from students, her mentor-teacher, and herself; and the literature she wanted to highlight. In another cluster, she organized her questions into categories and chose the ones she most wanted to discuss. Laurel posted these clusters around her computer and began to write the first draft of her "results."

Ian used his final synthesis statements from each category to organize his presentation. He put these in the order he wanted to use in his paper; he selected the ones he had the most data on and the most conviction about to focus on in his presentation. Using an unstructured outline format, he included under each selected synthesis statement the data and details to support the statement. From this outline, he began to put together his oral presentation.

➡ FIGURE 5.2: Prewriting Chart

The main points I want to make in my presentation	Connecting points from the data	Connecting points from the literature	Questions I still have from this area

Both of these examples highlight the first step in moving from data interpretation to presentation: organizing the interpretations into a format from which you can begin to actually put together your presentation. Use the prepresentation planner at figure 5.2 to organize your thoughts in a more linear way. Write concise statements for each heading; force yourself to be brief and to the point. If you already have this chart feel free to skip this exercise.

Printable CD Extra: Prewriting Chart

You can download a template of table 5.2 from the companion CD.

Now you are ready to actually begin writing the story of your research, organizing a portfolio, preparing for a research symposium, or creating alternative forms of representation. Skim through the following sections for an overview of the options. If you know which format you are going to use to go public, focus on the guidelines presented in the appropriate section.

The Research Paper: Writing Your Story

Writing the story of your action research can be a profound experience. This doesn't mean that it may not be difficult, but it can be another step of transformation as you organize the lessons learned, articulate the experiences, and finally share with others your new insights. Writer Anne Lamott (1994) describes this as "becoming conscious": "When you're conscious and writing from a place of insight and simplicity and real caring about the truth, you have the ability to throw the lights on for your reader" (p. 225). The process of writing your AR journey is an opportunity to "throw the lights on" and celebrate in sharing.

We recommend organizing your paper using nine major sections. These sections represent those commonly found in research papers. We've used these headings to introduce you to the tradition of research writing, but we have "tweaked" them to better represent preservice action research as presented in this text. The nine headings are:

Abstract

Introduction

What I've Learned from Distant Colleagues (also referred to as the *literature review* or the *theoretical framework*)

Clarifying My Action Research Project

The Road Map of My Action Research Project

The Story of My Action Research Project

Further Reflection and Continuing Questions About My Action Research Journey

References

Appendices

Of course, there are many other acceptable headings for organizing a research paper. Your program or course may require something different, or may skip some of the above headings altogether. We only offer the following template as a suggestion. Each of these headings is further described below.

Printable CD Extra: Annotated Manuscript Template and Examples

An annotated and downloadable template, and examples of completed action research projects, are available on the companion CD.

In addition to these nine headings, you will need to construct within each section your own *signposts* (Rankin, 2001) to further direct your readers. Signposts include the following:

Subheadings	These are especially useful in long sections of writing. Group these sections into smaller organizational units so your reader can follow along. For example, you might include subheadings that represent themes you found in your literature review. (Note: Many of our students report being taught to avoid using subheadings in formal writing. We require it as common practice in educational research texts.) Be consistent in your use of terminology and/or structure with subheadings throughout your paper—check with your professor for possible required stylistic preferences.
Transitional Paragraphs	These provide a road map to your readers, giving them direction about where the piece is going to go next. For example, in a transitional paragraph, you might state the purpose for the entire section and then introduce subheadings that will follow, and include a summary statement for the section.
Connecting or Linking Terms	Words such as *however, in addition,* and *furthermore* help link together ideas for the reader.

You will also want to start consulting the latest edition of the *Publication Manual of the American Psychological Association* or other style guides that may be required from now on in the writing of your draft manuscript. (Your university library most likely will have these but there are many easy-to-use online APA style guides to be found on the Internet (see, e.g., Dewey, 2003).

The Abstract

The abstract consists of a single, concise paragraph describing the purpose, procedure, and results of your study. Use no more than 200 words. Don't write the abstract until you are nearly finished writing the larger research paper. Then draft the abstract as a summary, and redraft it until it reads as clearly and concisely as possible.

The Introduction

The goal of the introduction is to combine information about the setting and the story behind the AR project into a smooth narrative that gets the reader engaged in the work's context; the critical question is also introduced here. This section is usually about three to five pages long. The reader should have a good idea what the paper is about before finishing the first page. In the introduction, be cognizant of the following:

Context   It is important to communicate to the reader a clear picture of the overall context of your AR project. The way you write the beginning of your paper lays the foundation (weak or strong) for the credibility and trustworthiness of your results and conclusions.

Storytelling   Instead of telling about your setting, illustrate it for the reader using stories and anecdotes taken from your notes, reflections, and data. Introduce major players in your analysis and results.

Active and Layered Description   Use multiple data sources to illustrate the setting and story behind the research. It must be clear to the reader that you are thoroughly immersed and engaged in your setting, and are therefore qualified to make credible analyses and interpretations. By referring to some data here you signal to the reader prior to the rest of the paper what type of research this is and how data was generally collected.

Your Story   It is also important to communicate to the reader a clear picture of yourself as the student teacher/researcher and how your own biases, experiences, and assumptions not only influence the study but also provided the fodder for your critical question. This may be woven into your illustration of context by including your own thoughts and memories. If there are key quotes that tell your story in another's words, consider including these quotes in this section. Make it clear how you arrived at your critical question.

Your Critical Question   Bring your narrative to a climax in which you lay out your critical question in detail. Explain briefly what your action(s) consisted of. Tell briefly what your conclusions look like—don't try to keep the reader in suspense.

How to Write Good Introductory Paragraphs

Opening paragraphs can be the most difficult to write. For some reason, the blank page of the computer monitor blinks ominously as we begin. Try using (and expanding on) a quote, telling a personal story, or even writing an invitation. Here are a few examples from our students.

Example 1

On the first day of school at a large suburban high school, a freshman English teacher welcomed 130 new ninth grade students as they nervously made the transition from middle school to the big new world of high school—from childhood to semiadulthood. With their eyes glazed they heard about the stringent requirements and responsibilities that were ahead, and I was surprised by a promise she made to them. Mrs. D. told the students that if they turned in every single assignment throughout the year, she would give them a passing grade—no matter how poorly they did on said assignments or tests. Surely this guarantee was far too generous, I thought. It's a "Get Out of Jail Free" card for students who don't meet standards!

Example 2

All study of human thought must begin by positing an individual who is attempting to make sense out of the world. —Howard Gardner, *Frames of Mind*

The car shuttered and lurched as she edged onto the highway just as the sun began to peak in its crown from behind the westward range, illuminating the sky to the east and the yellow lines ahead. A new day awaited, a day that marked the start of a teaching journey. She took a deep breath, accelerated . . . popped the car into fifth gear and paused momentarily to reflect on the golden events of the past, and the uncertain events that loomed close in the near future. Over, around, up and down mountainous and forest trails she'd trekked, identifying creatures great and small, green and otherwise with young, avid learners clamoring at her heels. After three years of experience teaching in the outdoors, she felt prepared for what lay ahead on this journey, but wondered exactly what she could expect from this new environment.

Example 3

Welcome to the Avi Coffee Shop. Come in, find your friends, pick up something interesting to read, and be ready when the maître d' stops by to bring you a snack. However, it will not be coffee and croissants. More likely it will be hot cocoa and a granola bar, or apple juice and popcorn. You are not at Starbuck's, you are in Mrs. Browning's fourth grade class. Friends, interesting literature, snacks, and great conversation are what Avi Coffee Shop is about; come on in and join in the conversation!

What I've Learned from Distant Colleagues

The goal of this section is to introduce the reader to the major issues and/or themes learned from distant colleagues in the literature surrounding your critical question. By broadening your readers' understanding of the major issue surrounding your research, you further solidify the credibility and trustworthiness of your work. This section is generally about three to five pages long.

We find that it is best to organize this section in one of two ways: either group the literature you are reviewing by themes or review the literature to provide an overview of the history leading up to the framework for your AR project. For example, one of our students organized her literature review according to these themes: (1) literature on the effectiveness of reading aloud; (2) strategies for increasing reading fluency and comprehension; and (3) meaningful reading fluency and comprehension assessment strategies. Another student organized her literature review as a historical overview of assessment in mathematics. Her review looked at the evolution of mathematical assessments to the present emphasis on problem solving.

Choose a format that will allow your readers to make the connection between your literature review and the AR study by establishing the theoretical foundation of the action, curriculum review, self-study, or ethnography you later describe in your AR paper. (Note: This section will contain the majority of your citations, although we suggest bringing in the voices of distant colleagues throughout your paper.)

Clarifying My Action Research Project

This is a concise one-page section focusing your reader on the essential elements of your AR project. Assume a more professional style and tone to precisely answer:

who is involved in the project

what the critical question is and what was implemented or analyzed

where the project took place (description of setting)

when the data collection occurred (dates of implementation and/or data collection, length of study)

how data collection was completed (these are brief statements—the next section gives this information in more detail)

why you conducted the study

limitations of the study

This subsection may seem redundant given that you have already revealed your critical question (CQ) and action(s) earlier. The intent here is to clearly focus your reader and to use a technical, professional tone that clearly defines the study before the reader begins the story of your research.

The Road Map of My Action Research Project

The goal of this section is to inform your reader about:

the interventions, analysis, or strategies you implemented

the data-collection strategies and sources you used

the contents of the data sets you collected

the methods you used to analyze, interpret, and deconstruct the data

changes you made in your research design

This section should be three to five pages long. Continue the professional tone of the "Clarifying My Action Research Project" section. This "Road Map" section is a technical piece of the paper in which the reader gets an inside view of your research process. The idea here is that someone else could do the same research in their classroom by following your detailed descriptions of methodology.

The Story of My Action Research Project

The goal of this section is to illustrate what you have learned as related to your critical question. Use your data to tell the story of your research and support your conclusions and emerging theories. This section is the heart and soul of your AR paper. This is where you tell *your* story. The section is rich in voice, style, and data. Remember this classic bit of writing advice: *show, don't tell,* as you write. Interweave important data into your narrative. Include tables, charts, and quotes from interviews and your observations and reflections. Use your data to illustrate your ideas, and to provide the readers the freedom to draw their own conclusions as well. Explain how you interpret your data. Support your interpretations with examples. Use multiple data sources to support major assertions or ideas. Include multiple voices and perspectives. Be sure to include other voices, such as those of critical colleagues, students, and distant colleagues (literature review). *Deconstruct your work*, providing counterexamples and alternative interpretations.

Two examples of writing are given below; one *tells* the story; the other *shows* the story. The voice in the first example is flat and somewhat detached; the second example includes a lively voice and style and makes the most of narrative structure. The examples are based upon an AR project to develop the artists' abilities of grade three students.

Example 1: Telling the Story

One student found it very difficult to give up the idea that "good" art is art that is a realistic depiction of what is observed. This student struggled in her art efforts; she often destroyed her work. During the self-portrait drawing assignment, however, she appeared to have a change of attitude. Although she accidentally created a hole in her picture from rubbing too hard, she found a way to incorporate the hole into her final self-portrait. I was very pleased, and encouraged her work and her ability to do this.

Example 2: Showing the Story

Rosie, the class perfectionist, was crushed: she had rubbed too hard and ripped a hole in her self-portrait. When asked for another paper, I reminded her of our class motto, "There are no mistakes—only opportunities." A little later, she came back with a finished portrait. Rosie had taken that hole, that "mistake," and purposefully ripped it a bit more, turning it into a halo! The ripped edges gave the portrait a unique and beautiful texture. "You know what?" she said, "That hole is my favorite part of the picture." Koster (2003) writes, "Art inspires students to question, wonder, and explore to discover unique combinations and solutions" (p. 132). That day, Rosie discovered a "unique combination and solution" as well as her artist self.

Further Reflection and Continuing Questions about My Action Research Journey

In this section, you bring themes together and begin the process of concluding your paper. Consider the following questions as writing prompts for this final reflection of your AR journey:

What are some of the most important lessons you will take into your teaching career?

What will you do differently next time?

What additional questions did this research project pose for you?

What was your action research journey like? How has this journey transformed your image of teacher, teaching, students, schools, learning? How have your paradigms been altered, confirmed, and/or challenged?

What have you learned about action research? How has your definition of AR changed? How do you see yourself using this process in the future?

How to Write a Memorable Conclusion

Conclusions are tough: how do you end a good date, or say good-bye after a long visit? More than likely, you will write your concluding paragraph several times before you are satisfied. An effective way to write the concluding paragraph is to use a quote, either from someone famous, your students, other participants, or from your own researcher's notebook. Another possibility is to end with a short story, a vignette, from your data that illustrates the central focus of the study. Sometimes, a combination works well.

In the example below, the student teacher had conducted an AR project about homework. In his classroom, students either did not turn in homework or they turned in poor quality homework. He attempted two different kinds of homework strategies to improve both quality and completion rates. However, he found that a reward system that gave students "free time" points for turning in homework regardless of quality trumped all his other homework strategies. This is how he concluded his piece:

To conclude my research I decided to ask the entire class one question. "Would you rather earn homework points by turning in an assignment that you know you could do better on or sacrifice the homework points but get the best score in the class on a big assignment?" Seventy-six percent of the class said they would choose the homework points. Only six of the 25 students polled would take the top score. Students are getting mixed messages. They're motivated to get the homework points even though we want them to produce their best work. They're motivated by the wrong thing—completing assignments no matter what the quality is. Absolutely, they still struggle to complete their work, but they do understand that completing work is what is valued regardless of the quality. More than anything else, I've learned that students are smart. They learn early on in the school year what is important, and most students strive to achieve that. As a teacher, I need to be aware of this and careful not to send a message to my students that I don't want them to receive. Students will provide us with the information we need to create the types of classrooms we want if we look for it. I credit the students for teaching me the lessons that I will take from this AR project, one of which is summarized by this quote: "The question educators need to ask is not how motivated their students are, but how their students are motivated" (Kohn, 1994, p. 3).

This conclusion returns to the heart of the action research study. It summarizes the main lesson the student teacher/researcher learned. And it encourages the reader to ask, "What kind of mixed messages do I send my students?" This makes for a memorable final curtain call!

References

Consult carefully with American Psychological Association style guidelines, or whatever other citation methods are required in your program, as they are another important element of trust-worthiness. Having proper references is important in ensuring that credit is given where credit is due, not only when directly quoting a source, but also when summarizing someone else's ideas or concepts. Make sure and attend to references carefully.

Appendices

A writer places in the appendices additional information that supports or illustrates points in the paper. Items in the appendices allow the reader to go deeper or gain a clearer view of what is being said in the main text. Appendices are important, but they are not a "dumping ground." For example, not all data goes in the appendices; however, a log of data sets may be appropriate. Not all student work would be placed in the appendices, but a sample that clarifies an assignment would be appropriate.

Possible inclusions in the appendices might be:

a log of data sets or specific items from a data set

assessments

surveys, questionnaires, and interview questions

letters sent to parents (including those used in obtaining informed consent from your students)

lesson plans

artifacts

Note that anything placed in the appendices must be referenced in the text of the paper. Check the appropriate citation guidelines on how to do this.

A Final Word on Writing

Take this final word of advice from author Ray Bradbury (1994) on writing: "If you are writing without zest, without gusto, without love, without fun, you are only half a writer. . . . For the first thing a writer should be is—excited. He should be a thing of fevers and enthusiasm" (p. 4).

This is most likely one of the last projects for your teacher-education program. Have fun! Be yourself! Enjoy! Become a teacher with both zest and gusto and let it show in writing your AR project.

The Portfolio: Showing Your Story

A portfolio is another demonstration of your AR journey. While portfolios share some organizational principles with formal papers, portfolios are much more visual and interactive, allowing the audience a closer, less-processed look at your research work. A collection of artifacts organized into a three-ring binder notebook or in electronic format allows readers to travel with you through the stages of learning. Your portfolio should demonstrate your ability to be reflective in using assessment data to better facilitate learning for students, and to answer questions you have about your teaching practice.

We recommend organizing your portfolio into the following categories:

Introduction

The Road Map of My Action Research Project

Discovery Documentation

Further Reflection and Continuing Questions About My Action Research Journey

Annotated Bibliography

The Introduction

This section functions as a narrative that provides an overview of the AR project. Write the introduction to your portfolio much as you would if writing the more traditional research paper. As part of the portfolio introduction, answer the questions *who, what, where, when, how,* and *why* (see the section "Clarifying My Action Research Project," above). The rest of the portfolio fills in the details of the overview presented in the introduction.

The Road Map of My Action Research Project

In this section, include a brief overview (one or two paragraphs) of how you collected data. Follow this with a chart or other visual image showing how the data was collected; an annotated timeline may be a good option. The visual image should demonstrate and support the trustworthiness of the data. Include a data-collection log that lists the data sets you collected.

Discovery Documentation

Communicate the essential themes of your AR journey in this section. You may include charts, graphs, and/or tables of data collected, pictures relating to the AR project, samples of student work, lesson plans, and reflections from your researcher's notebook. The secret to an effective "Discovery" section is organizing documentation in a meaningful way with appropriate narrative so that a reader can clearly understand the story you are telling. We think you will find it most effective to organize this section in chronological order, beginning with your first data set and moving through your student-teaching experience. (If you used a timeline for data interpretation, this is a good tool to return to in organizing this section.) Select the best documentation that best illustrates the primary discoveries you have made. You do not need to include *everything*; it is better to select for quality representation.

As an example, suppose you decide to illustrate the importance of assigning equally important roles to students during cooperative learning. To do this in your portfolio, you could choose one lesson you taught without clearly defined meaningful roles, and another where these roles were clearly defined. This subsection would begin with a brief narrative introduction. The introduction provides the reader a road map for reading the documentation that follows: the purpose of this subsection, a brief description of the two lessons, and a list of the artifacts to follow. The artifacts would include the two cooperative learning lessons (with the roles specified), pictures of students working on the two projects, sample student work, and, finally, selections from your researcher's notebook from each of the two lessons. Each artifact should be clearly labeled.

Sometimes student teachers need to demonstrate through a portfolio how they have met or are moving toward specific standards. If this is true, you may want to consider organizing this section around each standard, or specifically making the connection between the standard(s) and the content of each display in the introductions.

The depth of this section depends on the amount of data you have collected (in a short study, you may display the entire data set), the parameters determined by your teacher/education program, and the physical boundaries of a three-ring binder notebook. A variety of documentation will enrich this section, but all documentation should support the primary discoveries of your AR project.

Further Reflection and Continuing Questions About My Action Research Journey

This section of your portfolio is a written narrative summarizing major themes of your AR project, the process of action research, and questions you still have. Use the instructions from the previous section on writing an AR paper, Further Reflection and Continuing Questions about My Action Research, to guide you in completing this section.

The Annotated Bibliography

An annotated bibliography includes the citation of each source followed by a brief summary (one concise paragraph) of the source. The annotated bibliography should demonstrate your ability to find appropriate sources to support teaching and learning as demonstrated in your AR project. The connection between the citation and the AR project should be evident in each annotation.

The Annotated Bibliography: A Sample Entry

Daniels, H. (2002). *Literature circles: Voice and choice in book clubs and reading groups* (2nd ed.). Portland, ME: Stenhouse.

This is a practical guide to literature circles. It includes specific direction in preparing students for literature groups (both fiction and nonfiction), scheduling and managing groups, choosing materials, and specific grade applications. The source also includes principles and strategies for assessment. I found the structure of Daniels's literature circles to be useful in the early stages of my AR project.

Formatting the Portfolio

Organization is of utmost importance in a portfolio; items must be arranged in such a way that a reader can travel easily through your journey. Include a table of contents, title pages, and brief narratives as guides. Consider aesthetics as well. The use of color, borders, and different fonts can add to the overall professional and personal presentation. Aesthetic devices ought to complement, not overpower, the content. More is not usually better in this category. Be inventive, invite humor, allow your personality to shine through the documentation and illustrate the teacher you have become.

The Electronic Portfolio

We like the idea of electronic portfolios. They allow for more inventiveness by allowing the use of digital photography and movies, as well as using hypertext navigation to ease the readers journey through your work.

Printable CD Extra: Electronic Portfolios

A fuller description of tools and tricks for creating an electronic portfolio is included on the companion CD.

 ## Using Art Forms to Represent Your Story

Why would anyone want to make their AR presentation into an art project? Consider the following story. Christy completed her student teaching in an elementary classroom with a very diverse group of learners. Particularly troubling to her was how to bring some of the students who had difficult learning disabilities and emotional challenges into the classroom community. Her project was empathetic, compassionate, and deliberate in attempting to create an inviting, safe, and responsive classroom for all her students. Christy collected rich and interesting data but when it came time to interpret this data and organize it, Christy was stuck. None of the tools we suggested seemed to help. In working with Christy, we realized that she often used art to express herself in other assignments and projects. Her AR journal was full of symbolic drawings. So, Christy drew her interpretations, first as sketches, and then, as her final project.

Activity: Christy's Drawings–Media Vignette

Some of Christy's drawings can be viewed on the companion CD along with selections from her written text.

Dewey (1954) wrote, "The function of art has always been to break through the crust of conventionalized and routine consciousness. . . . Artists have always been the real purveyors of news, for it is not the outward happening in itself which is new, but the kindling by it of emotion, perception and appreciation" (pp. 183–184). There are many ways to represent as art the story of your action research: painting, sculpture, music, interpretative dance, fiction, storytelling, digital photography, and digital video, just to name a few. Artistic forms of representation can provide rich and expressive ways to tell your story, to capture that part of the experience that does not conform to words alone. The process of creating art can be particularly meaningful to both the artist and the audience as relationships between experiences, emotions, and literature are explored. In developing such representations, the guidelines at the beginning of this chapter should still be followed. How they appear in your presentation is a matter of your interpretation. Since art representations are still relatively new to academic culture, check with your professor or advisor for additional guidelines.

 ## Displaying Your Story Using Posters and Brochures

Research symposiums or other public settings are often the culminating venue for sharing AR projects. One format commonly used at such events is a "poster session." Poster board presentations are common at professional conferences. Creating a poster may be a good skill/art to develop as you move forward professionally.

The professional requirements of most poster board presentations include:

your name

the title of your research project

the name of your university and date of publication

the critical question(s)

the research design and select data

final reflection and continuing questions

Be attentive to spelling, punctuation, and mechanical errors. Include essential elements only; too many words make the board "busy." Artifacts or pictures of artifacts may be included. Remember, if you are displaying pictures of students, you should have permission to do so.

It's a good idea to provide your poster audience a short handout to go along with your poster. We recommend a trifold brochure for this purpose, a summary of your AR project. Trifold formatted brochures are printed front to back; templates are available on most word processing programs. The professional requirements of most brochures include:

your name

the title of your research project

the name of your university and date of publication

the critical question(s)

the research design and select data

final reflections and continuing questions

a bibliography of key sources

your contact information

Be attentive to spelling, punctuation, and mechanical errors. Include essential elements only; allow for enough unprinted space to make the brochure easy to read.

These are the professional requirements for a presentation board and brochure; but personal style should reflect who you have become as a teacher. Combine color, texture, symbols, and artifacts to represent your story and yourself as a teacher. Keep in mind how this intersects with the professional in making your presentation aesthetically appealing while representing you and your story.

Celebrating and Sharing: Finding Joy and Humility Through Action Research

We may find joy in celebrating each others' strengths, but there is also unleashing of joy when we join together in our humility —Rachel Kessler, *The Soul of Education: Helping Students Find Connection, Compassion, and Character at School*

Going public with your AR project is a time for celebration. As you share with your colleagues, there is strength in realizing how much you have learned, grown, become. There is also recognition of how much more there is to still discover. There is *joy* in both.

CHAPTER 6
LIVING ACTION RESEARCH AS A PROFESSIONAL EDUCATOR

 **Looping Back and Articulating What You Know**

Becoming a teacher…means more than acquiring technical knowledge and expertise. It means becoming a teacher morally, through one's commitment to the children one teaches and to the wider social purposes for which that teaching is done (Fullan, 1993; Sockett, 1987). It means becoming a teacher emotionally (Hargreaves, 1995a); through caring for and engaging passionately with others…Becoming a teacher also means becoming a teacher politically by having to negotiate and adjust to the continuing constraints of schooling (Schempp, Sparkes, & Templin, 1993).

—Andy Hargreaves and Noreen Jacka, "Induction or Seduction? Postmodern Patterns of Preparing to Teach"

Reread the epigraph above. How has your experience with action research prepared you to be a teacher along moral, emotional, and political dimensions? Who have you become as a teacher, and where might your continued self-evolution and reinvention take you? How do you see the art and science of action research as a scaffold that might support who you become as a professional educator? Respond to these questions in your notebook or journal; if possible, discuss them with your colleagues. Respond in writing, drawing, or by clustering your thoughts.

Action research can serve as a bridge between the world of student teaching and that of your new career as a professional educator. The skills, attitudes, and spirit of inquiry inherent in action research can be useful in meeting the challenges of your first year of teaching. "Teacher/action researcher" as a part of your professional identity can act as an ongoing scaffold as you become a teacher who is morally, emotionally, and politically astute. As you near completion of your teacher-education program (or at least the end of your action research project), take time in this final section to loop back through some of the primary themes of this text as you contemplate growing yourself as a professional educator.

Reviewing Major Themes of Student-Teacher Action Research

The role of your personal paradigm in influencing who you are as a teacher is a central theme of this textbook.

Begin by reflecting on what you have learned about your own paradigm, how your paradigm has changed, and how it might continue to transform you as an educator. Complete the following phrases through writing/drawing your own synthesis statements.

My paradigm for thinking about education has changed in these ways:

I can identify the following key influences on my paradigm for thinking about teaching:

The above translate into the teacher I have become as illustrated by:

These are areas within my paradigm through which I want to continue to question, grow, and explore:

Another major theme of this text is the role of cultural context in teaching. Who you are and how you are positioned (according to gender, race, ethnicity, and other defining categories) work alongside your values and beliefs (paradigms) to influence all of your perceptions and practices as a teacher. What have you learned about *context* during the action research process?

Complete the following phrases through writing, drawing, or clustering:

When I first began reading about cultural context (community and school values, socioeconomics, gender, religion, ethnicity, and other defining categories) in this book I thought:

I understand how context influenced my action research project and teaching in these ways:

When I accept a teaching position, this is what I want to remember about cultural context:

Reviewing Action Research Technique

Throughout the action research process, you have learned the art and science of observing students, interviewing or listening to students and other participants in the educational setting, and collecting artifacts or assessments to inform your teaching. Continued growth in these skills can strengthen the bridge between being a beginning teacher and being a teacher of influence.

Consider what you have learned and how you want to enhance these skills by responding to the following prompts. Use specific stories and/or examples when possible.

Observation

Complete the following statements:

This is what I have learned about making observations in the classroom (include some tools that have become favorites):

My observations can be useful and dangerous in these ways:

I find I am most willing to overlook:

The quick judgments I am most likely to make include scenarios like:

Interviews

Consider what you have learned about interviewing, listening, and seeking students' voices and other perspectives in completing the following statements. Use specific stories and/or examples when possible.

This is what I have learned about interviewing students and other participants in education (include tools that have become favorites:)

When interviewing students, I find I am most interested in the following:

I find it most difficult to listen to_____because:

Based upon my responses, this is what is useful and dangerous about the way I interview (listen to, seek other perspective from) others:

Artifacts: Collecting and Interpreting Assessment Documentation

 Consider what you have learned and how you want to grow your abilities to collect and assess artifacts by responding to the following prompts. Use specific stories and/or examples when possible.

What I have learned about collecting student artifacts as assessment:

What I have learned about the limits of assessments:

I consider the following critical points in designing, collecting, and interpreting student artifacts as assessment (and this is what makes them trustworthy):

In the future, I plan to grow my abilities in this area by:

Reconsidering Triangulation

Throughout this text, we have discussed triangulation as a means of building a trustworthy set of data. Triangulation, or actively seeking multiple perspectives and voices, can be a powerful tool in many teaching scenarios. For example, understanding a student who is constantly a behavior challenge in the classroom requires triangulation, or data gathering from many sources, such as parents and other teachers. When you hear a "rumor" about a district's decision regarding pension plans, you may want to "triangulate" what you hear by looking at several perspectives before you believe it entirely. When you perceive a lesson or unit to be a "disaster," triangulating the data may provide useful insight. When you hear, "Research says . . . ," keep triangulation in mind. Triangulation is the larger concept behind critical thinking: it is the act of suspending judgment while seeking multiple perspectives, voices, solutions, and possibilities. What have you learned about triangulation that you want to take with you into your first teaching position?

 Respond to the following prompts using specific examples and/or stories:

This is what I have learned about triangulation and its usefulness in the teaching/learning process:

This is what I have learned about triangulation and making classroom decision:

This is what I have learned about triangulation and assessing classroom climate:

Recall Hargreaves and Jacka (1995), who state that one must become a teacher *morally*, *emotionally*, and *politically*. We add to this list that a teacher must become a teacher *intellectually*. Loop back through your responses above: who do you want to continue to become *morally*, *emotionally*, *politically*, and *intellectually*?

 Action Research and Your First Year of Teaching

Who do they think they are, talking back to their teacher with such disrespect? When I was 8 years old, I would have never dreamed of speaking to an adult that way. Did I go to college for this?

—Patricia Anguiano, "A First Year Teacher's Plan to Reduce Misbehavior in the Classroom"

Anguiano (2001), a first year teacher and action researcher, wrote the above words in her journal. Her frustration with classroom management issues is an all-too-familiar story for many first year teachers who, faced with challenging situations, may wonder how they will ever teach the way they learned to teach in their teacher-education programs. You may already anticipate some of the same frustrations.

A case study of four first-year high school history teachers in different schools revealed four common areas of challenge: *instructional issues* (covering all required material), *behavior issues* (the fear of loosing control), *belief in students* (doubt in students' abilities), and *contextual factors* (isolation and lack of support) (Van Hoover & Yeager, 2004). As a student teacher you may have already experienced challenges in these areas; as a beginning teacher you will have more time to examine them and work toward resolutions. For example, first year teachers often struggle to find consonance with how they *see* their students and how they analyze and interpret students' behavior (Achinstein & Barrett, 2004). In other words, we (teachers) assume that they (students) think and regard school pretty much as we did as kids, and we expect them to behave and respond to us the way we would have behaved and responded. We *see* ourselves in our students, and interpret them accordingly. The problem is this: the internal lens through which we see our students can give us a distorted view, a view at odds with the culture of students, classroom, school, and/or community in which we teach. This cultural mismatch closes down possibilities for finding solutions, leaving the first year teacher feeling helpless to make positive changes, and vulnerable to cynicism and burnout.

In keeping in contact with our former students (and in recalling our own first years of teaching), we empathize with the shock that first year teachers often encounter. Moving from idealist visions of who one *desires* to be as a teacher into the first year of actually *being* a teacher may be a time of dissonance and confusion, but this is also what can make it a time of growth. Who you ultimately become as a teacher has much to do with how you choose to approach these and other "first year" challenges.

Anguiano (2001) conducted a small action research project to address her own challenges in understanding her students. She introduced strategies based upon her analysis of behaviors, and collected data. At the end of her five-week study she was able to write,

My students gained respect for me as a teacher because I was able to deal with misbehaviors in a way that did not take away instructional time. I also gained respect for myself as a teacher as I saw a positive response in my students' listening skills and ability to follow directions. (p. 55)

We applaud Anguiano's use of action research to find a solution to a challenge that might otherwise have degenerated into blaming children, doubting their abilities, or becoming so obsessed with "control" that authentic learning could not continue.

Getting Started in Your First Classroom

The skills of observing, listening, and collecting artifacts coupled with a paradigm informed by action research can position a first year teacher to successfully face a multitude of challenges. If you are anticipating your first teaching position, consider the weeks just prior to your first day in the classroom, as well as those initial first two weeks of teaching. How might you use the skills of action research as presented in this text?

We see the following possibilities; compare and contrast them with a list of your own making.

Once you have your first teaching position, return to chapter 2: Getting to Know Your Classroom Culture. Find out as much as you can about the context of your new position—and if you believe you are very familiar with this setting, it may be wise to test those assumptions—by using the activities described in chapter 6. Use this information to plan systems of organization, structures, and relevant lessons for the first two weeks of school.

During the first two weeks of school, use surveys to gather data about students' attitudes, learning styles, homework habits, interests, and strengths; complete essential academic assessment to establish the diversity of learning levels.

Be deliberate in planning for systems of management and structure based upon what you discover about your students and their community, as well as your own comfort levels and needs in this area. Be deliberate in teaching these systems. Finally, be deliberate in setting up ways to gather data concerning the effectiveness of these systems.

Although you may be exhausted after those first days, take time to write in your notebook or journal, sketch, cluster, or otherwise freewrite about your days; record both your own behavior and that of your students. Start a list of questions and resist answers or solutions that are too easy.

After the first two weeks, plan some time and space to analyze, synthesize, and deconstruct your data; let this data guide your next steps as a teacher.

Consult critical colleagues, both local and distant, to find encouragement and ideas.

This is a short list. As we have said before, a list can be dangerous, reducing what is complex and messy to overly simplistic answers and actions. Our list is an illustration of how to position yourself as a new teacher/researcher with a certain way of thinking, a particular teaching stance. If your days are hectic, you may say, "I don't have time for a frequency count chart!" But consider the alternative, which is trying one solution after another as if attempting to aim at a target while blindfolded. It may be worth it to adopt a more intentional approach suggested by action research.

The first year of teaching is about classroom management issues, rethinking big concepts like *control* and *authority*, and reframing what you believe about yourself and your students. Seeking multiple perspectives and the voices of critical colleagues, considering context, and developing the techniques of action research as a way of thinking and practicing can provide a road map allowing you to stay—for a long time, satisfied—in education.

Thinking about the First Year
Scenario 1

Fletcher's ninth grade language arts class threatens to drive him just a little crazy; it isn't that students are mean or even really disrespectful, but they are "everywhere at once," talking, laughing, and enjoying what seems like everything but the content, which is supposed to be Shakespeare. Fletcher isn't sure how he is going to get the class through four major plays during the semester. After one particularly frustrating day, Fletcher writes in his journal about what he *does* know: (1) students think Shakespeare is boring; (2) they reportedly "don't get it"; (3) most of the students are reading just at grade level or slightly below; (4) over two-thirds of the students have never seen a play; (5) students' behavior seems to decline just after directions have been given, when they are to read individually, and 10 minutes before class ends. Finally, Fletcher writes this question, "Why Shakespeare?"

Without coming to conclusions or providing possible solutions to this scenario, consider how action research techniques might be used to gather additional data and create an informed plan of action:

What techniques of action research are already being used in the scenario?

How might interview techniques be used to provide additional data on the dilemma?

How might observations be useful?

What artifacts might be deliberately collected and analyzed?

What additional perspectives or voices might be helpful in analyzing the situation?

What assumptions may need to be deconstructed?

Scenario 2

Dorrey never knew 22 first graders could be so "out of control." They never seem to stop moving or talking. Misbehavior significantly increases during math. The school's math curriculum incorporates multiple tactile and kinesthetic techniques, and Dorrey is amazed at what a first grader can do with a handful of colorful cubes. She asks a colleague to come and observe during a 30-minute math session. Here are some of the results of the observations:

Six different kinds of manipulatives were used during the 30-minute class period.

There were eight total transitions.

Children consistently began playing with manipulatives prior to listening to all of the instructions given by the teacher.

The lesson introduction did not appear to connect to the use of the manipulatives.

Children at two table groups appeared to be "bartering" with the manipulatives; children at a third table were constructing interesting designs.

The four English language learners did not follow any of the directions.

Dorrey mostly stayed at the front of the class and shouted over the children to various table groups.

Without coming to conclusions or providing possible solutions to this scenario, consider how action research techniques might be used to gather additional data and make an informed plan of action:

What techniques of action research are already being used in the scenario?

How might interview techniques be used to provide additional data on the dilemma?

How might observations be useful?

What artifacts might be deliberately analyzed?

What additional perspectives or voices might be helpful in analyzing the situation?

What assumptions may need to be deconstructed?

Your first year of teaching may very well include scenarios like these. Becoming a teacher who thinks and acts using action research principles early in your career can help you maintain the energy and enthusiasm necessary to happily remain in the teaching field. Be realistic about your goals. You won't likely do a formal action research project, but you can begin to think in this way now and grow your professional future.

Action Research, Energy, Enthusiasm, and Loving Your Job as a Teacher

Gandhi said, "We must be the change we wish to see in the world." I want to see students feeling excited about learning. I want to see students being engaged in school because it is relevant not only in content but also in technique. I want to see teachers who are skillful at employing varied techniques to appeal to the multiple intelligences of learners, using technology as a tool that allows for the pursuit of curiosity and encourages individual strengths to shine forth. This research has taken me giant steps toward becoming the change I want to see in the world of teaching. —Carley, a student teacher/researcher

Carley wrote the above reflection at the end of her action research project and her student-teaching practicum, one week prior to graduation from her teacher-education program. Like most of us in education, Carley is beginning her career idealistically. She is equipped with many skills, and is *ready* and *willing* to make a difference in the world through her role and contributions as a teacher. Her action research project has taught her ways to become the teacher she desires to be.

Even as Carley and her colleagues in the program contemplated graduation, they sensed that it would take determination to maintain their dream of being a teacher of influence. Consider their comments exiting their teacher-education program:

It is important to remember how this feels, this at-the-beginning feeling, and keep a part of it with us as we move through our careers.

The challenge is to keep learning, [to] continuously reflect, [and to] maintain a circle of peers to consult and confide in when the going gets tough.

Could it be that our biggest challenge as teachers is to remain as we are, and not become too obsessed with the details of our daily routine that could cause us to take the path of least resistance?

We agree that the biggest challenge may be getting bogged down in routine, mandates, testing requirements, losing that "at-the-beginning" feeling, or finding oneself too tired to contemplate even the idea of reflection. In fact, there is a fair amount of research that suggests this is exactly what happens to many teachers. "Burnout leads to teacher dropout. This condition has been referred to as 'battle fatigue'" (Hansen & Wentworth, 2002, p. 17).

What is your plan for combating "battle fatigue"? How did you see mentor-teachers coping with burnout and cynicism? What can you do to grow your idealism with experience and become a teacher who makes a difference?

We have found that action research can be effective in staving off dreary routine or finding oneself trapped as a teacher in a role, place, or job that no longer has passion or interest. Implementing action research as a way of living practice, as a way of thinking and being in the classroom empowers teachers to:

stay focused on students

keep a vision and enact choice

have a plan, or an approach to questions, conflicts, and dilemmas

continue to learn in areas of interest and passion

use data to make persuasive and powerful arguments on behalf of students

experience rewards through solutions and accomplishments

collaborate with like-minded colleagues to effect change

Cochran-Smith and Lytle (1993) have found that in school communities supporting teacher research, "teachers may be willing to confront their own histories, hear the dissonance within their own profession, and begin to construct working alliances with colleagues, students, parents, and communities" (p. 84). Stories of action research in school support this finding (Babkie & Provost, 2004; Hansen & Wentworth, 2002; Joyce, Mueller, Hrycauk, & Hrycauk, 2005; Lane, Lacefield-Parachini & Isken, 2003; Luna et al., 2004; Meyers & Rust, 2003; Mohr, Rogers, Sanford, Nocerino, MacLean, & Clawson., 2004; Raisch, 2005; Sax & Fisher, 2001; Senese, 2002, 2005). In this sampling of studies, teachers as researchers challenge their own assumptions about teaching while changing their practices; they effect change on school curriculum, programs, and policies, and through collaboration find renewed energy and vision. Ultimately, action research "establishes the teacher as the ultimate arbiter over what is to count as useful knowledge" (Elliot, 1994, p. 137), and having that kind of control over what counts and gets counted as knowledge can be just one more way of keeping idealism and passion alive.

An Illustration of What Living Action Research Can Be: Rachel's Story

We interviewed Rachel in her classroom on a sunny afternoon late in the school year. Rachel is a bilingual fifth year teacher in a large school district. Approximately 85% of the children attending the elementary school where she teaches come from backgrounds of poverty. An additional 75% of the students in her fourth grade class are English language learners, representing a continuum of language acquisition. Most of these children speak Spanish and have moved to the area from Mexico. Rachel's classroom is filled with drawings and artwork, all done by students; this is their shared and collaborative learning space.

You do not have to spend much time with Rachel to know that she is passionate about teaching, her students, and public education. Listen just a little longer and you come to understand that she is committed to democratic principles of education centered around facilitating education for all children so they might participate well in the larger society. For Rachel, action research is "what teaching is all about." She does action research both formally and informally as part of her teaching practice. As a fifth year teacher, Rachel remembers her first year of teaching as "really hard. It was a hard class and I didn't have a lot of support from colleagues. I wasn't ready to take a lot of risks that year. I worked on classroom management. We did a few good things that year. It took a lot just to do what the other teachers were doing. But by the next year, I was ready to take on some projects. I felt like I could risk more." And by the next year, she found like-minded colleagues both within and outside of her school community, including connecting with organizations like *Rethinking Schools*. Rachel continues to gain inspiration and encouragement from these colleagues and she teaches with passion for what is socially just and good. Her first formal action research project took place the year before our interview. Because the children in Rachel's classroom come from backgrounds of poverty, their homes are not filled with books or other reading material. Yet very close to where many of them live is a beautiful public library. Rachel began to wonder what would happen if she introduced her students to this open, public source and space of seemingly unlimited resources. How could access to a public library enrich her students' lives? Would this enthusiasm for print generate more ownership and use of their classroom library? If such rich literacy was available to her students and their families, might this be a benefit far beyond fourth grade?

Rachel decided to introduce the children to the public library in an intentional way. They visited the library, talked with the librarian, and each child received their very first library card—a kind of membership into the greater society's literacy club! Children learned how libraries are organized, and, critically (as Rachel discovered), they set about the task of organizing their own classroom library according to categories that were meaningful to them. They were proud of both the public space they came to know and the personal space within their classroom; classroom visitors were quick to be given a tour of the classroom library. Rachel documented her project with surveys and recorded how children and their families increased their use of the public library. In the end, children not only had access to the library as a resource, but knew how to use this resource, and *did* use it; they "owned" a skill for life.

During the school year of our interview, Rachel experienced another challenge. In fourth grade, students at the elementary school were to cover the science topics of electricity, life cycles, and water. Rachel created another action research project, a thematic unit about the nearby Columbia River combining these three science topics. In facilitating this unit Rachel wanted to make sure the children learned to be critical thinkers, entertained multiple ideas, read "facts" in context, and made informed decisions. She also realized that many of her students "didn't have a sense of place." Rachel hoped the unit would help students identify with their new home and come to "own" some of the controversial issues surrounding salmon and hydroelectric dams.

Because Rachel loves questions and is willing to engage in multiple perspectives, it followed that the unit began with children generating their own questions. From this beginning, children visited a dam and heard of the many benefits of hydroelectric power, but from a Native American speaker they also learned of the loss of culture and a way of life. They analyzed geology and land forms and considered the impact of dams on the environment, and finally, after so many facts and perspectives, they debated whether or not dams should continue to be utilized or breached. Rachel is willing to tackle controversial subjects with global and local complexities because she believes deeply in the fourth grader's abilities to think, learn, and participate. Controversial subjects, after all, require critical thinking skills.

During the unit, Rachel used techniques of action research informally by observing, interviewing, and collecting student work to access how students used critical thinking in reading, discussing, drawing, and writing about issues related to the dams. Rachel's documentation demonstrated that children are learning what is required by state standards (the required curriculum), fulfilling the requirements of the school and district. The unit also fulfills Rachel's learning goal: students are learning to be critical thinkers so they can better participate in a democracy as future active and engaged citizens.

Rachel continues to take risks on behalf of students. It isn't easy at her school, as "[t]here are a lot of pressures" since the children at the school often test below "acceptable" levels on standardized exams. There is a lot of emphasis on scores and basic skills, so visits to public libraries and science inquiry units must integrate reading, writing, and math as much as possible.

That's why Rachel didn't know if her garden project would ever happen. Yet she couldn't help but contemplate a little plot of soil within the schoolyard. "Can we do a garden?" she wondered, particularly given the pressures to raise the school's test scores. "What would happen if kids were growing things? Would they understand how things are tied together? Make connections?" Would they begin to connect salmon, red worm, plant, and human cycles together? It was one of those dreams Rachel didn't want to give up, so despite the fact that she doesn't know much about gardening, she began to collaborate with the children in her classroom. Together, they came up with questions, ideas, a list of "expert resources," and together, they are growing a garden.

For Rachel, action research is "taking risks and learning with the kids." It is about deepening an understanding of the world through seeking multiple perspectives and experiences. Action research gives her a vehicle to make her teaching dreams happen. It is about valuing controversy as a way of learning through conflict and thus gaining insight into ways of living and thinking outside of one's one paradigm. She practices this way of thinking for herself; she invites her fourth graders to join in the learning.

Not long ago, a friend sent Rachel a postcard with an old picture of the Berlin Wall being torn down. She shared the card and some of the history with her students. One of the fourth graders raised his hand and said, "That's like the wall between Mexico and the United States." Rachel thought about that comparison; it informed her again about the history of the children in her classroom. It made her wonder more about the variety of experiences of the students in her class and their individual stories of coming to live in this area. She took an opportunity during a summer break to travel to the Mexican-American border, to see the wall that divides, the eyes peering through and perhaps dreaming, or scheming of a way to cross over to the other side. She visited with deportees who have risked and will continue to risk everything to come to the United States. With her group, Rachel visited by day factories that provide employment and by night shanty towns of deep urban poverty where the workers can barely afford to live on their wages. Rachel is still processing this "ultimate" action research project, this inquiry into the place of her students' stories. Maybe she should undertake an inquiry unit into walls, something about the borders that divide us, real and otherwise, she thought. How would such a unit empower students?

In reflecting upon her five years of teaching, Rachel told us in our interview, "The first year I was so challenged, just how to get teaching in order and all of the management issues; it is easy to get boxed down by political pressures, testing, there is just a lot that is really challenging. But this is what keeps me going, these kinds of projects. They are things that I deeply care about, for real; it is not like I have to pretend to the kids that I am excited about learning with them. These topics are real, relevant, and important."

We hear in Rachel's words how action research allows a teacher to take a vision and transform that vision into a reality. In this way Rachel reminds us of why we teach, of why we believe deeply in education, and how we can stay energized in education through action research. Action research, for Rachel, is a way of living practice as "inquiry as stance" (Cochran-Smith & Lytle, 1999, p. 296). It is not something extra, but a way of being in the classroom in pursuit of democratic ways of teaching and learning. Purpel (1999) writes, "The major question that we need ask educators is not 'What is your philosophy of education?' but 'What is your philosophy of life and what are its ramifications for education?'" (p. 77). Learning to "live the questions" as a philosophy for life is to become a teacher/researcher of influence in education.

 Becoming an Agent of Change through Action Research

I began to think about the many ways, both great and small, in which we teachers advocate for the children in our care. Advocacy is about decision making and then moving forward to press a point home. On a daily, hourly basis, within the classroom context, we make choices that impact the lives of children and families, move forward with action plans, and thus transform the school itself from educator/service provider

to change agent. In my own teaching, I have always understood that beneath the lessons, the observations, the daily attention to detail (are the sponges damp?) lies the principle that education is fundamentally about change of the human condition. —Martha Torrence, "Teaching as Advocacy"

We become agents of change as teachers when we transform ourselves from "service providers" to teachers with an agenda and corresponding action plan. Shor (1992) defines such agency as "learning and acting for the democratic transformation of self and society" (p. 190); Aronowitz and Giroux (1985) define it as becoming a "transformative intellectual" (p. 45). Two of our students have noted that being a change agent means "having the courage (and the willingness to take the time and energy) to begin making small changes within my circle of influence," and "focusing on each student as the individual, finding out what they need, and meeting them there."

When we listen to Rachel's story, we hear the story of her evolution as a teacher: the first year was about classroom management, the second year about reaching out and beginning to take risks and making connections with like-minded colleagues. Rachel's first formal action research project was one *she* undertook and organized, but now Rachel's action research projects are collaborative efforts *with* students. One of our student teachers noted, "Every day I feel my focus shifting away from 'How am I doing as a teacher?' to how much [my students are] learning. . . . Are they 'getting it'? How do they feel today? What have I learned about my students today?" This shift in primary focus from self to students, and from students to local and global communities, is paramount to expanding one's sphere of influence and recognizing the role a teacher can have in transforming self, students, and society. But how does a teacher new to professional education get there? How can action research be the bridge to this kind of being a teacher?

In studying the action research projects of preservice teachers in our program and their continuous evolution as professional educators, we identify four critical and overlapping characteristics/skills that appear to propel them toward action, agency, and transformation: learning with community, the abilities to negotiate and think and act critically, and focused passion. These are outlined in figure 6.1.

Learning with Community

A crucial element of action research is having critical colleagues who can give perspective as a teacher seeks multiple solutions in practice and acts to effect change in school communities. This continues to be true for professional educators. Having critical colleagues, a community with which to learn, keeps one energized in teaching by raising relevant and authentic questions, bringing possibilities to the conversation, and ultimately shaping vision. Such colleagues

 FIGURE 6.1: Characteristics of Transformation

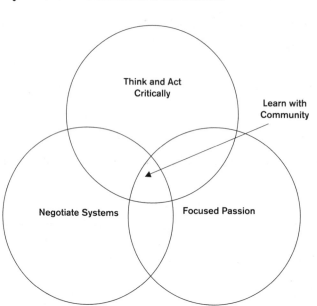

(both local and distant) can bring meaning to your career. Who this community is matters. McLaughlin (1993) has concluded,

The character of the professional community that exists in a school or a department—collegial or isolating, risk taking or rigidly invested in best practices, problem solving or problem shirking—plays a major role in how teachers see their work and their students and is why some teachers opt out, figuratively or literally, while many teachers persist and thrive even in exceeding challenging teaching contexts. (p. 98)

There are many voices or discourses that inform our identity as teachers (Britzman, 1991; Marsh, 2002; Phillips, 2002). Who you choose to engage with and who you choose to listen to may affect who you become as a teacher more than anything else. Early on, seek colleagues of influence who are positive, who offer encouragement, and who willingly engage with questions, ideas, and seek alternatives. These future critical colleagues (both local and distant) will influence how you negotiate, think critically, and even shape your passions and emotions (Zembylas, 2003). So teacher, beware! Choose your company mindfully.

Thinking and Acting Critically

To think and act critically is to live and practice action research on a daily basis by using observation, interviews (critical listening), and artifacts (assessment) to analyze, synthesize, and deconstruct the multiple voices and situations of the classroom and greater community. To think and act critically in this way is to seek to expand paradigms and spheres of influences through critical and transformative action plans. Students from our programs who understood and practiced this concept and skills as preservice teachers have gone on to be agents of change as professional educators. They have introduced innovative and successful programs, practices, and technologies; they have challenged systems of power on behalf of students.

Negotiating Systems

As a student teacher conducting action research as a guest in another's classroom, you have most likely needed to negotiate, to learn to work within the system. There is an art and science to negotiation that we identify with former students who become outstanding teachers. These teachers learn to negotiate by understanding concepts like those of *sacred, cover,* and *secret stories* (see chapter 1, Inside Track: Secret, Cover, and Sacred Stories). Such teachers learn to discern power dynamics at schools, among staff and administrators, and among students. Wise negotiators honor differences; they view conflict as an opportunity. By thinking and acting critically, they are able to negotiate for change.

Having Focused Passion

Passion is a powerful motivator for change. We have found that preservice teachers who are passionate about learning are passionate about others and education, and determined to work for a more just society find vision as professional educators. Passion/vision doesn't always equate with action, but when such teachers combine this with thinking and acting critically, skills of negotiation, and learning with community, they become agents of change in their school communities. In fact, they find vision within these other spheres, not just within themselves.

The result is action, agency, and transformation. This is a process, a journey, one in which we never arrive. This is living action research as practice.

Forming a Vision, Creating a Plan

A vision can give us meaning; a plan can keep us from feeling trapped. Both can keep us energized and joyful as teachers. Brainstorm responses to the following prompts. Then, complete the diagram shown in figure 6.2 using the responses. Keep the diagram and refer to it over the next several years as you teach. Just as in action research, be willing to change the plan as needed, yet doing this kind of vision planning now can provide a scaffold for you as you move toward your career in education.

Learning with Community

What characteristics are important to you in colleagues? What is your "ideal" teaching community? What kinds of questions do you want to ask during an interview? What distant colleagues can you continue to seek?

Thinking and Acting Critically

Review your responses earlier in this chapter. Make an assessment of your abilities to think and act critically (to observe, interview, collect artifacts; to analyze, synthesize, deconstruct). Where would you like to specifically focus on the next stages of being a teacher?

Negotiating Systems

Think back over your student-teaching experience. Consider situations where you did well and not so well at negotiating systems. What can you learn from this? Deconstruct your own behaviors during times of conflict. How do you approach conflict? How *could* you? What have you learned from your own experience and from the experiences of others about systems of power at school sites? What are your emerging theories for working with and around such systems?

Having Focused Passion

Brainstorm a list of the activities, ideas, content, and situations from student teaching and your teacher-education program that give you energy. Likewise, make a list of activities, ideas, content, and situations from student teaching and your teacher-education program that drain your energy.

When you talk about teaching, what issues, questions, ideas motivate you to increase the rate of your talk, the intensity with which you articulate your words, or actually raise your heart beat a bit?

Using these notes, complete the diagram in figure 6.2, giving yourself a vision of who you would like to continue to become as a teacher. Save your completed diagram; tuck it away in a place where you can find it again. Create notebook or journal entries from it, partake in dialogue with your colleagues about your plans, and continue to grow your vision of a teacher/researcher of influence.

⊙ Printable CD Extra: Plan of Action

➡ FIGURE 6.2: Plan of Action

This diagram is available as a downloadable template from the companion CD.

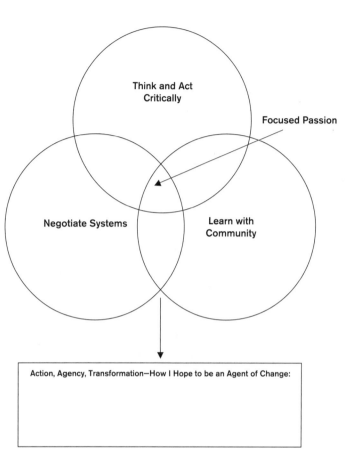

Finding Critical Colleagues

There are many publications and organizations providing support to new teachers; through these, search out distant colleagues from whom you might find inspiration, hope, and good teaching ideas. It is difficult to make suggestions, but in appendix I you will find a reference list of a few of our favorite publications, ones that we think may be helpful in creating a scaffold for your invention and reinvention of the teacher/researcher identity.

Beginning Again (and Always)

It is good to have an end to journey towards, but it is the journey that matters, in the end.
—Ursula K. Le Guin, *The Left Hand of Darkness*

We still love late August—that's the month in our community when school is beginning (again). We find ourselves drawn to aisles of department stores, checking out the latest in crayons and markers, playing with technogadgets, and anticipating that rush of the first day of school, the crush of students, schedules, and the promise of what might be. That's the beauty of school, though, at any grade level—one always gets another beginning as a teacher, a kind of guaranteed "do-over," another chance to *become*. It is not about arrival as a teacher; it is about the continuous looping of life, never back to the same place, but always another place, even though it may seem familiar. "From the beginning of, but also during their careers, teachers are engaged in creating themselves as teachers" (Coldron & Smith, 1999, p. 711). Or, you might think of it as continuous reinvention of self, as art giving birth to life. That's the French philosopher Michel Foucault's view (1984); we like his idea of continuing reinvention: it keeps the canvas interesting and alive.

At the beginning of this text, we wrote, "If this book could be more—if this book could touch, smell, argue, exclaim, sigh, even dance—then it might be more representational of action research as we have come to know it." What we hope is that you have come to know action research in this way as well—and, even more, as a way to continue to evolve and reinvent yourself as a teacher of influence.

Glossary

Action Research. For preservice teachers action research is a process of learning with community to think and act critically, recognize and negotiate political systems, and to focus passion to grow one's identity as a teacher. Such a process evolves out of desire to become a caring, intelligent, transformative educator and includes honing the art and science of planning, assessment, and a critical reflective practice that includes the interrogation of one's own paradigm while in active exploration of ways of thinking and acting beyond those said boundaries. The result of action research for preservice teachers is the beginning of a journey in becoming a teacher living the teaching/research life to simultaneously improve teaching practice, student outcomes, and systems of schooling to be more just and equitable for all children and adolescents.

Annotated Bibliography. A kind of bibliography that includes a short description of the work cited.

ANOVA. Analysis of variance; a procedure for determining if differences between two or more groups of scores is statistically significant.

Artifact. Any documentation gathered as "evidence" during a qualitative research project; may include written work, video, art projects, photographs, and/or other forms of performance.

Assessment. In education, the term is broadly applied to strategies, techniques, and/or methods for evaluating, comparing, contrasting, and/or reflecting on progress, performance, and/or development towards a set of criteria and/or goals.

Critical Colleague. A colleague in the research project committed to question, assist, support, and engage in dialogue with the researcher.

Critical Question. The primary question in an action research project.

Cultural Proficiency. "Esteeming culture, knowing how to learn about individual and organizational culture, and interacting effectively in a variety of cultural environments" (Lindsey, Robins, & Terrell, 2003, p. 85).

Curriculum Analysis. Action research methodology focused on analyzing curriculum with the goal of evaluating the curriculum for its weaknesses and strengths.

Data Set. A complete data set includes data from multiple sources such as: observation, interview, and artifact.

Deconstruction. This term is associated with Jacques Derrida, and denotes a way of thinking, of breaking down oppositional concepts to create alternative meanings.

Empirical Research. A term applied to research experiments using control and experimental groups, statistical analysis, and the control of variables to determine results.

Enlightenment. An intellectual movement associated with the 18th century (*the Enlightenment*); the belief that human reason can create a better world.

Epistemology. This term refers to "how people know what they know, including assumptions about the nature of knowledge and 'reality,' and the process of coming to know" (Sleeter, 2001, p. 213).

Ethnography. A research methodology first associated with the social sciences; a study of culture.

Experimental Research. A subset of empirical research; it attempts to establish cause-and-effect relationships among variables by carefully designing an experimental test, the results of which permit the researcher to reasonably claim the existence of a cause-and-effect relationship. Additionally, it limits its data to strictly quantifiable measurements to permit a rigorous, unambiguous, and mathematical analysis of results.

Field Experience. The time a student teacher spends in a mentor's classroom teaching; may also be referred to as *student teaching* or *internship*.

Informed Consent. The process of requesting and gaining permission from participants in a research study; informing participants fully of the research design and methods for data collection and evaluation.

Integrated Action Research. Action research methodology focused on trying out a specific intervention for some kind of student improvement.

Interview. A data-collection method associated with qualitative research; a way of engaging with participants to learn about their experiences, feelings, attitudes, histories, knowledges, and/or opinions.

Methodology. The approach one takes to research—the research design.

Methods. The techniques one uses to collect data during a research project.

Modernism. A time period and a paradigm or way of thinking generally associated with the mid-1800s to the mid-1900s; in research, this includes a strong belief in objectivity. World Wars I and II were significant events of this time.

Observation. A data-collection technique associated with qualitative research; the act of seeing or watching behaviors and actions in order to gain a greater understanding of a phenomenon.

Paradigm. The set unconscious philosophical assumptions that form the foundation of any body of practice (Kuhn, 1970).

Postmodernism. A time period and a paradigm or way of thinking associated with the later part of the 20th century; a rejection of modernism.

Preservice Teacher. This term refers to a student in a teacher-education program who is a "teacher in training" or is conducting "practice teaching" in a mentor's classroom; may also be called a *student teacher* or *intern*.

Qualitative Research. A broad category of research with a vast array of methodologies that generally rely upon some form of interview, observation, and/or artifact collection from which conclusions, additional questions, and/or results are formed.

Quantitative Research. Research that uses numerical data-collection techniques and is gener-

ally statistically based, meaning various computations of numbers are used to prove or disprove a hypothesis.

Quasi-Experimental Research Design. Quantitative research experiment in which research participants are not randomly assigned to experimental and control groups.

Reflexivity. When researchers inform their audiences about their historical, cultural, and geographical location, their personal involvement with the research, their biases (as they are aware of them), and of influences affecting the research design and analysis; a form of heightened critical awareness the researcher makes public.

Self-Study. A research methodology based upon studying oneself as a teacher in relationship to others; it is primarily focused on improving practice, and relies upon collaboration, multiple qualitative methodologies, and making the work public (Laboskey, 2004).

Statistically Significant. A confidence rating based upon the use of ANOVA procedures to determine the amount of difference between two or more groups of scores.

Student Teacher/Researcher. A student in a teacher/education program who is teaching as a guest in a mentor's classroom and is also conducting research.

Theory. Exploratory belief or hypothesis representing one's understanding of a phenomenon.

Triangulation. A strategy associated with qualitative research used to increase the credibility of the results; generally, triangulation refers to gathering data from at least three different sources in order to better respond to the research question.

Trustworthiness. A term applied to qualitative research when the research has met criteria based upon acceptable description in the literature of credibility.

References

Online Sources

Action research international. Retrieved June 2, 2005, from <http://www.scu.edu.au/schools/gcm/ar/ari/arihome.htm>.

Action research network. Retrieved June 12, 2005, from <http://actionresearch.altec.org/>.

Adams, J. (1995). Office of the president, Arctic Slope Regional Corporation, Barrow, Alaska. Retrieved July 10, 2005, from <http://arcticcircle.uconn.edu/ANWR/asrcadams.html>.

Brandt, D. S. (2005). Why we need to evaluate what we find on the internet. Retrieved May 1, 2005, from <http://www.lib.purdue.edu/itd/techman/eval.html>.

Brody, M. E. E. (2004) AR Expeditions. Retrieved June 13, 2005, from <http://arexpeditions.montana.edu>.

Collaborative action research network. Retrieved July 18, 2005, from <http://www.did.stu.mmu.ac.uk/carn/>.

Coon, C. E. (2001). Tapping oil reserves in a small part of ANWR: Environmentally sound, energy wise. Retrieved July 10, 2005, from <http://www.heritage.org/Research/EnergyandEnvironment/WM27.cfm>.

Dewey, R. (2003). APA research style crib sheet. Retrieved June 21, 2005, from <http://www.docstyles.com/apacrib.htm>.

EdChange: Professional development, scholarship and activism for diversity, social justice, and community growth. Retrieved June 12, 2005, from <http://www.edchange.org/multicultural/tar.html>.

Educational action research. Retrieved June 12, 2005, from <http://www.triangle.co.uk/ear/>.

Einstein, A. Retrieved June 27, 2005, from <http://www.quotedb.com/quotes/1348>.

Help save the arctic national wildlife refuge: Defenders of wildlife. Retrieved July 10, 2005, from <http://www.savearcticrefuge.org/learnmore.html>.

Madison metropolitan school district. Retrieved July 18, 2005, from <http://www.madison.k12.wi.us/sod/car/carhomepage.html>.

Merriam-Webster online dictionary. (2005). Retrieved May 25, 2005, from <www.Merriam-Webster.com>.

Rico, G. (2005). Writing the natural way: Turning the task of writing into the joy of writing. Retrieved July 9, 2005, from <http://www.gabrielerico.com/Main/AboutGabrieleRico.htm>.

Simmons, D., & Kame'enui, E. (2003). *A consumer's guide to evaluating a core reading program grades k–3: A critical elements analysis.* Retrieved March 1, 2003, from <http://www.pen.k12.va.us/VDOE/Instruction/Reading/ConsumerGuideReading.pdf>.

Stafford, W. (1993). Are you there Mr. William Stafford? Retrieved June 4, 2005, from <http://www.newsfromnowhere.com/stafford/wspoem04.html>.

Tanana Chiefs Conference, Inc., Board of Directors. (1990). Resolution no. 90-2. Protect porcupine herd—its ecosystem and the Gwitch'in way of life. Retrieved July 10, 2005, from <http://arcticcircle.uconn.edu/ANWR/tanana.html>.

Teaching today for tomorrow. Retrieved July 10, 2005, from <http://www.7oaks.org/ttt/>.

U.S. Department of Education. (2004). No child left behind. Retrieved January 21, 2005, from <http://www.ed.gov/nclb/landing.jhtml?src=pb>.

Voices from the field. (1999–2002). Retrieved July 10, 2005, from <http://www.alliance.brown.edu/pubs/voices/index.shtml>.

Vonnegut, K. J. (1970). Address to graduating class at Bennington college. Retrieved July 27, 2005, from <http://www.geocities.com/quotequeen81/speeches/vonnegut.html>.

Writing that works: 2000 issues notes. Retrieved July 9, 2005, from <http://www.writingthatworks.com/issuenotes/2000-authors/rico.htm>.

Text and Film Sources

Abraham, M., & Karsh, S. (Producers), & Hoffman, M. D. (Director). (2002). *The Emperor's Club* [Motion picture]. Hollywood, CA: Universal.

Achinstein, B., & Barrett, A. (2004). (Re)framing classroom contexts: How new teachers and mentors view diverse learners and challenges of practice. *Teachers College Record, 106*(4), 716–746.

Anguiano, P. (2001). A first year teacher's plan to reduce misbehavior in the classroom. *Teaching Exceptional Children, 33*(3), 52–55.

Arhar, J. M., Holly, M. L., & Kasten, W. C. (2001). *Action research for teachers: Traveling the yellow brick road*. Upper Saddle River, NJ: Merrill Prentice Hall.

Arminio, J. L., & Hultgren, F. H. (2002). Breaking out from the shadow: The question of criteria in qualitative research. *Journal of College Student Development, 43*(4), 446–460.

Armstrong, F., & Moore, M. (Eds.). (2004). *Action research for inclusive education: Changing places, changing practices, changing minds*. London: RoutledgeFalmer.

Aronowitz, S., & Giroux, H. (1985). *Education under siege: The conservative, liberal, and radical debate over schooling*. South Hadley, MA: Bergin & Garvey: Bergin-Garvey.

Atkinson, P., & Hammersley, M. (1994). Ethnography and participant observation. In N. K. Denzin & Y. S. Lincoln (Eds.), *Handbook of qualitative research* (pp. 248–261). Thousand Oaks, CA: Sage.

Atwell, N. (1987). *In the middle: Writing, reading, and learning with adolescents*. Portsmouth, NH: Boynton/Cook.

Avildsen, J. G. (Producer/Director). (1989). *Lean on me* [Motion picture]. Hollywood, CA: Warner Brothers.

Babkie, A. M., & Provost, M. C. (2004). Teachers as researchers. *Intervention in School and Clinic, 39*(5), 260–268.

Ballenger, C. (Ed.). (2004). *Regarding children's words: Teacher research on language and literacy*. New York: Teachers College Press.

Banks, J. A. (1997). *Educating citizens in a multicultural society*. New York: Teachers College Press.

Bass, L., Anderson-Patton, V., & Allender, J. (2002). Self-study as a way of teaching and learning: A research collaborative re-analysis of self-study teaching portfolios. In J. Loughran & T. Russell (Eds.), *Improving teacher education practices through self study* (pp. 56–69). London: Routledge.

Beijaard, D., Meijer, P. C., & Verloop, N. (2004). Reconsidering research on teachers' professional identity. *Teaching and Teacher Education, 20*, 107–128.

Bisplinghoff, B. S., & Allen, J. (Eds.). (1998). *Engaging teachers*. Portsmouth, NH: Heinemann.

Bloom, L. R. (2002). Stories of one's own: Nonunitary subjectivity in narrative representation. In S. Merriam & associates (Eds.), *Qualitative research in practice: Examples for discussion and analysis* (pp. 289–309). San Francisco: Jossey-Bass.

Bradbury, H., & Reason, P. (Eds.). *Action research*. London: Sage.

Bradbury, R. (1994). *Zen in the art of writing*. Santa Barbara, CA: Joshua Odell Editions.

Britzman, D. P. (2003). *Practice makes practice: A critical study of learning to teach* (2nd ed.). Albany: State University of New York Press.

Bullough, R. V. J. (1992). *Emerging as a teacher*. London: Routledge.

Bullough, R. V. J., & Gitlin, A. D. (2001). *Becoming a student of teaching: Methodologies for exploring self and school context* (2nd ed.). New York: RoutledgeFalmer.

Burnaford, G., Fischer, J., Hobson, D. (Ed.). (2001). *Teachers doing research: The power of action through inquiry*. Mahwah, NJ: Lawrence Erlbaum Associates.

Butler, J. (1997). *Excitable speech: A politics of the performative*. New York: Routledge.

Campbell, L., Campbell, B., & Dickinson, D. (2004). *Teaching and learning through multiple intelligences* (3rd ed.). Boston: Pearson/Allyn & Bacon.

Carr, K. (2005) The "Ten Most Beautiful" Experiments Interpreted by Novice Students. *The Physics Teacher 43*, November 2005, 533-537.

Carr, W., & Kemmis, S. (1986). *Becoming critical: Education, knowledge, and action research*. London: Falmer.

Chaudhry, L. N. (2000). Researching "My people," researching myself: Fragments of a reflexive tale. In E.

A. St. Pierre & W. S. Pillow (Eds.), *Working the ruins: Feminist poststructural theory and methods in education* (pp. 96–113). New York: Routledge.

Clandinin, D. J., & Connelly, F. M. (1994). Personal experience methods. In N. K. Denzin & Y. S. Lincoln (Eds.), *Handbook of qualitative research* (pp. 413–427). Thousand Oaks, CA: Sage.

Clandinin, D. J., & Connelly, F. M. (1995). *Teachers' professional knowledge landscapes.* New York: Sage.

Clandinin, D. J., & Connelly, F. M. (1996). Teachers' professional knowledge landscapes: Teachers' stories—stories of teachers—school stories—stories of schools. *Educational Researcher, 25*(3), 24–30.

Clandinin, D. J., & Connelly, F. M. (2000). *Narrative inquiry: Experience and story in qualitative research.* San Francisco: Jossey-Bass.

Cochran-Smith, M., & Lytle, S. L. (1999). Relationships of knowledge and practice: Teacher learning in communities. In A. Iran-Nejad & P. D. Pearson (Eds.), *Review of research in education* (Vol. 24, pp. 249–305). Washington, D.C.: American Educational Research Association.

Cochran-Smith, M., & Lytle, S. L. (Eds.). (1993). *Inside/outside: Teacher research and knowledge.* New York: Teachers College Press.

Coladarci, T., Cobb, C. D., Minium, E. W., & Clarke, R. C. (2004). *Fundamentals of statistical reasoning in education.* Hoboken, NJ: John Wiley & Sons.

Coldron, J., & Smith, R. (1999). Active location in teachers' construction of their professional identities. *Journal of Curriculum Studies, 31*(6), 711–726.

Corey, S. M. (1953). *Action research to improve school practices.* New York: Bureau of Publications, Teachers College, Columbia University.

Cort, R. W., Field, T., & Nolan, M. (Producers), & Herek, S. D. (Director). (1995). *Mr. Holland's Opus* [Motion picture]. Hollywood, CA: Hollywood.

Coyne, M. D., Kame'euni, E. J., Simmons, D. C., & Harn, B. A. (2004). Beginning reading intervention as inoculation or insulin: First-grade reading performance of strong responders to kindergarten intervention. *Journal of Learning Disabilities, 37*(2), 90–104.

Crotty, M. (1998). *The foundations of social research.* Thousand Oaks, CA: Sage.

Dana, N. F., Yendol-Silva, D. (2003). *The reflective educator's guide to classroom research: Learning to teach and teaching to learn through practitioner inquiry.* Thousand Oaks, CA: Corwin.

Daniels, H. (2002). *Literature circles: Voice and choice in book clubs and reading groups* (2nd ed.). Portland, ME: Stenhouse.

Darwin, C. (1859). *On the origin of the species.* London: J. Murry.

Denzin, N. K., & Lincoln, Y. S. (2003). Introduction: The discipline and practice of qualitative research. In N. K. Denzin & Y. S. Lincoln (Eds.), *The landscape of qualitative research: Theories and issues* (2nd ed., pp. 1–45). Thousand Oaks, CA: Sage.

Denzin, N. K., & Lincoln, Y. S. (Eds.). (2003). *The landscape of qualitative research: Theories and issues* (2nd ed.). Thousand Oaks, CA: Sage.

Derrida, J. (1983). The time of a thesis: Punctuations. In A. Montefiore (Ed.), *Philosophy in France today* (pp. 34–51). New York: Cambridge University Press.

Dewey, J. (1934). *Art as experience.* New York: Minton, Balch.

Dewey, J. (1954). *The public and its problems.* Athens, OH: Swallow.

Dudley-Marling, C. (1997). *Living with uncertainty.* Portsmouth, NH: Heinemann.

Eisner, E. (2002). What can education learn from the arts about the practice of education? *Journal of Curriculum and Supervision, 18*(1), 4–16.

Eisner, E. W. (1998). *The enlightened eye: Qualitative inquiry and the enhancement of educational practice.* Upper Saddle River, NJ: Prentice-Hall.

Elam, D. (1994). *Feminism and deconstruction.* New York: Routledge.

Elbow, P. (1998). *Writing with power: Techniques for mastering the writing process* (2nd ed.). New York: Oxford University Press.

Elliot, J. (1991). *Action research for educational change.* Milton Keynes, England: Open University Press.

Elliot, J. (1994). Research on teachers' knowledge and action research. *Educational Action Research, 2*(1), 133–137.

Ellis, C., & Bochner, A. P. (2003). Autoethnography, personal narrative, reflexivity: Researcher as subject. In N. K. Denzin & Y. S. Lincoln (Eds.), *Collecting and interpreting qualitative materials* (pp. 199–258). Thousand Oaks, CA: Sage.

Ellsworth, E. (1997). *Teaching positions: Difference, pedagogy, and the power of address*. New York: Teachers College Press.

Feldman, A., Paugh, P., & Mills, G. (2004). Self-study through action research. In J. Loughram, M. L. Hamilton, V. K. LaBoskey, & T. Russell (Eds.), *International handbook of self-study of teaching and teaching education practices* (Vol. 2, pp. 943–977). Dordrecht, Netherlands: Kluwer Academic.

Felman, S. (1987). *Jacques Lacan and the adventure of insight: Psychoanalysis in contemporary culture*. Cambridge: Harvard University Press.

Fine, M., Weis, L., Weseen, S., & Wong, L. (2003). For whom? Qualitative research, representations, and social responsibilities. In N. K. Denzin & Y. S. Lincoln (Eds.), *The landscape of qualitative research* (2nd ed., pp. 167–207). Thousand Oaks, CA: Sage.

Fletcher, R. (1993). *What a writer needs*. Portsmouth, NH: Heinemann.

Foucault, M. (1972). *The archaeology of knowledge* (A. M. Sheridan Smith, Trans.). New York: Harper Colophon.

Foucault, M. (1984). On the geneology of ethics: An overview of work in progress. In P. Rabinow (Ed.), *The Foucault reader* (pp. 340–372). New York: Pantheon.

Frank, C. (1999). *Ethnographic eyes: A teacher's guide to classroom observation*. Portsmouth, NH: Heinemann.

Gall, M. E., Borg, W. R., & Gall, J. P. (2003). *Educational research: An introduction* (7th ed.). Boston: Allyn and Bacon.

Gardner, H. (1993). *Creating minds: An anatomy of creativity seen through the lives of Freud, Einstein, Picasso, Stravinsky, Eliot, Graham, and Gandhi*. New York: Basic.

Gardner, H. (2004a). *Frames of mind: The theory of multiple intelligences* (20th anniv. ed.). New York: Basic.

Gardner, H. (2004b). *The unschooled mind: How children think and how schools should teach*. New York: Basic.

Gay, G. (2002). *Culturally responsive teaching: Theory, research, and practice*. New York: Teachers College Press.

Gee, J. P. (2001). Identity as an analytic lens for research in education. In W. G. Secada (Ed.), *Review of research in education* (Vol. 25, pp. 99–125). Washington, D.C.: American Educational Research Association.

Geertz, C. (1973). *The interpretation of cultures*. New York: Basic.

Gergen, M. M., & Gergen, K., J. (2003). Qualitative inquiry: Tensions and transformations. In N. K. Denzin & Y. S. Lincoln (Eds.), *The landscape of qualitative research: Theories and issues* (2nd ed., pp. 575–610). Thousand Oaks, CA: Sage.

Giroux, H. A. (2003). *The abandoned generation: Democracy beyond the culture of fear*. New York: Palgrave.

Gitlin, A. (2000). Educative research, voice, and school change. In B. M. Brizuela, J. P. Stewart, R. G. Carrillo, & J. G. Berger (Eds.), *Acts of inquiry in qualitative research* (pp. 95–118). Cambridge, MA: Harvard Educational Review.

Gitlin, A. (2005). Inquiry, imagination, and the search for a deep politic. *Educational Researcher, 34*(3), 15–24.

Gningue, S. M. (2003). The effectiveness of long-term vs. short-term training in selected computing technologies on middle and high school mathematics teachers' attitudes and beliefs. *Journal of Computers in Mathematics and Science Teaching, 22*(3), 207–224.

Goldberg, N. (1990). *Wild mind: Living the writer's life*. New York: Bantam.

Goodlad, J. I. (2004). *A place called school* (20th anniv. ed.). New York: McGraw-Hill.

Gorard, S. (2001). *Quantitative methods in educational research: The role of numbers made easy*. London: Continuum.

Gore, J. (1993). *The struggle for pedagogies: Critical and feminist discourses as regimes of truth*. New York: Routledge.

Graves, D. (2001). *The energy to teach*. Porsmouth, NH: Heinemann.

Greene, M. (2001). Reflections on teaching. In V. Richardson (Ed.), *Handbook of research on teaching* (4th ed., pp. 82–89). Washington, D.C.: American Educational Research Association.

Habermas, J. (1972). *Knowledge and human interests*. Boston: Beacon Press.

Haberman, M. (1991). The pedagogy of poverty versus good teaching. *Phi Delta Kappan, 73*(4), 290.

Haft, S., Witt, P. J., & Thomas, T. (Producers), & Weir, P. (Director). (1989). *Dead Poets Society* [Motion picture]. Burbank, CA: Touchstone.

Hamilton, M. L. (2005). Researcher as teacher: Lessons modeled by a well-remembered scholar. *Studying Teacher Education, 1*(1), 85–102.

Hansen, J. J., & Wentworth, N. (2002). Rediscovering ourselves and why we teach. *High School Journal, 85*(4), 16–22.

Haraway, D. (1996). Situated knowledges: The science question in feminism and the privilege of partial perspective. In E. F. Keller & H. E. Longino (Eds.), *Feminism and science* (pp. 249–263). New York: Oxford University Press.

Harding, S. (1996). Rethinking standpoint epistemology: What is "strong objectivity"? In E. F. Keller & H. E. Longino (Eds.), *Feminism and science* (pp. 235–247). New York: Oxford University Press.

Hargreaves, A. (1994). *Changing teachers, changing times*. New York: Teachers College Press.

Hargreaves, A. (1999). The psychic rewards (and annoyances) of teaching. In M. Hammersley (Ed.), *Researching school experiences: Ethnographic studies of teaching and learning*. London: Falmer.

Hargreaves, A., & Jacka, N. (1995). Induction or seduction? Postmodern patterns of preparing to teach. *Peabody Journal of Education, 70*(3), 41–63.

Heidegger, M. (1972). *What is called thinking?* New York: Harper & Row.

Howard, G. R. (1999). *We can't teach what we don't know: White teachers, multiracial schools*. New York: Teachers College Press.

Hubbard, R. S., & Power, B. M. (2003). *The art of classroom inquiry: A handbook for teacher-researchers* (Rev. ed.). Portsmouth, NH: Heinemann.

Jarrett, R. L., & Odoms-Young, A. (2005). Now that I have it, what do I do with it? Exploring techniques for interpreting, writing up and evaluating qualitative data. *Congress of Qualitative Inquiry*. University of Illinois at Urbana-Champaign.

Johnson, R. B. (1997). Examining the validity structure of qualitative research. *Education, 118*(2), 282–291.

Joyce, B., Mueller, L., Hrycauk, M., & Hrycauk, W. (2005). Cadres help to create competence. *Journal of Staff Development, 26*(3), 44–49.

Kemmis, S., & McTaggart, R. (1988). *The action research planner* (3rd ed.). Geelong, Australia: Deakin University Press.

Kemmis, S., & McTaggart, R. (2003). Participatory action research. In N. K. Denzin & Y. S. Lincoln (Eds.), *Strategies of qualitative inquiry* (pp. 336–396). Thousand Oaks, CA: Sage.

Kessler, R. (2000). *The soul of education: Helping students find connection, compassion, and character at school*. Alexandria, VA: Association for Supervision and Curriculum Development.

Kidd, S. M. (2003). *The secret life of bees*. New York: Penguin.

Kincheloe, J. L. (2003). *Teachers as researchers: Qualitative inquiry as a path to empowerment* (2nd ed.). London: Routledge Falmer.

Kohn, A. (1999). *The schools our children deserve: Moving beyond traditional classrooms and "tougher standards."* Boston: Houghton Mifflin.

Kozol, J. (1985). *Death at an early age: The destruction of the hearts and minds of negro children in the Boston Public Schools.* New York: New American Library.

Kozol, J. (1992). *Savage inequalities: Children in America's schools* (1st Harper Perennial ed.). New York: Harper Perennial.

Kozol, J. (1995). *Amazing grace: The lives of children and the conscience of a Nation.* New York: Crown.

Kozol, J. (2001). *Ordinary resurrections: Children in the years of hope* (1st Harper Perennial ed.). New York: Harper Perennial.

Kozol, J. (2005). *The shame of the nation: The restoration of apartheid schooling in America.* New York: Crown.

Krakauer, J. (1997). *Into thin air.* New York: Villard.

Kranzler, G. (2003). *Statistics for the terrified* (3rd ed.). Upper Saddle River, NJ: Prentice Hall.

Kuhn, T. (1970). *The structure of scientific revolutions* (2nd ed.). Chicago: University of Chicago Press.

LaBoskey, V. K. (2004). The methodology of self-study and its theoretical underpinnings. In J. J. Loughran, M. L. Hamilton, V. K. LaBoskey, & T. Russell (Eds.), *International handbook of self-study of teaching and teacher education practices* (Vol. 2, pp. 817–869). Dordrecht, Netherlands: Kluwer Academic.

Lacy, C. (1977). *The socialization of teachers.* London: Methuen.

Lamott, A. (1994). *Bird by bird: Some instructions on writing and life.* New York: Anchor Books.

Lampert, M. (2000). Knowing teaching: The intersection of research on teaching and qualitative research. In B. M. Brizuela, J. P. Stewart, R. G. Carrillo, & J. G. Berger (Eds.), *Acts of inquiry in qualitative research* (pp. 61–72). Cambridge, MA: Harvard Educational Review.

Lane, S., Lacefield-Parachini, N., & Isken, J. (2003). Developing novice teachers as change agents: Student teacher placements "against the grain." *Teacher Education Quarterly, 30*(2), 56–68.

Lather, P. (1991). *Getting smart.* New York: Routledge.

Lather, P. (1992). Post-critical pedagogies: A feminist reading. In C. Luke & J. Gore (Eds.), *Feminisms and critical pedagogy* (pp. 120–137). New York: Routledge.

Lather, P. (1994). Fertile obsession: Validity after poststructuralism. In A. Gitlin (Ed.), *Power and method: Political activism and educational research* (Vol. 34, pp. 36–60). New York: Routledge.

Lather, P. (2004). This is your father's paradigm: Government intrusion and the case of qualitative research in education. *Qualitative Inquiry, 10*(1), 15–34.

Lewin, K. (1948). *Resolving social conflict: Selected papers on group dynamics (1935–1946).* New York: Harper.

Lincoln, Y. S. (2002). *On the nature of qualitative evidence.* Paper presented at the annual meeting of the association for the study of Higher Education, Sacramento, CA.

Lincoln, Y. S., & Denzin, N. K. (2003). The seventh moment: Out of the past. In N. K. Denzin & Y. S. Lincoln (Eds.), *The landscape of qualitative research: Theories and issues* (2nd ed., pp. 611–640). Thousand Oaks, CA: Sage.

Lincoln, Y. S., & Guba, E. G. (1985). *Naturalistic inquiry.* Beverly Hills, CA: Sage.

Lincoln, Y. S., & Guba, E. G. (2003). Paradigmatic controversies, contradictions, and emerging confluences. In N. K. Denzin & Y. S. Lincoln (Eds.), *The landscape of qualitative research: Theories and issues* (2nd ed., pp. 253–291). Thousand Oaks, CA: Sage.

Lindsey, R. B., Robins, K. N., & Terrell, R. D. (2003). *Cultural proficiency: A manual for school leaders* (2nd ed.). Thousand Oaks, CA: Corwin.

Linn, R. (1996). *A teacher's introduction to postmodernism.* Urbana, IL: National Council of Teachers of English.

Loughram, J. J. (2004). A history and context of self-study of teaching and teacher education practices. In J. J. Loughram, M. L. Hamilton, V. K. LaBoskey, & T. Russell (Eds.), *International handbook of self-study of teaching and teacher education practices* (Vol. 1, pp. 7–39). Dordrecht, Netherlands: Kluwer Academic.

Luna, C., Botelho, M. J., Fontaine, D., French, K., Iverson, K., & Matos, N. (2004). Making the road by walking and talking: Critical literacy and/as professional development in a teacher inquiry group. *Teacher Education Quarterly, 31*(1).

Marsh, M. M. (2002). The shaping of Ms. Nicholi: The discursive fashioning of teacher identities. *Qualitative Studies in Education, 15*(3), 333–347.

McCotter, S. S. (2001). The journey of a beginning researcher. *Qualitative Report, 6*(2), 1–22.

McLaughlin, M. W. (1993). What matters most in teachers' workplace context? In J. W. M. Little & W. Milbrety (Eds.), *Teachers' work: Individuals, colleagues, and contexts* (pp. 79–101). New York: Teachers College Press.

McNiff, J. (1988). *Action research: Principles and practice.* Basingstoke: Macmillan.

McNiff, J., Lomax, P., & Whitehead, J. (2003). *You and your action research project* (2nd ed.). London: Routledge Falmer.

McTaggart, R. (1997). *Participatory action research: International context and consequences.* Albany: State University of New York Press.

McWilliam, E. (1995). *In broken images: Feminist tales for a different teacher education.* New York: Teachers College Press.

Meyer, H., Hamilton, B., Kroeger, S., Stewart, S. & Brydon-Miller, M. (2004). The unexpected journey: Renewing our commitment to students through education action research. *Education Action Research, 12*, 557–574.

Meyers, E., & Rust, F. (Eds.). (2003). *Taking action with teacher research.* Portsmouth, NH: Heinemann.

Mills, G. E. (2000). *Action research: A guide for the teacher researcher.* London: Prentice Hall International.

Mohr, M. M., Rogers, C., Sanford, B., Nocerino, M., MacLean, M. S., & Clawson, S. (2004). *Teacher research for better schools.* New York: Teachers College Press.

Moore, A. (1999). Beyond reflection: Contingency, idiosyncrasy, and reflexivity in the initial teacher education. In M. Hammersley (Ed.), *Researching school experience: Ethnographic studies of teaching and learning.* London: Falmer.

Moore, J. (2003). Hiking Colorado's Sangre de Cristo Wilderness. Helena, MT: Falcon.

Moore, K. D. (1995). *Riverwalking: Reflections on moving water* (1st Harvest ed.). New York: Lyons & Burford.

Moore, K. D. (2004). *The Pine Island paradox.* Minneapolis: Milkweed Editions.

Nieto, S. (2003). *What keeps teachers going?* New York: Teachers College Press.

Noffke, S. E. (1995). Action research and democratic schooling: Problematics and potentials. In S. E. Noffke & R. B. Stevenson (Eds.), *Educational action research: Becoming practically critical* (pp. 1–10). New York: Teachers College.

Noffke, S. E., & Stevenson, R. B. (Eds.). (1995). *Educational action research: Becoming practically critical.* New York: Teachers College Press.

Oliver, M. (1994). *White pine: Poems and prose poems.* San Diego, CA: Harcourt Brace.

Oliver, M. (1997). *West wind: Poems and prose poems.* Boston: Houghton Mifflin.

O'Reilley, M. R. (1998). *Radical presence: Teaching as contemplative practice.* Portsmouth: Boynton/Cook.

Palmer, J. A. (2001). *Fifty modern thinkers on education: From Piaget to the present.* London: Routledge.

Palmer, P. J. (2003). Teaching with heart and soul: Reflections on spirituality in teacher education. *Journal of Teacher Education, 45*(5), 376–385.

Patton, M. (2002). *Qualitative research and evaluation methods* (3rd ed.). Thousand Oaks, CA: Sage.

Paulsen, G. (1989). *A winter room.* New York: Bantam Doubleday Dell Books for Young Readers.

Pearson, D. P. (2004). The reading wars. *Educational Policy, 18*(1), 216–252.

Phillips, D. K. (2001). Learning to speak the sacred and learning to construct the secret: Two stories of finding space as preservice teachers in professional education. *Teaching Education, 12*(3), 261–278.

Phillips, D. K. (2002). Female preservice teachers' talk: Illustrations of subjectivity, visions of "nomadic" space. *Teachers and Teaching: theory and practice, 8*(1), 9–27.

Purpel, D. E. (1999). *Moral outrage in education.* New York: Peter Lang.

Raisch, M. (2005). Action research aids Albuquerque. *Journal of Staff Development, 26*(3), 50–52.

Ralston, A. (2004). *Between a rock and a hard place.* New York: Atria.

Rankin, E. (2001). *The work of writing: Insights and strategies for academics and professionals.* San Francisco: Jossey-Bass.

Reinharz, S. (1992). *Feminist methods in social research.* New York: Oxford University Press.

Richardson, L. (2003). Writing: A method of inquiry. In N. K. Denzin & Y. S. Lincoln (Eds.), *Collecting and interpreting qualitative materials* (pp. 499–541). Thousand Oaks, CA: Sage.

Rico, G. (2000). *Writing the natural way.* New York: Jeremy P. Tarcher/Putnam.

Rilke, R. M. (1934). *Letters to a young poet* (M. D. H. Norton, Trans.). New York: W. W. Norton.

Rowling, J. K. (2000). *Harry potter and the chamber of secrets.* New York: Scholastic.

Rudduck, J., & Hopkins, D. (Eds.). (1985). *Research as a basis for teaching: Readings from the work of Lawrence Stenhouse.* London: Heinemann Educational.

Salas, K. D., Tenorio, R., Walters, S., & Weiss, D. (Eds.). (2004). *The new teacher book: Finding purpose, balance, and hope during your first years of the classroom.* Milwaukee, WI: Rethinking Schools Ltd.

Sax, C., & Fisher, D. (2001). Using qualitative action research to effect change: Implications for professional education. *Teacher Education Quarterly, 28*(2), 71–80.

Schaller, G. B. (2003). Arctic legacy. In S. Banerjee (Ed.), *Arctic national wildlife refuge: Seasons of life and land, a photographic journey* (pp. 62–69). Seattle, WA: Mountaineers.

Schon, D. A. (1990). *Educating the reflective practitioner* (2nd ed.). San Francisco: Jossey-Bass.

Schulte, A. K. (2002). *"Do as I say."* Paper presented at the Fourth International Conference of the Self-Study of Teacher Education Practices, Herstmonceux Castle, East Sussex, England.

Senese, J. C. (2002). Energize with action research. *Journal of Staff Development, 23*(3), 39–41.

Senese, J. C. (2005). Teach to learn. *Studying Teacher Education, 1*(1), 43–54.

Shank, G. D. (2002). *Qualitative research: A personal skills approach.* Upper Saddle River, NJ: Merrill Prentice Hall.

Sharpes, D. K. (2002). *Advanced educational foundations for teachers: The history, philosophy, and culture of schooling.* New York: Routledge Falmer.

Shor, I. (1992). *Empowering education: Critical teaching for social change.* Chicago: University of Chicago Press.

Simpson, D., Bruckheimer, J., Rabins, S., & Foster, L. (Producers), & Smith, J. N. (Director). (1995). *Dangerous Minds* [Motion picture]. Hollywood, CA: Hollywood.

Sleeter, C. E. (2001). Epistemological diversity in research on preservice teacher preparation for historically underserved children. In W. G. Secada (Ed.), *Review of research in education* (Vol. 25, pp. 209–250). Washington, D.C.: American Educational Research Association.

Smith, A. G. (1997). Testing the surf: Criteria for evaluating internet information resources. *Public-Access Computer Systems Review, 8*(3).

Smith, F. (1998). *The book of learning and forgetting.* New York: Teachers College Press.

Smith, J. (1993). *After the demise of empiricism: The problem of judging social and educational inquiry.* Norwoods, NJ: Ablex.

Spivak, G. C. (1993). *Outside in the teaching machine.* New York: Routledge.

St. Pierre, E. A. (1997). Nomadic inquiry in the smooth spaces of the field: A preface. *Qualitative Studies in Education, 10*(3), 365–383.

St. Pierre, E. A. (2001). Coming to theory: Finding Foucault and Deleuze. In K. Weiler (Ed.), *Feminist en-*

gagements: Reading, resisting, and revisioning male theorists in education and cultural studies (pp. 141–163). New York: Routledge.

St. Pierre, E. A., & Pillow, W. S. (Eds.). (2000). Working the ruins: Feminist poststructural theory and methods in education. New York: Routledge.

Stenhouse, L. (1975). An introduction to curriculum research and development. London: Heinemann.

Stenhouse, L. (Ed.). (1980). Curriculum research and development in action. London: Heinemann.

Tidwell, D., & Fitzgerald, L. (2004). Self-study as teaching. In J. J. Loughram, M. L. Hamilton, V. K. La-Boskey, & T. Russell (Eds.), International handbook of self-study of teaching and teacher education practices (Vol. 1, pp. 69–102). Dordrecht, Netherlands: Kluwer Academic.

Tilden, F. (1977). Interpreting our heritage (3rd ed.). Chapel Hill: University of North Carolina Press.

Todd, S. (Ed.). (1997). Learning desire: Perspectives on pedgagogy, culture, and the unsaid. New York: Routledge.

Torrence, M. (Summer 2002). Teaching as advocacy. Montessori Life, 14(3), 13.

Van Hover, S. D. Y., (2004). Challenges facing beginning history teachers: An exploratory study. International Journal of Social Education, 19(1), 8–26.

Weber, S., & Mitchell, C. (1995). "That's funny, you don't look like a teacher": Interrogating images and identity in popular culture. London: Falmer Press.

Weedon, C. (1987). Feminist practice and poststructural theory. New York: Blackwell.

Weiler, K. (1988). Women teaching for change: Gender, class and power. New York: Bergin and Garvey.

Wells, G. (Ed.). (2001). Action, talk, and text: Learning and teaching through inquiry. New York: Teachers College Press.

White, T. H. (1966). The once and future king. New York: Berkley.

Whitehead, J. (1989). Creating a living educational theory from questions of the kind, "How do I improve my practice?" Cambridge Journal of Education, 19(1), 1–11.

Whitehead, J. (1993). The growth of educational knowledge: Creating your own living educational theories. Bournemouth, England: Hyde.

Whitt, E. J. (1991). Artful science: A primer on qualitative research methods. Journal of College Student Development, 32, 406–415.

Willig, C. (2003). Discourse analysis. In J. A. Smith (Ed.), Qualitative psychology (pp. 159–183). Thousand Oaks, CA: Sage.

Wink, J. (1997). Critical pedagogy: Notes from the real world. New York: Longman.

Yatvin, J. (2003). I told you so! The misinterpretation and misuse of the national reading panel report. Education Week, 42(33), 44–56.

Zeichner, K. M., & Gore, J. (1995). Using action research as a vehicle for student teacher reflection: A social reconstructionist approach. In S. E. Noffke & R. B. Stevenson (Eds.), Educational action research: Becoming practically critical (pp. 13–30). New York: Teachers College Press.

Zeichner, K. M., & Liston, D. P. (1996). Reflective teaching: An introduction. Mahwah, NJ: Lawrence Erlbaum Associates.

Zeichner, K. M., & Noffke, S. E. (2001). Practitioner research. In V. Richardson (Ed.), Handbook of research on teaching (4th ed., pp. 298–330). Washington, D.C.: American Educational Research Association.

Zembylas, M. (2003). Emotions and teacher identity: A poststructural perspective. Teachers and Teaching: theory and practice, 9(3), 213–238.

Zukav, G. (1980). The dancing Wu Li Masters. New York: Bantam.

Appendix A: Personal Paradigm Self-Test/Scoring Guide

How to score:

1. Add the times you checked numbers 2, 4, 5, 8, 9, 11, 14, 16, & 18. This is your "modern" score.

2. Add the number of times you checked numbers 1, 3, 6, 7, 10, 12, 13, 15, 17, 19. This is your "post-modern" score.

What your scores could mean:

If your totals are different by more than 3, it means you have a propensity for one paradigm over the other.

If your totals on both are less than 4, you are pretty noncommittal. You may find that your views swing one way or the other as you become a teacher.

If you scored more than 7 in either modernism or postmodernism, you appear to have a very strong propensity for that paradigm.

Appendix B: Data Set/Teacher Images

Pictured Teacher's Gender

Male	Female
7	25

Pictured Teacher's Ethnicity

White	African American	Native American	Asian American	Latino	Other Ethnicity
28	4	0	0	0	0

Other Observations

Teacher Centered in Picture	Teacher Not Centered in Picture	Nontraditional Educational Setting	Students Teaching Students
31	1	0	0

APPENDIX C: DATA SET/TEACHER GIFTS AND CLOTHING

Item for Sale	Primary Colors Used in Pictured Scene	Age of Pictured Student	Symbols Pictured	Slogan
Pin	Bright red, green, blue, yellow	Primary grades	Apple, chalkboard	Together we can make a difference
Pin	Bright red, green	Primary grades	Apple	2 teach 2 touch lives 4 ever
Pin	Bright yellow, red	Primary grades/diverse	School bus	
Pin	Bright red, green, yellow, black		Apple, heart, pencil	I love to teach
Pin	Bright red, green, yellow		Apple, pencil	
Pin	Bright red, green, yellow, black	Primary grades/diverse	Paintbrush, heart	Love comes in all colors
Pin	Bright red, green, yellow, blue, black	Primary grades/diverse		
Pin	Bright red, green, yellow		Traditional schoolhouse with bell and apple	Up with learning
Pin	Bright blue, grey		Computer	
Pin	Bright red, green, yellow	Primary grades	Chalk board	Math is for everyone
Scarf	Black background; yellow, red, green		School bus, star, numbers (1, 2, 3), ruler, apple	
Scarf			Handprints	
Scarf	Bright blue, red, yellow, green	Primary grades	Flags of the world, globe,	Children first
Denim Jumper	Bright red, yellow, blue, green		Apple, globe, bell, numbers (1, 2, 3), coffee cup	
Jumper with Matching Sweater	Black background; red, white		Apple, chalk board, 1, 2, 3	
T-shirt	Bright red, white, blue	Primary grades	American flag	
White Denim Overalls	Bright red, green		Letters (A, B, C)	
Beach Accessories	Bright red, blue, green, yellow		Adult women reading books	Summer reading!
Denim Jacket	Bright red, blue, green, yellow		Rulers, schoolhouse, apples, bells	
Jumper	Bright red, blue, green, yellow	Primary grades		
Green Denim Jumper	Bright red, yellow, black		Apple, ruler, chalk board, numbers (1, 2, 3)	
Necktie	Black background; red, blue	Primary grades; mostly boys/diverse		
Necktie	Dark blue background; red, blue		Apple, books, numbers	
Necktie	Dark blue background; red, blue, yellow		Numbers	Math!
Necktie	White background; red, yellow,		Apple, flag, school bus, scissors, clock	
Necktie	Black background; white, red		Computers, equations	
Necktie	Black background; white		Albert Einstein, equations	
Necktie	Blue background; red		Computers	
Necktie	Dark blue background; Red, yellow		Sun, apple, pencil, cat, numbers	
	Purple background; blue, yellow		Chemistry beakers	
	Black background; Red, green		Books	Read

APPENDIX D: DATA SET/TEACHERS ACCORDING TO HOLLYWOOD

Movie	Setting: Location, Grade Level, Gender of Students	Descriptive Words and/or Quotes from the Teacher/Principal	Descriptive Words, Students and School	Teacher or Principal, Gender, Ethnicity	Teacher/Principal Positioning and Stance	Observations: Light and Color
Lean on Me	Inner city, high school, female and male	Extraordinary, Tough love, Last hope	Strife-torn, Troublemakers, Strivers	Principal Male African American	Authoritative Finger pointing at students	Red background, black silhouette of principal, students
Dead Poets Society	Private school for boys; secondary	Inspiration, Extraordinary, Passionate, Charismatic, "Changing lives forever," "Carpe Diem, lads!"	"Crew cuts, sports coats, and cheerless conformity"	Teacher Male White	In center of picture being lifted by students	Students are in red sports coats; teacher in white shirt
Dangerous Minds	Inner city, high school, female and male	Changes lives, Feisty, Frustrated, Loves, "Defies all the rules," "Cajoles and tricks them, even bribes them,	Impenetrable facade, Tough, Inner city, "desperate to connect with someone who cares"	Teacher Female White	Center, arms crossed, stern, in leather jacket; students in background	Light is focused on teacher
Mr. Holland's Opus	High school; location cannot be determined.	Musician and composer, Reluctant teacher, Contagious passion	(Not described)	Teacher Male White	Center in suit; surrounded by students in graduation regalia	Light from above shines on teacher
The Emperor's Club	Private school for boys; secondary	Determined to reach (student), Inspire, Impassioned, Principled, "Makes a difference," Role of teacher to "mold pupil's character"	Challenging authority	Teacher Male White	Prominent in picture; students' raised hands in foreground; beneath, game of baseball	

APPENDIX E: DATA-COLLECTION TOOLS EXPLORED

The following data-collection tools are detailed in this appendix:

E1:   Note Taking/Note Making

E2:   Anecdotal Notes

E3:   Logs, Checklists, and Rating Scales

E4:   Mapping

E5:   Shadowing

E6:   Surveys, Questionnaires, and Attitude-Response Scales

E7:   Formal, Informal, and Focus-Group Interviews

E8:   Sociograms

E9:   Multiple-Intelligence Approaches to Interviews

E10:   Artifact Collection

Printable CD Extra: "Data-Collection Tools"

Templates for several of these tools can be found on the companion CD.

Note-Taking/Note-Making

Overview

Note taking/note making is an ethnographic approach to observation.

When doing note taking/note making, the observer writes what she sees and hears, attempting to record without judgment.

Note making is completed after observation; it is when and where the observer raises questions and records hunches and analysis.

Variations and Uses

Note taking/note making of your teaching and classroom may be done by a mentor-teacher or other supervisor. A lesson may also be videotaped and then observed for note taking/note making.

There are many variations depending on the desired outcome. For example, time increments may be added to the observation form. Sometimes, only specific items are observed, for example, only questions might be recorded. One way we have used this strategy is to divide the observation into two categories: "What the Teacher Does" and "What the Students Do." Consider the purpose of the observation and then decide the specifics.

→ TABLE E.1: Note Taking/Note Making of Video Observation, Self

Observations	Note Making
1. Daily Science—students working on it. Some talking. 3 minutes for DS.	Giving too much time for daily science.
2. Gabe enters room. Takes off jacket and organizes earphones.	Gabe tardy from Phil Johnson's advisory group.
3. Asking questions during daily science. Using lots of words like *appropriate, classify.*	Yes I talk a great deal. Feel tension in getting control. Adjust daily science to get kids more involved?
4. Noise from outside in the hall during daily science. Sixth graders.	Distracting—Keep door closed.
5. David makes a comment for tundra.	David's comments tend to go on and on, but the class has been quite respectful of what he has to say. He is a wealth of information, that's for sure.
6. Jamie makes comment.	I have a difficult time listening to one kid talk and not losing the rest of them.
7. Jonathan asks to sharpen pencil.	Temporary cease fire.
8. I clarify potential and kinetic energy to review from yesterday.	This talk went fairly well. Kids seemed to get it at the time, but know that there are many who are still confused.
9. I ask questions. Breanna has hand up. I don't call on her. She sets her head down on the table.	Favoring hand-raisers. Begin calling on those that don't have hand up to more equitably distribute attention to all kids.
10. David answers question.	Called on David again. Struggle with this because he raises his hand a lot and I call on him a great deal because I want everyone to feel included. I don't want to not call on him because he always knows the answers.
11. Breanna raises hand again. I allow people to call out to get through the lesson.	Ignoring people with hands raised. Allowing loud folks to answer questions, dictate flow of class.
12. I circulate around the room. Gabe yells out "dangerous" energy. I ignore it.	First detectable "smart" remark by Gabe goes ignored.
13. I am using lots of words to explain energy conversion. Students yelling out in class.	My actions say that I don't care if you yell out in class. What cannot be seen by my outward appearance is the growing frustration within. I'm getting harried and frustrated at myself for my resistance in addressing it. Truly, it was no longer the child's problem, but my own.

Note taking/note making can be used for a variety of purposes. It can be used to observe a whole class lesson, small groups, or only for specific teaching events. Used over time, note taking/note making can show progress and reflect or identify process.

Note taking/note making becomes easier and more efficient with practice! Experiment with the method even in nonschool settings, as this will increase your effectiveness with the strategy.

Example

See table E.1. Carrie completed this note taking/note making while watching a videotape of herself teaching a science lesson in a middle school classroom.

Anecdotal Notes

Overview

Taking anecdotal notes is a way of collecting critical moments and recording them in the midst of a busy classroom (table E.2).

Anecdotal notes are an effective way to collect data concerning specific students, small groups of students, or for use in a self-study as a quick reflection device.

When taking anecdotal notes, write down quick descriptions or quotes and then come back to them later for interpretation. Complete the analysis and interpretation in the margins, and then in your researcher's notebook more formally.

Variations and Uses

Some teacher/researchers have found that Post-it sticky notes and a clipboard are a good way to record anecdotal notes. The notes can then be easily organized at a later date.

Another variation is to actually set up a chart with space for notes. For example, if there are five science lab groups in the classroom, organize a chart with two columns and five rows. Use the chart and a clipboard to collect the notes. There are a number of possible ways to set up such anecdotal charts; again, consider the purpose and devise and revise the kind of chart that works best in your teaching situation.

Anecdotal notes are best done deliberately. Collect the notes over time to show progress and process. As with all data-collection strategies, you will improve with practice.

➜ FIGURE E.1: Example: Anecdotal Notes

Date: January 14

Time: 9:45

Event: Computer lab simulation, 9th grade

Group 2 having problems: can't decide who gets to actually key in the information on computer. R. insists it is his turn. M. says R. always gets to do this. I asked for a peer mediator to step in and left the group …

Group 3, doing well. They've already got data entered. I can hear group 2 still bickering.

Groups 1 & 5 appear to be on-task. J. is wondering--what group is he supposed to be in?

Back to group 2: R & M have resolved the matter for now. Group may be behind in assignment.

Example: Kelly's Notes

In the example in figure E.1, Kelly designed a chart with all of her students' names. She recorded anecdotal assessment notes about the math lesson. Note how she also recorded the context for the observation by describing the lesson.

Counting by 2s Grid to Penguin Pairs Chart

The worksheet included two charts. The first was a 100s chart with only the even numbers. In the first rows the even numbers were present as dotted lines that the students were to trace over. Farther down the chart fewer and fewer numbers were provided and students were to continue writing in only the even numbers. The second chart consisted of two columns; the first listed numbers 1–20. Students were to complete the second column by entering the number of penguins in 1 pair, 2 pair, 3 pair, and so on. On the day before this worksheet was assigned, students had created a chart with a growing pattern of penguin pairs. The chart ended after row 8.

Observations from Work Time:

Seemed to have difficulty understanding that chart showed results of skip counting: EB, RW, LW; DM—did at beginning but seemingly struggled with concept until arrived at meaning.

➡ **TABLE E.2: Anecdotal Notes**

AM	Finished	Seemed to have good CU, skipped 16 on PP chart (# of penguins), asked st to review—pointing at specific error; self-corrected and changed that & following incorrect answers
AL	Did not finish	Small-motor fatigue evident; after 40, I alternated rows to write numbers; st. provided information; still only got to 70; did not get to pairs/penguin chart
AG	Did not finish	Ended at 84, did not do PP chart
AS	Finished	One of first finished, CU apparently strong as we reviewed together
AB	Did not finish	Ended at 88, did not do PP chart
CC	Finished	CU strong
DF	Finished	Evident difficulty with understanding at beginning, understanding seemed to emerge as work progressed; need 1:1 to check for understanding
DM	Finished	Solidified meaning as worked; complained of getting stuck at 16 on PP chart (student-created penguin chart went as far as 8 pairs), but worked through it to complete chart
DN	Finished	CU, evidence of self-correction
EB	Did not finish	Ended at 38, but traced only, did not fill in missing even numbers; did not do PP chart
EW	Finished	CU strong, finished quickly and completely accurate
JF	Did not finish	All of skip counting, did not do PP (Penguin Pairs) chart
LW	Did not finish	Traced all numbers, did not fill in all missing evens; did write in some odds; did not do PP chart
MC	Did not finish	Ended at 80, did not do PP
MK	Finished	CU, accurate
NW	Did not finish	All of skip counting, did not do PP chart
RW	Did not finish	Stopped at 76, did not do PP chart
TJ	Finished	Seemed to have CU, lots of reversals on PP chart
TT	Did not finish	All of skip counting, did not do PP chart

Logs, Checklists, and Rating Scales

Logs: Overview

A log is a running record of events. A log may be a detailed list of events throughout an entire period or day. It may be a list of class activities only or it could include interactions with students, routine classroom procedures (taking attendance, lunch count, etc.). Phone conversations, responses to e-mail, conferences, and/or other daily events are recorded.

The simplest way to organize a log is by recording the date and time at the top of any page and then noting the events through the specific time period data is being gathered. Keep the log in your researcher's notebook.

Logs are useful in accessing time and placing other data in context.

Checklists: Overview

A checklist is a structured form of observation. It is perhaps the most efficient way for a busy classroom student teacher/researcher to collect observational data. The checklist focuses the teacher/researcher to record specific kinds of behaviors, occurrences, and responses.

The simplest kinds of checklists record "yes" or "no" in response to specific kinds of statements or questions or use slash marks to record the number of times a behavior or occurrences happens. Checklists can be more sophisticated and may use a combination of ways to record the data.

Checklists are most useful when they are recording meaningful and focused data. You may need to use a checklist several times, analyze the data, and then revise the checklist to make it more useful.

Checklists are best used multiple times, over time. Used in this way, they document progress and/or patterns of behavior.

Checklists: Variations and Uses

Checklists can be completed by the teacher/researcher, a mentor-teacher, a supervisor, or students.

The more items on the checklist, the more the checklist will demand of the observer; choose the items carefully.

Analyze the results of the checklist the same day the observations are made.

A variation of a checklist uses a rating scale (tables E3 and E4).

Rating Scales: Overview

A rating scale is a variation of a checklist. It is also used as an observational tool but adds a value according to a continuum rather than just recording "yes/no" or the specific times an event occurs.

Rating Scales: Variations and Uses

Checklists with rating scales can be used by the teacher/researcher or any other observer. Students may also use this tool.

➡ TABLE E.3: Checklist

Sixth Grade Literature Circle Observation Checklist Date: October 15						
Student	Prepared	Listened	Used Book Examples	Made Personal Connections	Asked Questions	Eye Contact
A	Y	Y	✓ ✓ ✓	✓ ✓ ✓	✓ ✓ ✓	Y
B	Y	Y	✓	✓		Y
C	N	Y		✓	✓ ✓	Y

➜ TABLE E.4: Combination Checklist

Sharing Circle
Date: 11/12*　　　**Time: 12:00–12:15**

Name	Shared	Time	Distraction	Comment
A	✓	5 sec.		Liked Sammy the Snake activity
B			✓ ✓ ✓	
C	✓	1 min.		Talked about Mrs. W's class book
D			✓	
E	✓	3 sec.		Enjoyed reading and pattern activity
F	✓	5 sec.		Shared routine activity—favorite
G	✓	3 sec.		

*Show and Tell today; students were able to pick one thing they enjoyed about today and would like to share with the rest of the class.

Checklists need to be developmentally appropriate for age, grade, and language levels if used by students.

Like any observation tool, the checklist should be analyzed just after being used and revised if necessary to collect meaningful and focused data.

Rating scales may be designed as categories:

• How often did the student participate in the cooperative group lab?

• (Never) (Seldom) (Occasionally) (Frequently) (Always)

Rating scales may be designed using a number system:

• Student participates in the cooperative group lab.

• 1 = rarely . . . . 5 = actively

Rating scales can also be designed to use pictorial representations; this is particularly useful when young children are doing their own observations.

Anecdotal rating scales can be useful for a teacher monitoring small group work (see table E.5).

→ TABLE E.5: Anecdotal Rating Scale

First Grade: Story Retelling			
Child's Name _____		Date _____	
Literacy Target	Demonstrates Difficulty	Adequately Performs Task	Demonstrates Excellent Comprehension
Accurately Retells Story (Plot)			
Describes Characters			
Describes Setting			
Makes Personal Connections to Text			

Mapping

Overview

Mapping is a general term applied to any observational strategy where behavior or movement is recorded and later analyzed. For example, a teacher/researcher may draw a diagram of the classroom and map the movement of students, or he may note table or lab groups and chart the on-task behavior of students.

Mapping may be difficult for a teacher/researcher to do, depending upon how involved he must be in the lesson.

Mapping is a useful way to gather specific kinds of behavioral data.

Variations and Uses

Mapping can be used in combination with anecdotal notes. This can be an efficient and useful way for involved teacher/researchers to collect data. The teacher/researcher maps a diagram of their classroom with a seating chart. Anecdotal notes are kept for individual students or groups of students on the chart.

In figure E.2, the student teacher/researcher provided her university supervisor with a seating chart to record on- and off-task behaviors during a small group math lesson. The observer checked students' behavior every five minutes. Besides on- and off-task behavior, the observer noted when students left their table groups and other anecdotal data. When compared with other such observations, the student teacher/researcher was able to see certain patterns of behavior emerge. For example, most students who were confident in their math abilities assisted other students who struggled. However, when the higher-ability students did not feel confident in the math tasks, they tended to leave their small groups and ask the teacher. They did not ask the other students in their group, nor did they help these students on these occasions.

 **FIGURE E.2:** Mapping

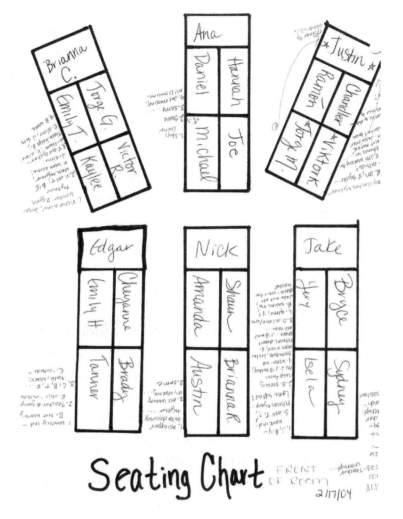

Shadowing

Overview

A shadow study is primarily used to gather data on a single student. A teacher/researcher may shadow a student throughout an entire school day or for any given class period or content instruction.

Although there are many variations, shadow studies typically use a form of note taking/note making: time increments are noted, the student's behaviors and particular expressions or responses recorded, and environmental considerations noted as well. Later, note making is completed; the teacher/researcher theorizes and raises questions about the behaviors.

Shadows can also be recorded using a log system.

Variations and Uses

Shadowing is a good way to learn about students whose experiences may be different from your own, or students who are given various labels such as "learning disabled," or "having attention deficit disorder." Teacher/researchers often make assumptions about such students. Gathering data through a shadow study often reveals insights that might otherwise be overlooked.

Shadowing is also a good way to learn about specific groups of students, particularly those you are going to student teach. It allows a teacher/researcher to become more aware of "life in school."

Example

Anne wanted to teach middle school but didn't feel like her own middle school experience in a private school with an environmental emphasis was "typical" of the middle school where she was going to student teach. Anne spent considerable time the first two weeks of her placement doing a shadow study of five students. She followed them throughout the school day to gain insight into a "normal" day of a 12-year-old at her school.

Surveys, Questionnaires, and Attitude-Response Scales

Overview

Surveys, questionnaires, and attitude-response scales are used to collect data primarily about students' perceptions, feelings, or attitudes about skills, concepts, or other classroom issues. These data-collection strategies can be effectively and efficiently used by classroom teachers when there isn't time or opportunity to visit with each individual student.

When writing surveys, questionnaires, and attitude response scales, it is particularly important to craft good questions that will generate the kind of data you wish to collect. This may take some practice, so plan to revise whatever survey you craft, based upon your analysis of the data generated.

Often, teacher/researchers write more than one question to gain insight into the same issue. They restate the question, sometimes in a positive way and then in a more negative way, to ensure consistency in the response.

Surveys, questionnaires, and attitude-response scales are often used as pre- and post-assessment in a unit, or used over time to demonstrate progress and/or process. The teacher/researcher analyzes this data for patterns and for changes in attitudes or perceptions.

Surveys, questionnaires, and attitude-response scales should be tallied. Patterns and aberrations are then noted.

If there are students who speak other languages rather than that of the dominant culture, it is important that the surveys, questionnaires, and attitude-response scales are provided in their language.

Variations and Uses

Surveys, questionnaires, and attitude-response scales often use descriptive phrases:

I enjoy reading on my own.

(Strongly Agree) (Agree) (Disagree) (Strongly Disagree)

Surveys, questionnaires, and attitude-response scales sometimes use Likert Scales:

Reading a good book is a great way to spend the evening.

No . . . . Yes

Surveys, questionnaires, and attitude-response scales may use pictorial representations; these are especially good for younger children (see figure E.3).

Surveys, questionnaires, and attitude-response scales may employ user-friendly language:

The discussion today concerning globalization . . .

    . . . didn't interest me

    . . . raised important questions for me

    . . . made me angry

    . . . made me feel hopeful

FIGURE E.3: Student Evaluation Example

Student Evaluation

Name_____

1. I like to share in class   ☺ ☺ ☹

2. I feel comfortable in our class to share   ☺ ☺ ☹

3. I feel that other students listen when I share   ☺ ☺ ☹

4. I like working with others   ☺ ☺ ☹

Surveys, questionnaires, and attitude-response scales may use number representation:

For the following questions, please use this rating scale to respond:

1— Strongly Disagree

2— Disagree

3— Undecided

4— Agree

5— Strongly Agree

_____ Music is an important part of my life.

_____ I listen to many kinds of music.

_____ I like to study with music in the background.

Formal, Informal, and Focus-Group Interviews

Overview

The interview group is the most direct form of inquiry. In the formal, informal, and focus-group interviews, the teacher/researcher asks the participants for their insights and feedback. The critical piece of an interview, like a survey, questionnaire, or attitude-response scale, are the questions asked. Spend time constructing the questions; make sure they are focused and will provide the kind of data that will be most helpful to you.

The skills of the interviewer are the skills of many great teachers we know: interviewers listen intently, they observe for nonverbal messages, and they know how to follow up on cues from the interviewee. Effective interviewers and teachers are genuinely interested in hearing what others have to say; asking the questions is not just a requirement or routine. Finally, effective interviewers and teachers recognize they have assumptions about how students, parents, and others will respond so they work to listen around those assumptions.

Variations and Uses

The *formal interview*, as it suggests, involves a preset group of questions. The teacher/researcher asks these questions one-on-one and uses the same group of questions for all students. Responses are recorded via notes or audiotape. Formal interviews often provide more in-depth data. For example, Sheena's action research project centered on describing how community forms among high school drama students. She conducted formal interviews with each member of the cast. This was an effective choice, since the one-on-one setting gave students space to talk more completely about their place in the drama "family."

During an *informal interview*, the teacher/researcher begins more of a conversation with the student by asking a question and then allowing the interview to follow the responses of the student or other participant. Student teacher/researchers new to informal interviews must still be deliberate in conducting these interviews. It is useful to have preformed questions to guide the conversation as needed. The informal interview may use mapping, an anecdotal note format, or even a chart with students' names on one side and a note column on the other side to record student responses. As a form of classroom assessment, informal interviews can be very valuable, since a teacher/researcher may walk around the classroom, stop at various desks, and inquire of students in a natural way, such as, "What math problem solving strategy did you use today? How did you use this strategy? Can you explain it to me?"

Focus-group interviews are another effective way for a teacher/researcher to inquire of students during the busy classroom day. A focus group is really a small group centered on a particular topic. Responses are recorded via notes or audiotape. Typically, a cross-section of the student population is most useful, although attention should be given to group dynamics; some small groups of students are more comfortable conversing together than others. The teacher/researcher may have a prescribed set of questions to ask the focus groups or she may ask a single leading question and then allow the dialogue to flow. We have seen student teacher/researchers use focus groups in many ways. Michael's fifth grade focus group met often at lunchtime during the math-based service-learning project. This is where Michael learned how students were processing not only the math concepts, but also sorted through group dynamics. Cindy's focus group included the small group leaders from the student social studies teams. By checking in with the leaders, she gained insight about how the class was developing community, along with their development of concepts.

When an interview is audiotaped, it is often useful to make a transcription of the interview. Transcriptions take time, but the benefit is being able to read through the words spoken, highlight patterns, raise questions in the margins, and better analyze the interview. Not all interviews warrant this kind of analysis; however, additional insights may be gained through this strategy.

Sociograms

Overview

Sociograms are another type of formal interview used to chart relationships within a classroom. Hubbard and Power (2003) describe sociograms in detail; to summarize, they suggest these steps:

Develop questions to ask each student, such as "If you could invite anyone in this class to your birthday party, who would you ask? Rank your choices one, two, three." Or "Who is good at math problem-solving in this class?" Or "To whom would you share a secret in this class?" Or, "With whom would you like to be in a cooperative learning group?"

Interview young children individually; older children may complete a response sheet.

Have students respond quickly—you are after an initial response.

Complete a tally sheet of responses. Assign a point value to each response: first choice receives 3 points, second choice receives 2 points, third choices receive 1 point.

Now chart the point values for each student and patterns of relationships and power will emerge. (pp. 73–78)

Hubbard and Powers (2003) identify students with terms like *cliques* (for those groups of students who choose each other), *stars* (for students who are chosen most often), and *isolates* (for students who are not selected by other students); other categories may also emerge. They also offer this very wise and ethical advice:

You must use some caution in doing sociograms for a class. This is one data source that should not be open to students. *You also need to disguise the names of students in all of your sociogram figures and charts.* (p. 76)

Example

Christy was a student teacher–researcher whose action research projects focused on developing community among children seemingly separated by language and gender. The sociogram was an effective tool both used at the beginning and end of her research to aide in accessing community among their students.

An example of Christy's first sociogram is in figure E.4. She also charted the data according to boys and Spanish-versus English-speaking students so she could better analyze the group dynamics according to gender and language.

→ **FIGURE E.4:** Girls' Sociogram

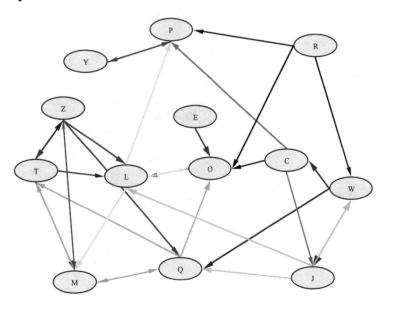

Solid black line: Spanish speakers

This early analysis identified potential leaders as well as isolates that Christy targeted during community-building activities.

Interview questions Christy used:

1. If you could pick any student from class to come over to play at your house, who would you choose?

2. If you could pick any student from class to come over to your house to spend the night, but student 1 was sick, who would you choose?

3. If you could pick any student from class to go to the zoo, but student 1 and 2 were sick, who would you choose?

Multiple-Intelligence Approaches to Interviews

Overview

Interview strategies are dependent upon students' (or other participants') ability to verbally respond to questions. However, we have learned from Gardner's (2004a; 2004b) research that the ability to verbally respond is just one way of expressing attitudes and perceptions, and of problem solving. A multiple-intelligence approach to interviews allows students or other participants to respond to questions in multiple ways.

These are just some of the possibilities (table E.6). We recommend Campbell, Campbell, and Dickinson (2004) as an additional resource for considering multiple ways students might respond to interview questions.

Having students of all ages draw a response as an interview can often be insightful (see figure E.5). Cindy asked her fifth grade students to draw a picture of an ideal community. After

→ TABLE E.6: Multiple-Intelligence Approaches to Interviews

Verbal-Linguistic	Logical-Mathematical	Kinesthetic	Visual-Spatial	Musical	Interpersonal	Intrapersonal
Storytelling	Venn Diagrams	Role Play	Flow charts	Music as Analogy	Global Perspectives	Metacognition
Word Webs	Analogies	Dance	Clustering	Poetry	Collaborative Responses	Journal Responses
Letter Writing	Forming Questions as a Response	Creative Drama	Guided Imagery	Rap	Class Meetings	Reflective Drawings
	Graphs/Charts	Play	Visual Arts			

drawing, she asked the students to write a paragraph about the community. Note how the drawing supports the interview responses and make possible some response where language is not adequate. If translation is possible, allow students to respond in the language they are most comfortable using.

Marta designed a "Head, Hand, and Heart Student Self-Evaluation" (see figure E.6) for use throughout her action research project. Children became more proficient in using the tool, as the project went on for several months. They could draw, or write words or sentences in response to a question Marta gave them; she also gave students the opportunity to act out their responses in small groups.

Artifact Collection

Overview

The term *artifact* conjures up images of items set in special light and under protective glass in museums. In fact, artifacts for teacher/researchers are similar. Artifacts are any documents, projects, arts, or other such items that the teacher/researcher sets aside to study more carefully. Artifacts tell a different story than an interview or an observation; artifacts tend to speak for themselves as evidence.

FIGURE E.5: Student Drawing as Interview

"Esta es mi comunidad en ensta comunidad esiste la amistad la alegria nos apoyamos unos a los otros tambien podemos salir ala calle ir al mar sin nigun peligro. Tambien en mi cominidad posemos divertirnos con la arena cuando estamos de vacasiones o tambien nos divertimos en la escuela."

This is my community. In my community there is friendship and happiness. Everybody helps each other and we can go out in the street without danger. Also in my community we can have fun playing at the beach in the sand when we're vacationing or we have fun at school.

FIGURE E.6: Head, Hand, and Heart Student Self-Evaluation

Artifacts can be any kind of student-produced work: portfolios, exams, daily homework, artwork, projects, videotaped or audiotaped productions, and student records and/or rewards.

Artifacts can be produced by the teacher/researcher in the form of lesson plans, notes, articles, dialogue logs, and phone messages.

Artifacts can be school documents, such as policy manuals; community newspapers may also serve as important artifacts.

Artifacts can confirm or disaffirm patterns in the data. Learn to analyze artifacts well. Record analysis in your researcher's notebook.

Variations and Uses

Digital cameras are a friendly teacher/researcher's tool. Use such cameras to record all kinds of student work and/or other documentation. This is a simple way to collect such documentation and allows the teacher/researcher to return work to students in a timely manner.

Use photography, videotapes, and audiotapes to collect different kinds of artifacts. For example, an audiotape recorder in the midst of a small student group can be useful in a number of ways! Pictures will also allow you to remember the context for your study when you are analyzing the data later.

Be deliberate in considering what kinds of artifacts will best support your action research project best.

Example

See figure E.7. Kelly scanned into her computer a copy of not only this first grade student's attempt at problem solving, but also her instructional intervention.

→ **FIGURE E.7**: Example of Artifact Collection

"Four friendly number flowers and two leaves. How many petals and lobes? How many stems?"

To the left is the sticky note on which I showed my problem solvinig solution that I discussed with student who created the problem above.

Appendix F: Research Design Templates

The following research design templates are included in this appendix:

F1: Integrated Action Research Design

F2: Curriculum Analysis Action Research Design

F3: Ethnography Action Research Design

F4: Self-Study Action Research Design

◎ Printable CD Extras: Action Research Design Templates

Downloadable action research design templates are available on the companion CD

F1: Integrated Action Research Design

1. Project Overview

1.1. The critical question(s) of my action research project:

1.2. The setting for this action research project:

> brief description of community, school (class, race, mission, values, urban/rural)

> brief description of participants

> brief description of the classroom where the action research project will take place

> how this context matters to the study

> my comfort level with this context

1.3. The story behind this action research project:

> why I am interested in this area

> what my own experiences are with this area

> how my own values, beliefs, and sense of what "good teaching" is, are represented in this action research project

> what my biases are

> how my position as a student teacher influences the project

> how this information matters to this study

1.4. A synopsis of the problem, dilemma, and/or issue, centering this action research project:

1.5. A synopsis of the strategy to be used, the intervention to be tried, the innovation to be implemented, the evaluation to be conducted, or other action to be applied in the study:

1.6. Timeline for the action research project:

1.7. A list of common themes in the literature regarding this action research project:

1.8. Reference list for the action research project:

2. Methodology: How the Problem, Dilemma, and/or Issue Will Be Addressed

2.1. Data and documents to be collected:

> observations described

> interviews described

> documents and artifacts to be collected

2.2. Description of researcher notebook:

> how it will be organized

> when entries will be made

> timeline of planned critical analysis points

> appendices (what additional data I will collect to give context to my journal entries)

2.3. How I will include others in the interpretation of my action research project:

> professional colleagues
>
> critical colleagues
>
> students

2.4. Brief statements of how the data and documents will be analyzed:

> analyze (parts): how the categories of data and documents will be analyzed
>
> synthesize (whole): how all of the data and documents will be scrutinized
>
> deconstruct (assumptions): what assumptions have been made and what are "other" possible interpretations

2.5. How this design deliberately plans for trustworthiness:

2.6. How I am gaining appropriate permissions:

2.7. Possible interruptions, distractions, and difficulties, and the plan for dealing with these:

3. Conclusions and Possibilities

3.1. Statement of how I will share what I have learned:

> written document
>
> public forum

3.2. What actions I expect/hope to be the result of my action research project:

F2: Curriculum Analysis Action Research Design

1. Project Overview

1.1. The critical question(s) of my action research project:

1.2. The setting for this action research project:

> brief description of community, school (class, race, mission, values, urban/rural)
>
> brief description of participants
>
> brief description of the classroom where the action research project will take place
>
> how this context matters to the study
>
> my comfort level with this context

1.3. The story behind this action research project:

> why I am interested in this area
>
> what my own experiences are with this area
>
> how my own values, beliefs, and sense of what "good teaching" is, are represented in this action research project
>
> what my biases are
>
> how my position as a student teacher influences the project
>
> how this information matters to this study

1.4. The specific curriculum (name, publisher, stated goals) I will be analyzing:

1.5. The specific categories and/or other strategies I will use to analyze this curriculum:

1.6. Timeline for the project:

> Part 1: Curriculum Analysis
>
> Part 2: Teacher Interviews
>
> Part 3: The Curriculum in the Classroom

1.7. A list of common themes in the literature supporting the categories used in analysis:

1.8. Reference list for the action research project:

2. Methodology

2.1. How I will document my curriculum analysis:

    analysis described

    observations described

    interviews described

    documents and artifacts to be collected

2.2. Description of researcher notebook:

    how it will be organized

    when entries will be made

    timeline of planned critical analysis points

    appendices (what additional data I will collect to give context to my journal entries)

2.3. How I will include others in the interpretation of my journey to become a teacher:

    professional colleagues

    critical colleague

    students

2.4. Brief statements of how the data and documents will be analyzed:

    analyze (parts): how the categories of data and documents will be analyzed

    synthesize (whole): how all of the data and documents will be scrutinized

    deconstruct (assumptions): what assumptions have been made and what are "other" possible interpretations

2.5. How this design deliberately plans for trustworthiness:

2.6. How I am gaining appropriate permissions:

2.7. Possible interruptions, distractions, and difficulties, and the plan for dealing with these:

3. Conclusions and Possibilities

3.1. Statement of how I will share what I have learned:

    written document

    presentation

3.2. What actions I expect/hope to be the result of my action research project:

F3: Ethnography Action Research Design

1. Project Overview

1.1. The critical question(s) of my action research project:

1.2. The setting for this action research project:

    brief description of community, school (class, race, mission, values, urban/rural)

    brief description of participants

    brief description of the classroom where the action research project will take place

    how this context matters to the study

    my comfort level with this context

1.3. The story behind this action research project:

    why I am interested in this area

    what my own experiences are with this area

    how my own values, beliefs, and sense of what "good teaching" is, are represented in this action research project

    what my biases are

    how my position as a student teacher influences the project

    how this information matters to this study

1.4. Why I have chosen this particular ethnographic area of interest:

1.5. A synopsis of what I hope to learn in this ethnographic study and how I plan to use what I learn:

1.6. Timeline for this action research project:

1.7. A list of common themes in the literature regarding this action research project:

1.8. Reference list for this action research project:

2. Methodology

2.1. How I will document my ethnographic study:

> observations described

> interviews described

> documents and artifacts to be collected

2.2. Description of researcher notebook:

> how it will be organized

> when entries will be made

> timeline of planned critical analysis points

> appendices (what additional data I will collect to give context to my journal entries)

2.3. How I will include others in the interpretation of my ethnographic study:

> professional colleagues

> critical colleague

> students

2.4. Brief statements of how the data and documents will be analyzed:

> analyze (parts): how the categories of data and documents will be analyzed

> synthesize (whole): how all of the data and documents will be scrutinized

> deconstruct (assumptions): what assumptions have been made and what are "other" possible interpretations

2.5. How this design deliberately plans for trustworthiness:

2.6. How I am gaining appropriate permissions:

2.7. Possible interruptions, distractions, and difficulties, and the plan for dealing with these:

3. Conclusions and Possibilities

3.1. Statement of how I will share what I have learned:

> written document

> presentation

> portfolio

> brochure

> other

3.2. What actions I expect/hope to be the result of my action research project:

F4: Self-Study Action Research Design

1. Project Overview

1.1. The critical question(s) of my action research project:

1.2. The setting for this action research project:

> brief description of community, school (class, race, mission, values, urban/rural)

> brief description of participants

> brief description of the classroom where the action research project will take place

> how this context matters to the study

> my comfort level with this context

1.3. The story behind this action research project:

why I am interested in this area

what my own experiences are with this area

how my own values, beliefs, and sense of what "good teaching" is, are represented in this action research project

what my biases are

how my position as a student teacher influences the project

how this information matters to the study

1.4. The vision I have of myself as a teacher by the end of this project:

1.5. The specific steps I plan to take toward becoming this teacher:

1.6. Timeline for the project (the cycle to be used in self-analysis):

1.7. A list of common themes in the literature regarding development in this area:

1.8. Reference list for the action research project:

2. Methodology

2.1. How I will document my journey to become a teacher:

observations described

interviews described

documents and artifacts to be collected

2.2. Description of researcher notebook:

how it will be organized

when entries will be made

timeline of planned critical analysis points

appendices (what additional data I will collect to give context to my journal entries)

2.3. How I will include others in the interpretation of my journey to become a teacher:

professional colleagues

critical colleagues

students

2.4. Brief statements of how the data and documents will be analyzed:

analyze (parts): how the categories of data and documents will be analyzed

synthesize (whole): how all of the data and documents will be scrutinized

deconstruct (assumptions): what assumptions have been made and what are "other" possible interpretations

2.5. How this design deliberately plans for trustworthiness:

2.6. How I am gaining appropriate permissions:

2.7. Possible interruptions, distractions, and difficulties, and the plan for dealing with these:

3. Conclusions and Possibilities:

3.1. Statement of how I will share what I have learned:

written document

presentation

3.2. What actions I expect/hope to be the result of my action research project:

Appendix G: Gaining Permissions/Letter Template

Printable CD Extra: Parent Letter Template

This letter template is also available on the companion CD.

[Date]

Dear Parent or Guardian:

[Introduce who you are and your role in the classroom:]

I would like to introduce myself. I am Ms. Nancy Marshall and I will be student teaching this term in Mr. Albert's fourth grade classroom. I am delighted to have this opportunity to learn with Mr. Albert and your child.

[State the objective of the project:]

During my student teaching, I will be studying my own practice of becoming a teacher through an action research project. Specifically, I want to learn more about ways to make homework meaningful.

[Discuss the strategies that will be implemented:]

I plan to implement a number of strategies to enrich the homework experience.

[Discuss the data to be collected:]

During this project, I will monitor homework assignments, survey students about homework, and observe class projects involving homework to better understand this issue. This data will be collected during the normal course of class routine and work.

[Give a timeline for the project:]

I will be collecting data for this project between December 1 and March 5.

[Explain how the project will be made public:]

I will present this project to the faculty and my peers at my university in April.

[Explain how confidentiality will be maintained:]

Throughout the report that I write, pseudonyms will be used for the community, school, and all students.

[Explain lack of risk to students:]

Data generated by students will be part of the teaching and learning process and will help me to be a better teacher and to provide a better education to your child. There is no risk in participation.

[Explain the response needed:]

Please sign the permission slip below, indicating whether I may or may not use the data generated during the normal school day from your child's work.

[Optional: Permission for videorecording/photographing:]

I would like to make videorecordings and/or take digital photographs for this project. These will be used to create a class CD at the end of the project, and as parent or guardian you will receive a copy of this CD. I would also like to use the CD during my presentation. Please indicate if I have permission to use videorecordings and/or photographs of your child in my report.

[Provide contact information:]

Sincerely,

Ms. Nancy Marshall

[Give e-mail address and/or school phone number]

[Give mentor-teacher's e-mail address and/or phone number]

[Provide a slip to be signed by parent/guardian, to be returned by the student:]

Please check yes or no below, along with your signature, and have your child return this slip to school. Thank you!

_____Yes. You may use data generated by my child to be used in your research project.

_____No. Please do not use data generated by my child in your research project.

_____Yes. You may use videorecordings and/or photographs of my child in your research presentation.

_____No. Please do not use videorecordings and/or photographs of my child in your research presentation.

_____   _____

Signature of parent and/or guardian   Date

APPENDIX H: PRACTICE DATA SET/NINTH GRADE BIOLOGY

Printable CD Extra: Data Set

This and other data sets are also available on the companion CD.

Background Information

The Critical Question

How can small groups be effectively used to increase students' content comprehension in science?

This large high school is located in a growing bedroom community of an urban area.

The mixed gender/ability groups were chosen by the student teacher/researcher.

The Project

Four students work together to use an organelle from a cell and attempt to use the unique structure and function of that organelle and its importance to the life of the cell to develop a cure for cancer by altering the way the organelle functions. The groups are instructed to give a Microsoft PowerPoint presentation describing their proposal for a cure and to turn in a portfolio of their group work over the course of the project.

The following data set includes:

a chart and graph showing the average grade of individuals in each lab group

a chart and graph showing compiled group responses to a survey about the project

a chart showing final group scores on group lab project

the survey given to students

observations by the student teacher/researcher during the lab

an analytical memo written by the student teacher/researcher

Read through the data set with these questions in mind:

How do the data inform or not inform the student teacher/researcher about critical factors that may influence small group work?

How do the data work together or not work together to provide insights into teaching and learning in this classroom? What additional data might you seek if you were the student teacher/researcher?

Is there any evidence that the small group work is increasing student comprehension of science? Based upon your response, what might you plan to do next if you were the student teacher/researcher?

Read through the student teacher/researcher's analytical memo with these questions in mind:

What, if anything, do you think is missing in the memo?

What advice might you give to the student teacher/researcher?

→ TABLE H.1: Practice Data Set

Action Research Data Set #2				
Groups Chosen During Data Set #2				
	Average Class Grade Before Group Project			
Group 1	Above average			
Group 2	Average			
Group 3	Below average			
Group 4	Mixed			
Responses to Cancer Group Project Survey				
	Group 1	Group 2	Group 3	Group 4
Group Function/Time Use	3.7	3.3	3.7	4.4
Perceived Educational Value	3.0	3.8	4.0	3.4
Attitude/Interest	2.9	3.0	3.7	2.9
Comfort with Project	3.5	4.0	3.8	3.9
Access to Technology	3	4	2	3
Cancer Project Group Score				
	Project Grade			
Group 1	90%			
Group 2	84%			
Group 3	75%			
Group 4	83%			

*Note: this table shows the average group response to a set of interview questions answered after the completion of the project. Each member of each group was given the same interview sheet and asked to answer questions on a scale of 1–5. Responses are organized to show all groups' ratings together for each category of question response.

→ TABLE H.2: Practice Data Set*

Group	Average Grade Before Project
Group 1	Above Average
Group 2	Average
Group 3	Below Average
Group 4	Mixed

*Note: This table shows the average grades for each group at the beginning of data collection for data set #2. The rating represents an average of all four members of each group. Most groups were generally homogeneous with the exception of group #4.

Data Set #2: Observation and Interview

January 10, 2005; conducted in the library

Group #1

Student A

Spent much of the class period working on the project. First half of work time was spent meeting with group to assign responsibilities and clarify directions. Worked on computer for the last half of the work time.

Student B

Worked on project during much of the work time. Worked on the computer for the second part of the work time.

Student C

On task for most of the work time except for a few times near the end of the class period. Spent much of the first part of the time meeting with group.

Student D

On task for a lot of the work time but distracted and was distracted by another student during the last 5 or 10 minutes of class. Spent the first part of the work time in a meeting with the group to talk about the project.

Group Function (Interview)

This group was working and communicating well with one another about the project and indicated that they were working well together. A couple of the group members expressed frustration that the other two members sometimes distract each other (boyfriend and girlfriend) and don't get as much accomplished as they should. This group was formed by a combination of two groups, which may result in this phenomenon.

Group #2

Student A

Working on the project and talking with group intermittently throughout the period.

Student B

Sitting on the floor, not working on a computer. Occasionally talking with her group about the project but generally did not appear to be working on project most of the time.

Student C

Working on the project on a computer much of the time but also spent quite a bit of time talking with other students. The talking was split between the project and other topics.

Student D

Working on the project intently for much of the class period. She interacted with group members as necessary but mainly seemed focused on getting some work done on the project.

Group Function (Interview)

Group attitude (morale) seemed to be good and there seemed to be little confusion about the requirements of the project or deadlines. Members seemed to be satisfied with how their group was working together.

Group #3

Student A

Spent most of the period looking for research information on the computer. Was rarely off task (if ever) during the period.

Student B

Spent most of the period working on the project, but did not appear to have a specific task that he was working on so it didn't appear that he accomplished very much during the period. May not be entirely clear on the requirements of the assignment.

Student C

Sitting on the floor for much of the period while her group worked on computers. Did not appear to be engaged to a significant degree in the project.

Student D

Spent most of the time working on the computer but did not appear to have a clear direction of what to work on. Did not seem to be working with his group on the project.

Group Function (Interview)

It is interesting that this group seemed to work well together but did not seem to be getting much done even though they were working. They seemed to indicate that each member of the group is doing his or her part of the work but it was unclear that they actually understood what they were supposed to be doing. This group also indicates that they work well with one another.

Group #4

Student A

Worked on project some of the time but sometimes spent time talking with group members about her frustration with her class grade.

Student B

Spent most of her time working on the project but occasionally talked with another classmate.

Student C

Worked on project most of the time, but sometimes chatted with group.

Student D

Sometimes worked on project, often appeared distracted by group members talking with one another.

Group Function (Interview)

This group seemed to have lots of questions about how the project was supposed to work. They got along well with each other but were surprised when I told them that their presentation was due at the end of the week. Overall this group seemed to feel as though they functioned well, and they indicated that they were satisfied with their group function.

Analytic Memo by Student Teacher/Researcher

As I continue in my attempt to answer the question, "How can small groups be effectively used to increase students' content comprehension in science?" I have been collecting data in an attempt to shed more light on the ways in which groups function and how they can be used best. In this most recent round of data collection it seems that the results I have obtained will hopefully be able to provide a clearer picture of the direction in which this research is headed (figure H.1). The data will be analyzed thematically here as I will look at the general categories of my data and make comparisons among groups based on that data. Four groups have been chosen for study during this data set; this has helped to streamline the data collection and interpretation process. The project described here involves groups of four students working to use an organelle from a cell and attempting to use the unique structure and function of that organelle and its importance to the life of the cell to develop a cure for cancer by somehow altering the way the organelle functions. Groups will then give a Microsoft PowerPoint presentation describing their proposal and will turn in a portfolio of their work over the course of the project.

The groups chosen should give a good cross-section of the class as they exhibit the entire range of academic achievement (from below average to above average) in this class. The first category to be examined here is group time use/group function. There are several interesting items that can be mentioned here as all groups rated themselves above a 3 on a scale of 1 (low) to 5 (high). Group #2 scored itself lower than the other groups, but my observations show that they were more on task than some of the other groups that scored themselves higher. Group #4 scored itself the highest of all groups in this first category, while my observations do not necessarily concur: group #4 does function well socially, but often this social behavior works to the detriment of the group's progress. I am pleased to note that all groups rated themselves above 3 in this category, and so it seems there were no major problems in this category. On another note, based on my observations, it does seem that stronger leaders in groups #2 and #3 might result in more productive groups.

It seems that an important aspect of a group project is the groups' perception of its educational value to each student. Again all groups rated the educational value of the project at or above 3, and while there is 1 point of variation between the groups' responses here, based on observation and the final project grade there does not seem to be much connection between this and on- or off-task behavior or the quality of the final product. So it seems there must be another factor that needs to be considered and accounted for, which results in the difference in group performance.

As we examine the attitude/interest of each group in this project it should be noted here that I have encountered the first scores of below 3 (posted by 3 of the 4 groups). The exception to

➡ **FIGURE H.1: Survey Questions**

Interview from Data Set #2

Name _____

Period _____

Group/Organelle _____

As you think back about our Cancer project, try to think about how well your group worked
and how well you contributed to your group:

Answer the following statements by circling the appropriate response:

1. My group got along and worked well together

    1 2 3 4 5   1 = not well   3 = okay/average   5 = very well

2. Working in a group made it easier to complete this project

    1 2 3 4 5   1 = made it harder   3 = about the same   5 = much easier

3. My group spent the majority of our time in class working on the project

    1 2 3 4 5   1 = strongly disagree   3 = neutral   5 = strongly agree

5. My group spent the majority of our time in class *not* working on the project

    1 2 3 4 5   1 = strongly disagree   3 = neutral   5 = strongly agree

6. I am satisfied with how my group worked on this project

    1 2 3 4 5   1 = not satisfied   3 = satisfied   5 = very satisfied

7. How many computers are at your home currently? _____

    How many of them are connected to the internet? _____

    Do you have PowerPoint? _____

8. What is your general comfort level with PowerPoint? _____

    1 2 3 4 5   1 = low comfort   3 = some comfort   5 = high comfort

9. What is your interest level in this project?

    1 2 3 4 5   1 (No Interest)   3 (Some Interest)   5 (High Interest)

10. What is the educational value of this project?

    1 2 3 4 5   1 (No Value)   3 (Some Value)   5 (High Value)

11. How would you compare the educational value of this project to other group projects in this class?

    1 2 3 4 5   1 (Not as Valuable)   3 (Just as Valuable)   5 (More Valuable)

12. How would you compare your interest level in this project to other group projects you have done in this class?

    1 2 3 4 5   1 (Less Interesting)   3 (Just as Interesting)   5 (More Interesting)

13. How would you rate your general attitude before you started this group project?

    1 2 3 4 5   1 (Bored)   3 (Neutral)   5 (Excited)

14. How would you rate your general attitude during this group project?

    1 2 3 4 5   1 (Bored)   3 (Neutral)   5 (Excited)

15. How would you rate your general attitude after you have completed this group project?

    1 2 3 4 5   1 (Bored)   3 (Neutral)   5 (Excited)

16. How would you rate your comfort level with this group project?

    1 2 3 4 5   1 (No Comfort)   3 (Some Comfort)   5 (High Comfort)

17. How do you feel about being involved in future group projects?

    1 2 3 4 5   1 (No Interest)   3 (Some Interest)   5 (High Interest)

What else do you want me to know?

this trend was group #3, which scored its attitude/interest above 3.5. The interesting thing here is that although this group seems to have been interested in the project, this did not translate into the quality of the final product or the direction of the group (as seen during observation—more will be noted on this in the next section). On the other hand, groups #1, #2, and #4 scored nearly identical in this section but scored differently on their projects and so we continue to search for a factor that is important to the final outcome of the project.

Often it seems that a group's comfort or understanding of their task is important, so next we will examine groups' comfort with the project. All groups rated relatively high (between 3.5 and 4.0), so again at first this does not seem to be connected with the project score/performance. Upon review of the observation notes, however, it does seem that my notes for group #3 do not match their assessment of their own comfort with the project. During the in-class work time on the project, group #3 did not seem to have much direction for its project and did not seem to really understand what it was attempting to do and did not know who was going to do what task. Many of the same comments could be made about group #2, although a couple of the group members here did seem to have a basic understanding of what was going on. I also observed group #4 asking lots of questions about the project, which I first assumed to be indicative of their lack of understanding of it, but I now believe that their questions may have come from a basic understanding of the project.

As this project was intimately tied to technology, the access to technology was another area of inquiry. One of the first things to jump out of the data in this section is that group #2 rated themselves high (4) while group #3 rated their access as low (2). When these findings are compiled with observational data the connection seems to become more significant. While group #2 did not yield a very high score on the project, this was not due to their lack of access to technology or the low quality of their presentation but was instead due to their failure to turn in a significant portion of their portfolio for the project, which resulted in their missing points. On the other hand, group #3 (based on observation) had a difficult time with technology during both the research and presentation-preparation phases of the project. Group #3 also indicated that most of its members did not have Internet access at home and no one had a version of Power-Point that was compatible with the version on the computers at school. It seems likely that these factors combined may have contributed to the low project score for group #3. On another note, it must be said that groups #1 and #4 had the same access to technology, and neither had access to PowerPoint at home, but group #1 scored higher than group #4 so there must be another factor that needs to be considered when considering small-group projects. Another question may also need to be addressed here: Is it reasonable to ask for the use of specific technology (such as Microsoft PowerPoint) for a particular project, or does this adversely affect some groups? In many ways I believe the answer to this is no because I believe that enough time was given for the project, but perhaps there needed to be more scaffolding and structure so groups could work more effectively during the time they were given.

As I have been considering how all of this data seems to fit together I have noticed that the final product grades of each of the groups may show that the groups achieved at levels similar to those of the individuals who comprised their group. It does seem that the group score may be shifted up slightly from the previous grades of individuals within the group however. The data do show group #1 with the highest score (90%) and its members also had above-average grades individually before the start of the project, while group #3 had below-average grades before the project and scored 75% (although it should be noted that the group scores for every group generally represented an improvement on the grades of most individuals within the group with only a few exceptions).

After all of this it seems there are a few issues that need to be addressed. First, it is entirely possible that groups may still bias their responses to survey/interview questions because they are afraid of negative consequences on their grades; it is also possible that students tend to avoid giving 1's and 5's as scores, although I think enough of these were recorded that I believe this is not the case. I have noticed a very obvious connection in the data (which was discussed in the previous paragraph) and am curious if this may be a connection to the research of Hogan (1999), who suggested that the manner of group formation (student choice vs. teacher choice) should be driven by the complexity of the assignment. In this case the more complex the task the more control students should have over the selection of groups. During the continuation of this research I may experiment with some different group-formational techniques. Another important point I have noticed is that the groups who seemed to be effective (especially group #1) had good leaders, and I am curious if the leaders just do much of the work out of concern for their own grade or if the group actually improves due to the leader. I suspect some of the former but I imagine the latter has a role as well.

APPENDIX I: SELECTED REFERENCES

Here are a few of our favorite resources:

Graves, D. (2001). *The energy to teach*. Portsmouth, NH: Heinemann. Graves is a wise and well-experienced mentor from afar. In this book, he guides teachers through a series of activities and thus provides space in which to rethink practice. This is action research/self-study; the strategies for thinking about what gives you energy as a teacher are invaluable, and we use them still.

Nieto, S. (2003). *What keeps teachers going?* New York: Teachers College Press. Nieto tells the story of veteran teachers in urban schools who love their jobs, and are passionate about students and communities. If you are tired of the tale of the "burned-out teacher," turn to these teachers.

Salas, K. D., Tenorio, R., Walters, S., Weiss, D., and Lynn, L. (2004). *The New teacher books: Finding purpose, balance, and hope during your first years of teaching*. Milwaukee, WI: Rethinking Schools. This book includes authentic questions like, "What do I do when I've made a mistake with a child?" and "Do I have to spend money on my own supplies?" It is honest, inspirational, and written by teachers who practice justice and action research in their classrooms. It is a quick read; you can select sections that are most pertinent to you.

Professional organizations usually have local affiliates and sponsor local conferences. What can be better as a teacher than to spend a day with colleagues, talking ideas and issues, and having a real lunch? Furthermore, many professional organizations sponsor mentorship programs for first year teachers. Check them out! We list just a few here, but professional organizations exist for most content areas.

National Council for the Social Studies (http://www.socialstudies.org)

National Council of Teachers of English (http://www.ncte.org)

National Council of Teachers of Mathematics (http://www.nctm.org)

National Science Teachers Association (http://www.nsta.org)

Rethinking Schools (http://www.rethinkingschools.org)

The present volume will, we hope, be a useful guide to you as you continue practicing action research as a teacher. There are many other excellent resources for additional perspectives and ideas on action research, particularly for a classroom teacher. We recommend the following, and encourage you to seek these out:

Dana, N. F., & Yendol-Silva, D. (2003). *The reflective educator's guide to classroom research: Learning to teach and teaching to learn through practitioner inquiry.* Thousand Oaks, CA: Corwin.

Frank, C. (1999). *Ethnographic eyes: A teacher's guide to classroom observation.* Portsmouth, NH: Heinemann.

Hubbard, R. S., & Power, B. M. (2003). *The art of classroom inquiry: A handbook for teacher/researchers.* Portsmouth, NH: Heinemann.

INDEX